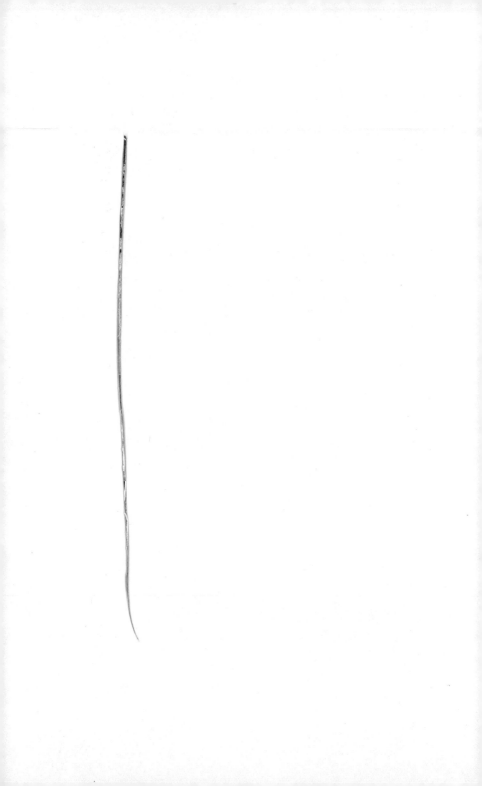

THE
STUDY OF
LITERATURE

by
GEORGE
WATSON

Allen Lane The Penguin Press

First published in 1969

Allen Lane The Penguin Press
Vigo Street, London W1

SBN 7139 0087 3

Printed in Great Britain by
Hazell Watson & Viney Ltd, Aylesbury, Bucks

for Sheila and Peter Stern

CONTENTS

Preface   9

Part I   *The Theory of Criticism*
    1   The Liberty of Judgement   15
    2   Reason and Value   29
    3   The Language of Verse and Prose   47
    4   The Literary Past   66
    5   The Theory of Kinds   84
    6   Comparative Literature   102
    7   The Editorial Art   120

Part II   *Other Disciplines*
    8   Linguistics   141
    9   Psycho-analysis   156
   10   Sociology   172
   11   The History of Ideas   192
   12   The Idea of Cultural History   209

        Select Bibliography   221

        Index   231

PREFACE

This book, which is a rationale of literary history, was stimulated by a situation which may appear to some excessively characteristic of English studies in the English-speaking world. Whether this is so or not, I hope its argument will be found available to students of other modern literatures, and of the ancient literatures as well. The situation I speak of lies in the paradox that, whereas literary history flourishes as never before in the late twentieth century, especially in a quantitative sense, the principal theorists of literature in the present age, whether aesthetes, moralists, formalists, mythologists, literary advocates of structural linguistics and the rest, have almost universally neglected and even condemned in their theories the historical foundations of literary studies. The gap between theory and practice could hardly be wider, and it is tempting to enquire how such a situation has arisen and whether it can survive.

In an absolute sense, at least, there may be only two possibilities of resolving such a situation. Either the theorists are wrong; or else schools and universities ought to attend more literally to what they have to say, and ought even to abandon the historical study of literature, with its characteristic concepts of periods, influences and schools, together with much of its patient search for the factual basis of historical assertion and its traditional objectivity. My own view is the first of these. I believe that recent theorists have been largely wrong, that they can be shown to have been so, and that the millions who continue to read literary history and who accept it, often unreflectively enough, as an objective discipline and a massive aid have good reasons for doing what they do.

It seems inevitable, then, that this book should invite the

disagreement of those who accept the cult of the contemporary relevance of the poetic past. This study is avowedly based on the conviction that Western literature does not derive its significance from the ways in which it may chance to bear upon present problems: that its finest powers of instruction, in fact, often lie precisely in the fact that, like much of what remains of the human past, it is simply different from the present. If the best end of literary study were merely to confirm or refine our sense of what we already know, or think we know, then it would be vastly less significant than it is. An obsession with the effects of literature, with 'response', whether moral or aesthetic, has often lain at the deep roots of some of the more characteristic assumptions of modern literary theory. It has certainly helped to encourage the reader to go to literature for the sake of what he could get out of it for himself; and the most intense of literary debates have often been concerned with whether one ought to seek this effect rather than that. And yet those who value literature hardly need to be promised an effect upon themselves, powerful as the effects of literature often are, and they may justifiably feel something like contempt for those who habitually exaggerate the educational need to make literature appear interesting, since they know it to be interesting in itself.

It is probable that views like these, though hardly a part of the consensus of literary judgement, may sound less wildly unfashionable than they might have done ten or twenty years ago. Indeed there are scattered signs that the anti-historical mood of literary theory in the earlier twentieth century is now approaching its close. But it is even clearer that our view of the past cannot be the Victorian view, and the second part of this book considers how certain humane disciplines largely outside literature have in the present century modified, for better or worse, our estimate of what the poets did. This is evidently the most perilous part of my undertaking, since it has encouraged me to infiltrate areas of knowledge where my passport is not strictly in order. It hardly needs to be said in my own defence that the chapter on linguistics which appears below is not primarily meant for linguists, or the chapter on sociology for sociologists, and so on through the concluding chapters of the book. If at times I have trespassed into teaching them their business, I hope the trespass is at least clearly marked. I have written here essentially for those whose concern is with literature. Nobody who reads for long will be in much doubt that this book is composed by someone who teaches English in an English university. What I know of other disciplines is inevitably little more than what a traveller knows of a landscape he sees from the window of his train. If it is remembered that the questions posed in these last chapters concern the advantages that an acquaintance with other disciplines might in the present historical moment offer the student of literature, this may help to diminish some of the more immediate objections to the procedures I have adopted here. It seems too evident to be worth mentioning, except in a preface, that subjects as established as linguistics, sociology and the rest do not exist in order to serve literary studies, and that the view I have taken of them here is explicitly an external one. And equally, I hope I have not seemed to propose easy solutions. Certainly there is no clear cause for optimism among those who declare themselves alarmed at the pace of specialization and concerned for the unity of human knowledge. No one has so far demonstrated a ready means of solving this problem in any system of advanced education. The practical alternative to specialization, at this level, may easily prove only the dire alternative of handbook knowledge and the trivialities of second-hand scholarship. I have tried to show here how relations between disciplines might be attempted; but the prospects of creative links between the humane disciplines remain problematical in outline and puzzling to predict in detail. The future, in all likelihood, is a matter of provisional arrangements subject to rapid replacement rather than formal ties between advanced disciplines. My concern with interrelationships needs to be cautiously qualified at all points by just such a sense of the provisional as this.

No sense of caution, however, governs my gratitude towards those who have helped with this book. This has proved an endeavour that owes nothing to any grant or foundation, and everything to a university where teaching and writing go hand in hand. I owe more than can easily be expressed to the members of a graduate and undergraduate seminar at Cambridge on the theory of criticism conducted for students of English, classics, philosophy and modern languages with Mr Renford Bambrough. The English Faculty Colloquium at Cambridge discussed an earlier version of Chapter 10, to the great benefit of that chapter. In private conversations concerning various aspects of the book, Mr Hugh Sykes Davies, Professor Graham Hough, Mr J. A. Crook and Dr David L. Frost, among others, have brought willing aid, both by agreement and by agreement to differ. And Mrs P. Parsons has once more deciphered my hand and typed the whole.

George Watson
St John's College, Cambridge
January 1968

Part 1
THE THEORY
OF CRITICISM

1

THE LIBERTY
OF JUDGEMENT

To study literature in any sense beyond the elementary is to
perform a literary act; and literary criticism is so largely involved
in creativity, and so much, at its best, an aspect of the creative
act, much as creation itself often involves a judgement of existing
works, that at certain crises of argument it must seem rash to
distinguish one from the other at all. But most literary study falls
well short of formal literary criticism and fails to invite rewarding confusions of this sort. At the worst it may be altogether
alien to the creative act. Indeed the contrast might be expressed in
bolder terms. To create is almost necessarily an act of liberty. No
state, however tyrannical, has ever made a practice of forcing
men to write – though many have forced them not to write.
Poverty may prove a stimulus to authorship as often as it provides
a constraint. But the study of literature, by contrast, though at
best a free act, and of value only when it is free, may in practice
be something much less than that. It can be, and often is, simply
enforced; and since enforcement is commonly practised upon
the young, it may be fastidious to object on any libertarian
grounds. But even where the student of literature is a responsible
being, it is still in no way inevitable that his enquiry should be
his own. A tyrannical teacher may dominate him; and the
student, out of mistaken servility, may even wish for nothing
better than that. Or, out of idleness or indifference, he may
simply acquiesce in judgements which he has not troubled
through reflection to make his own.

The creation of literature, in fact, is in its nature free; but only
some critical acts are so. In this study I hope to show what free
acts of literary judgement might be like, and how other historical

disciplines in the existing state of knowledge could serve them. In delimiting the problems in these terms, it is true, a question has been deliberately begged: that the study of literature is itself a historical study. And certainly it is in no way self-evident that it is so. The early twentieth century, indeed, was marked in the English-speaking world by a surprisingly sudden and successful campaign to diminish or even annul the sense of the past in literary study. The roots of this reaction lay in Victorian moralism and aestheticism, but the anti-historical movement spread quickly from the early essays of T. S. Eliot, where literary history is sometimes ridiculed in parody, to the treatises of I. A. Richards in the late 1920s, and by this route into the academic criticism of the United States in the 1930s and 1940s, where it came to be known as the New Criticism. It is also a plain fact, though in no way a conclusive one, that since the forties the study of literature has tended to move back into something like the Victorian pattern of historical emphasis confidently discarded by advanced opinion between the World Wars. For whatever reason, the case against history is not now felt to have been made; though equally, the drift back into literary history has occurred without manifestoes and with a remarkable absence of self-consciousness. Few have bothered to pronounce the New Criticism dead, still less to proclaim a successor. It is rather that historical studies of literature are silently in vogue, while 'pure' analysis already has a dated air. But the reasons why this has occurred, and the conditions governing the new situation, are still open to debate.

If the study of literature shows signs of having been restored to its dignity as a historical discipline, it may still be controversial to claim that it is one and the same with the discipline called literary history, or that (unless in a spirit of paradox or of consciously limited endeavour) there can henceforth be no other form of study than this. This bolder and more vulnerable claim is also part of my thesis here, though I do not mean to suggest that literary study can only be conducted on a vast canvas, as in the nineteenth century, or that the only prospect is to recount the histories of whole literatures or of whole classes of literature. History, after all, does not need to be narrative at all, and the historical lens may be as powerful or as concentrated as opportunity permits and as the case demands. It is simply that the quality of literary response has been permanently changed by the vast expansion of historical evidence over the past two hundred years. In the centuries of intellectual history before the historical explorations of nineteenth-century Europeans, it was certainly possible to believe, as Dryden, Voltaire and Johnson all believed, that human nature has been the same in every age and under every climate. Anyone who attempted to believe that today, unless in a merely residual sense, or who tried to behave as if he believed it – by treating Shakespeare, for instance, as if he were a contemporary dramatist – would be pretending to an ignorance that no twentieth-century man is capable of maintaining except as an awkward pose. One may choose to walk on one's hands, simply to show that it is possible: but it will always seem easier to walk the other way up. In much the same way, Western man cannot for long pretend to be unaware that the life of the past was qualitatively distinct from the present – that the Greek tragedians and their first audiences, for instance, or Shakespeare and his, saw the moral and political world in some ways differently from the ways in which we see ours, and that twentieth-century man possesses historical experiences which they lacked. It is no objection to suggest what is indeed incontrovertible – that our knowledge of the past is fitful and inaccurate. What the historian does may be as subject to error as any other human activity, and there are vast numbers of historical questions to which he may never find the answer. But it can equally be said of most human enquiries of an advanced and complex kind that they will never achieve finality. Objections like these neglect the simple truth that it is a positive merit of historical study to emphasize the fallibility of human judgement: just as it was a positive demerit of the dogmatic literary systems to underrate it.

But then the last and most desperate battle against the historical spirit is unlikely to be contested from positions as weak as these. It is more likely to be undertaken by passionately honest men who fight, as they believe, in an urgent and enlightened cause, and one which they most commonly call education. It is often urged, and especially by educational theorists, that literature exists primarily for the education of the young, and nobody who argues in these terms will easily be convinced that the modern vernacular literatures of Europe, such as the English, the French, the German or the Russian, were demonstrably written for a different purpose, and that their academic use is essentially an afterthought, a phenomenon as recent as the years since the First World War. It is still tempting to protest that, however that may be, the principal function of literature now and in the future must be educational; and that in such matters the needs of the student must be preferred before any cause of historical truth. If the debate takes on its most familiar pattern, the word 'relevance' will probably be used at this point; and it is notable that in such contexts the word is used, so to say, in a one-way sense, as if literary study were in more urgent need of proving itself relevant to the student than to the work of literature. The derisive term 'academicism' may follow almost at once; and the implication will have been fully made that anyone who cares for the past more for what it was than for what it can do for modern man is failing in a moral duty. Few of those, probably, who allow themselves to employ such arguments have any clear notion how precious the academic spirit is, how rare (even in academies) the disinterested love of truth can be, and how deprived a society forced to live without it. Such societies, all the same, are an easy journey away, and it is instructive and easy to study the deadening hand of totalitarianism in those states where free enquiry is not allowed to flourish.

It may be as well to concede to such views, however, that the main function of the literature of the past is now for better or worse educational. The massive part which literature plays in education is admittedly an afterthought in civilization, and contradicts much that we know about the original impulse by which literature was created; but it is fair to say that no one is ultimately bound by such considerations, salutary as it may be to recall them from time to time. Shakespeare's attitude to the present use of his plays in schools and universities would no doubt be one of mocking amazement; and Milton, if he could know that interest in his epics is no longer primarily theological, would be contemptuous in the last degree. But universal literary education seems for all that to have become one of the irreversible aspirations of mankind, and it need not prove a disaster. What is more decisive here is to recall that education cannot afford to become an enclosed intellectual system in which students are taught what seems to their elders to be best for them. It is a prime aspect of the academic duty towards knowledge to teach what is there to be taught. If a university undertakes to teach literature, it cannot escape the conclusion that much that is good in literature is irrelevant in the cant and familiar sense of that word. A teacher who taught otherwise would, in the end, be teaching a lie. And it would be a lie insulting to the intellectual sturdiness of his pupils.

The demand for relevance to the modern condition amounts to a demand that the student should be confirmed in the existing values of his own civilization, or at least in an approved selection from among them, and that he should never be offered the possibility of adopting another. Literary study conceived in these confined terms could easily degenerate into a mere training in orthodoxy, with the heresies well marked out by warning notices. It could demand of the student not only that he should remain the prisoner of some ideal of his own society, but that he should show himself servile enough to congratulate himself upon refusing to escape. 'Perverse as it seems to say so,' a famous critic once said, 'I sometimes find myself wishing, when dealing with these matters of poetical criticism, that my ignorance were even greater than it is.'* The temptation not to know can exceed even the temptation of knowledge. But it is not an impulse to be boasted of.

The misconception which encourages the shrinkage of knowledge into a dwindling list of approved authors has at times threatened to lead literary studies into one or another blind alley of ignorance and complacency. Fortunately, they have always re-emerged: in fact the resource and resilience of literary studies within human memory has proved astonishing. The Fascist view of literature triumphed only for a decade or two; the Marxist is now felt to be possible in intelligent debate only in a highly qualified and attenuated form. But the attempt to destroy historical foundations earlier in the century still continues to demonstrate some of the heavy costs of deliberate ignorance. Isolated as he often is from the kindred historical disciplines, the student of literature can at times show himself capable of easy convictions. He may still be heard confidently to hold a view of philosophy unknown to philosophers in any age, of language unknown to linguists, of social history unknown to the social historians. It is natural consequence of the anti-historical reaction that, as literary studies now attempt to re-enter history and to resume their natural place among the other disciplines, they should find the place unfamiliar and the scenery greatly changed. Our knowledge of the past is not what it was in the early years of the century, when literary history last showed much confident life. A new accommodation is needed. It is true that the literary student is in no sense bound to believe what historians of one sort or another may tell him: they are as fallible as he is, and it is right that

* Matthew Arnold, *On Translating Homer: Last Words* (1862).

they should listen as well as teach. But bland assumptions that the study of literature is 'of course' and rightly the 'central discipline' in a university are wildly out of place. 'In schools of English,' as a professor of English announced in a recent inaugural lecture, 'we tend, I think, to go around saying that there's nothing like leather, that the English school should be the centre, the core, etc. etc. *We are right, of course....*'* Perhaps the remark is ironic; in that case, it can bear a heavier irony than the context seems to allow. It is not only that to announce any subject, let alone one's own, to be 'central' involves one in a presumptuous and indefensible claim to be acquainted with them all. More pertinently, it involves one in the present instance in a self-centred misunderstanding of the isolation into which literary studies have been allowed to fall.

That isolation may best be described by reviewing the rise of modern literary studies in British universities around the turn of the century. Edinburgh, with its eighteenth-century chair of rhetoric, and later London, came first with the academic study of English; and by 1890 Oxford and Cambridge were still without English schools. It was natural that the new discipline should look to classical studies for its model; and in a questionnaire published in the *Pall Mall Gazette* in 1889, Gladstone, Pater, Matthew Arnold and others all recommended that English should be studied along with the classics, and even within the existing schools of classics, or not at all. The university departments of English that multiplied in British universities in the years around the First World War almost inevitably reflected the state of late Victorian classical scholarship in a new vernacular dress; and the Oxford and Cambridge schools of English, though only two among many, represented in convenient antithesis two distinct and even contrasting reasons traditionally offered in that age for the study of the ancient literatures. The first, which held that the intensive study in detail of a defunct civilization, its language and its institutions, was the supreme mental discipline for the young, led naturally into an Oxford emphasis on philology and Old English – a language which even possessed the disciplinary advantage of being inflected. The second, which emphasized the moral improvement to be derived from a study of carefully selected classical texts, adapted itself into

* Richard Hoggart, *Schools of English and Contemporary Society: an Inaugural Lecture delivered in the University of Birmingham on 8 February 1963* (Birmingham, 1963). My italics.

a Cambridge emphasis upon the poetry of the Metaphysicals, the nineteenth-century novel and the poems and essays of T. S. Eliot.

Few universities, if any, still preserve one or the other of these prescriptions inherited from the Victorian classics in a state of purity. But much of the debate centering upon literary studies in the present century has been concerned with the rival merits of the two, often to the exclusion of a simple truth: that to recommend the study of literature either for the sake of its mental discipline or its moral improvement is to recommend it for its effects upon the student and not for itself. Literature is undeniably likely to take effect upon the reader, whatever his motive for reading. That has never been in question. Even if Plato, or the exponents of mental discipline, or the Crown in the trial of *Lady Chatterley*, have at times exaggerated or simplified the effects of literature, those effects are none the less an observable fact of literary experience. Plenty of readers will step forward to testify with perfect truth that their lives have been changed by a book. Others will talk, in broader but still convincing terms, of response, of an enrichment of sensibility, of a broadening of intelligence which they owe to a literary education. But it does not follow that the study of literature is best justified in terms of its effects upon the student. Much of the weakness and incompleteness of such arguments, in all probability, arise from the special social conditions in which they are over-hastily conducted. Such defences, whether employed by Victorian classicists or by twentieth-century scholars of the great vernacular literatures, are often summary excuses in reply to challenges offered by hostile inquisitors. They arise from unnatural, stand-or-deliver discussions in which, most often, the teacher of literature is pressed to answer questions like 'What is the use of studying this?' It would be best of all if arguments were never allowed to reach situations as unrewarding as this; advisable, if they do, to refuse to answer a question so inaptly framed. A brief and direct answer, whether 'mental discipline', 'moral improvement' or any other conceivable counter, is necessarily vulnerable and probably damaging. A skilful prosecutor at this point of cross-examination can make nonsense of the case for literature proposed in such terms by demanding whether the witness, if offered an alternative study which could be demonstrated to have similar effects on the student to the effect named (arithmetic, moral philosophy, or the like), would then concede that literature was not worth studying. No one should allow himself to be placed in the position of the medieval historian who defended his profession on the grounds that a study of medieval history is helpful to an understanding of the modern world. The plain fact is that, if it is the modern world that we want to understand, then it is the modern world we should study. And if it is moral improvement or mental discipline that we want, then it is in no way obvious that literature will provide it best.

The truth is that excellence is self-validating, and that those who cannot see this are not capable of recognizing excellence for what it is. Only a man without a literary sense, or one in whom a passing mood of depression had usurped the place of judgement, would ask whether literature is worth studying. The question is rarely, if ever, an honest enquiry after information. To consent to answer such a question is to betray intelligence. When we volunteer reasons for the study of literature without being challenged to do so, we collaborate with a hostile scepticism that is rarely concerned with learning the truth. The inheritance from classical studies, indispensable as it has been in laying the foundations of the only way of studying literature known to Western man, has undoubtedly proved misleading in this particular. The study of literature is not to be judged by its effects upon those who pursue it. But this (to repeat) is not to deny that it may genuinely conduce to mental discipline, moral improvement, and much besides.

The fact of literary excellence, in the last resort, is what the study of literature seeks to examine, and it is another nail in the coffin of the sceptical view to say that, if the sceptic seriously wants an answer to his question 'What is the use of studying poetry?', then he can only approach an answer by way of the very study whose utility he doubts or denies. But the search for excellence in literature is often and easily misunderstood. It is sometimes thought of as a characteristic that distinguishes it from other historical studies such as the political, the social, or the constitutional; and some would even claim that it is this concern for excellence or value which is the ultimate mark of the literary critic, and one which proves him something other than a historian – regardless of how free he may make with historical procedures for his own purposes. It is proper to the historian, so the argument runs, to be concerned simply with what happened, whether he approves or not. Sheer scale for him is enough. The French and Russian revolutions are big historical events because they affected the lives of many millions for decades, regardless of whether for good or ill; the latest South American *coup d'état* is a relatively minor historical event, for similar reasons; whereas the literary student cares passionately for works which caused scarcely a ripple in their age, such as the poems of Blake, Hölderlin, or Hopkins. He cares for excellence in itself.

This is the subtlest of all anti-historical arguments in the field – the most plausible, the most winning and perhaps the most dangerous, since it is an error that comes so close to being true. Large parts of the case have to be conceded at once. It is entirely just that the literary student cares for excellence for its own sake. Even total neglect, and a consequent total absence of influence, would not deter his interest if he thought a newly discovered work to be a masterpiece. And many historians would agree that scale means priority in the writing of history. But if it is so, let it be remembered that it is so only in a sense too crude to count. The most frigid, the most 'scientific' historian has his judgements of value too. He would not value the massacre of a thousand men with the massacre of a thousand insects. The killing of the North American bison, though they doubtless outweighed in a literal sense the human dead of the frontier wars, does not for him outweigh the human event in significance. The historian may as an individual choose to treat as significant only those men of affairs who in the most worldly sense succeeded, but he is not bound to do so by the terms of his office as historian, and most would surely agree that Burke, who succeeded in no political cause and scarcely held office at all, was a more momentous figure in political history than some men who actually became Prime Minister. When historians declare, sometimes with a cynical air, that they are concerned with what happened, not with what should have happened, they are exaggerating for useful effect an emphasis which is genuinely present in their work, though hardly in so pure a state as they sometimes imagine; but they are also unwittingly drawing attention to an analogy with the work of the literary historian. For the literary historian too tries to tell what happened in literature. And when he commits himself, by comment, selection, or silence, to the view that some literary events are more important than others, he is behaving as other kinds of historian behave. History is always interpretative, after all, if only by virtue of its duties of selection; and a selection of evidence not involving judgements of value would in any discipline be worthless.

But then no assumption is more inviting and more perilous for the literary student than that matters of value are in some way his special concern: special, that is, in the sense that they affect other and comparable studies less. An attitude of defence is commonly adopted in such matters when no defence is necessary: the student in the humanities is hastily inclined to vindicate himself in reaction against what he supposes to be the greater prestige of the scientist in this age – and within the humanities the literary student is inclined to vindicate himself against the historian, economist and the like – on the grounds that he at least performs the ultimate civilized mission of maintaining standards of value. Let others discover facts, like Mr Gradgrind: he makes judgements; and the making of judgements, though perhaps difficult to justify as an academic discipline, impossible to computerize and rarely susceptible to massive subsidy by international foundations, still demands most of the individual in sheer distinction of mind. Many a literary student matches his frayed cuffs with a defiant gleam of conviction in the eye, and is inclined to confuse seriousness with poverty and the cultivation of literature with an air of joylessness. And many a scientist is an accomplice in the innocent fraud, and leaves his expensive laboratory daily with the air of one who deals only in facts and is content to leave opinions to others. Both views are an odd mixture of arrogance and humility. The student of literature can certainly forget his pride; plenty of others besides himself are concerned with the defence of Western values. It is not even obvious that literature is the supreme civilized function: the English, especially, are oddly disposed to forget that the world may owe at least as much to English political institutions as to English literature. And he can forget his humility too – or rather, his aching suspicion that the study of literature is somehow not a pursuit of a body of knowledge which, like other disciplines, grows in mass and in clarity. Judgement-making is an essential part of any intellectual activity. The historian, the economist, and the scientist in his laboratory are as surely concerned with issues of value as he.

And equally, the student of literature need not take pride or despair in supposing that there is some disqualifying oddity in the way in which literary knowledge is sought and attained. Let us neglect for the moment those easy cases where the literary historian behaves exactly like historians in general, as when he attempts to ascertain the date of Shakespeare's birth; or even a case of higher literary content, as when he tries to establish the order in which Shakespeare wrote his plays – a case in which he would certainly have to prove himself an acute analyst of Shakespearean language. The purest literary case, perhaps, is that of practical criticism, where the student shows what there is to be seen in a given poem. I use the deliberately general formula of 'showing what there is to be seen', since any formula more precise would be likely for just that reason to prove less accurate. 'Explaining what the poem is about', for instance, though it might represent the greater part of the operation, and might often provide the best point of entry, would still not account for everything that might usefully happen, such as an apt attention to formal properties like metre. It is notable at once that such literary demonstrations necessarily take place within a frame of reference. There will certainly be things to be seen in a poem which will not be thought worth mentioning, if only the shapes of the letters on the page and the colour of the paper. And there will often be things worth over-emphasizing, in the sense that they will occupy a larger proportion of a discussion or critical essay than they occupy in the poem itself. Problems may need to be discussed as much because of their complexity as because of their importance. But in all these respects, and in many others, the interpretation of literature can be shown to resemble other interpretative tasks in other disciplines. And it resembles them, above all, precisely in that it is concerned with showing what is there to be seen. What is there, after all, was there before the critic showed it to be there, and before the reader independently observed it to be there; otherwise we should hardly speak of showing, but rather of adding or inventing. And the features observed in the poem would be there whether observed or not. Criticism is not a matter of free attribution in which critics compete to find the most arresting interpretations. It is always, in principle, open to the reader to object that what the critic claims to have shown is in fact not there at all.

It may be objected that the demonstrative act of criticism, even if scrupulously conducted within an accepted frame of reference and widely accepted as demonstrative, none the less transforms what it touches. Suppose the critic conducts the student through Keats's 'Ode to a Nightingale', and the student sees not only what his unaided efforts have always allowed him to see, but what the critic has shown him to be present as well. There is a clear sense in which the critic has changed the poem; and the student, in gratitude, may even speak of his seeing the

poem for the first time. Those who claim to believe that literary
study is a free-for-all in which every man is entitled to his own
opinion are inclined to miss the resemblance that such cases
bear to historical and scientific processes. Seeing the object
afresh, more fully or (by a pardonable exaggeration) 'for the
first time' is much like what the scientist enables us to do. If I
am ignorant of botany, the botanist may instruct me about the
species and properties of a tree I have seen in my garden a thousand times; and though it will still be the same tree, I may none
the less speak with real accuracy of seeing it afresh. The study of
literature, in these large instances, is like the study of other areas
of human knowledge. It shows what is to be seen; and yet what
is to be seen may be something one has seen and failed to notice a
thousand times.

And certainly, when we notice things by the demonstrative
processes of criticism, whether our own or another's, we are
not proceeding in a manner logically different from the ways of
the historian or the scientist. The commonest assertions of difference, at least, do not bear examination. It is sometimes thought
that scientists proceed by first collecting their facts and then
drawing conclusions from them in the form of general laws,
though probably no philosopher of science any longer believes
in this account. (It is remarkable, however, how many scientists
and students of literature still believe in it.) And it is sometimes
suggested that the literary critic behaves, or ought to behave, in a
manner parallel to this mythical account of how scientists work –
first collecting all the facts about the poem, and then 'arriving
at a judgement' about it. Any close examination of an actual
experience of reading reveals this to be a fairy-tale. Judgement is
not the end of criticism, if only because in the complex conditions
which obtain in discussing great works there is no 'end' to
criticism in either sense of the term: no single purpose in view,
and no point at which the discussion can rightly be called
exhausted. In any case, the collection of facts does not precede
in time the possession of judgement, either in the library or in
the laboratory. Facts are collected because a judgement has already been made concerning their probable value and use. The
critic of Milton does not begin by collecting all the known facts
concerning *Paradise Lost* and its author. If he did, he would
never be done. His procedures are the familiar procedures of
trial, error and re-trial, of positions assumed, secured or abandoned, of hypotheses tested and sometimes won. He arrives not at a

judgement, though indeed he is constantly in judgement, but at a wider and yet still imperfect understanding.

This is not to say that judgements are in their nature fragile or infirm. It is surprising how many students of literature suppose that facts are what we have for certain and judgements what we may argue about. 'Facts are sacred, opinions free. . . .' And yet if anyone were to deny the judgement that the *Iliad* is a great poem, we should all know what to think of the freedom of his opinions. The strictly factual question whether the *Iliad* was written by one man or more, on the other hand, is genuinely open to doubt. It would be easy to multiply examples of cases in which judgements are established and deniable only by idiots, and where certain facts are perhaps forever unknowable. Unless new evidence is discovered, it will never be known for certain in which order Shakespeare's plays were written – a question of directly literary as well as biographical concern. But the question whether Shakespeare was or was not a great dramatist is scarcely open to debate at all.

And yet if certain facts and judgements concerning literature are forever established, how can the initial assumption of this chapter be maintained: that the study of literature at its best is a free act, and of value only when it is free? Some will think the claim overstated at the best; and it has already been conceded that it is possible, even common, to use literature as an illiberal discipline. The schoolboy who is taught to see *Oedipus* as a mass of grammatical forms, or *Hamlet* as a series of textual problems, is certainly studying literature after a fashion. The reasons for thinking such instruction inferior to the business of 'showing what is there to be seen' have already been set out: the grammatical forms are decidedly not all there is to be seen in *Oedipus*, though they are admittedly there among the rest. On the contrary side, there are more or less deterministic arguments for denying that literary study can ever be free, and such arguments may be arranged in ascending order of generality: that in the choice of what we read, since no man can read everything, we are subjected to pressures of suggestion over which we have no control, including the academic device of the set book; that the discussions of literature which guide our study are conducted by others, so that we are inevitably subject to the climate of literary opinion in which we live; that, in a still wider sense, the totality of our views about human existence, including religious and political views, are scarcely chosen freely; and that, even if they are so, they colour our literary judgement in an extra-literary way, so that the free discussion of literature soon ceases to be free, and indeed soon ceases to be literary at all.

This is not offered as a parody of an argument, though it is necessarily a bald summary; and it is not offered as less than a formidable obstacle to the view that literature, to the extent that it is to be regarded at all as a tool of education, is best seen in a liberal light. It is a battery of arguments which few will endorse as a whole but many in part. Marxists, Fascists, and all who see individual man as subject to history and to impersonal forces, will subscribe to much of it. So will moralists of the keener breed. A full reply would involve a general account of what it is like to commit a free act in a real situation. Certainly the advocate of free choice is under no necessity to disown either the known facts of an academic discipline or the factors which have made the individual what he is. To do so is to demand a clear impossibility – in effect to concede that no act of judgement, literary or other, could ever be considered free. If the determinist wants to win consent on these terms we may safely offer consent at once, for we have conceded nothing of any value in admitting that choice is limited by situation. To believe that man is a responsible being capable of making his own choices does not, in all conscience, require a view of man as a creature existing outside the web of circumstance. Human liberty in an absolute sense is always limited: the most free of free men is not literally able to do as he pleases. But those who prize individual decision and choice are unlikely to be so uninstructed in their faith that they cannot on such a challenge answer Marxists and others in clear terms. They know that liberty is the more precious because it is impossible to possess it utterly. They are more conscious than their opponents of confinement within systems of established values, unquestioned assumptions and naïve acceptance of habitual ideas. The critical act is not a single event of self-liberation, like the unbinding of Prometheus, but a task that exceeds a lifetime. It is best to recognize at the start that to such a task there can in a single lifetime be no end.

2

REASON AND VALUE

Rilke tells a story of a minor nineteenth-century man of letters who died in the act of correcting a hospital nurse who happened to have mispronounced a word in his hearing, and comments approvingly: 'He was a poet, and hated the approximate.'* Most people, and even most professional judges of literature, find his comment on the story disturbing, and that is what it is meant to be. It is not commonly thought that accuracy is high among the poetic virtues, or even that it is properly to be numbered among them at all. 'Information is true if it is accurate. A poem is true if it hangs together,' as E. M. Forster once wrote, perhaps without much fear of contradiction. 'Information is relative. A poem is absolute.'† A work of literature might suffer from a kind of internal inaccuracy, in the sense that the parts might fail to hang together. But it cannot in this view be inaccurate in any other way. It may happen to be about something; but if it is, it is often felt that it does not matter much what it is about, or whether it reports it faithfully or not.

And yet the formalist doctrine of the poem as a 'heterocosm', or world of its own, is surprisingly modern; and Rilke's view, paradoxically framed as it is, is far more traditional than Forster's. The Ancients knew the Homeric poems in large part as history, and would certainly have thought of them as less valuable (though not necessarily valueless) if shown as a whole to be otherwise. Aristotle's doctrine of poetry as an imitation of reality certainly demands that it should be conceived of in some clear sense as true, and not merely true to itself: this is the weight of his defence of poetry against Plato's attack. Medieval man would

---

* R. M. Rilke, *Aufzeichnungen des Malte Laurids Brigge* (Leipzig, 1910).

† E. M. Forster, *Anonymity* (1925), reprinted in his *Two Cheers for Democracy* (1951), p. 91.

have been puzzled and outraged at the notion of a corpus of literature existing independently of any reference to anything but itself; and though some Renaissance critics seem at first glance to hold heterocosmic doctrines of poetry, their writings do not bear out this interpretation under careful examination. Scaliger in his *Poetices* (1561) speaks of the poet as one who 'produces another nature altogether' from the world of the five senses, and praises the Greeks for having called the poet a maker or creator. But Sidney in his *Apologie* (1595) has probably interpreted Aristotelian doctrine with justice when he represents the poet as one who deals with Nature in her ideal forms, showing not what is but what might best be: 'he goeth hand in hand with Nature, not enclosed within the narrow warrant of her gifts, but freely ranging only within the zodiac of his own wit. . . . Her world is brazen, the poets only deliver a golden.' Renaissance doctrine here effortlessly rejoins its ancient source: 'Poesy therefore is an art of imitation, . . . a representing, counterfeiting, or figuring forth – to speak metaphorically, a speaking picture.'

It is often supposed that the contrary doctrine of the absolute poem is an early Romantic invention, but this is certainly a mistake. Wordsworth offers his autobiographical *Prelude* in unequivocal terms as an account of what actually occurred, 'The Growth of a Poet's Mind', and in the concluding lines addressed to Coleridge he proposes a poetic programme that is directly didactic:

> . . . *what we have loved,*
> *Others will love, and we will teach them how;*
> *Instruct them how the mind of man.* . . .

Schiller, Shelley and Hugo often saw poetry as propaganda in humane and liberal causes. Coleridge, in a subtle and difficult passage in the first chapter of the *Biographia Literaria* (1817), tells how as a schoolboy he had learned that 'poetry, even that of the loftiest and, seemingly, that of the wildest odes, had a logic of its own as severe as that of science; and more difficult, because more subtle, more complex, and dependent on more, and more fugitive, causes'. It is true that 'a logic of its own' is a phrase oddly open to opposite interpretations, according to emphasis; but the rest of the passage, and indeed the rest of the *Biographia*, emphasize the deep underlying relation between the world of Nature and the world of poetry, 'fugitive' as may be the causal elements that connect them. Certainly there are minor predictions of modern formalism in the eighteenth and early nineteenth centuries; but the real source of the doctrine as a continuing tradition was more probably provided by the rigid scientism of the Positivists and others in the mid and late nineteenth century, when an excessively formal view of human knowledge, based upon strict mathematical and quantitative models, seemed to deny to literature all hope of verification. Coleridge's subtle, complex logic and fugitive causes did not seem defensible to Comte or Mill; and twentieth-century successors such as I. A. Richards and Susanne Langer have accepted the Victorian view that poetry, at the best, is only a formal structure of 'emotive' value. 'A poem is absolute'; 'a poem should not mean but be'. . . it would be easy to multiply the many restatements of what has since become one of the great literary superstitions of the age.

And yet the Western world has continued to behave as if literature were a form of knowledge, even in the act of denying just that. Novels are extensively read, among other reasons, for the information they offer about human conduct – information often available in no other form. The great poets of the century, such as Eliot in *The Waste Land*, offer views of Western civilization which visibly affect the convictions and behaviour of those who accept them. Those who 'read the Bible for its prose', if they exist at all, are rarely caught in the act of doing so, and Gibbon's *Decline and Fall*, which has often been cited as an example of a work designed as fact to survive only 'as literature', is seldom if ever read from beginning to end by persons with no interest whatever in Roman and Byzantine history. Literary formalism is a fashionable doctrine that does not work. But it maintains a continuing vitality as a theory, a kind of abiding plausibility, for so long as our notion of what knowledge can be like remains constricted and needlessly exacting. *The Waste Land* affected the mind of its age; but it is accepted as a great poem, it may be protested, even by those who regard Eliot's view of Western secular society as a desert to be an act of betrayal and sabotage. Its first line, 'April is the cruellest month', is an evident untruth; and so on. Probably there will always be those who see human discourse in these limited terms, never calling a spade anything but that, and profoundly convinced that to behave otherwise is always to be less than honest. To show the table-thumper to be wrong is an elaborate process, but it is one that has long since been shown to be within the range of criticism. The cruelty of April in Eliot's poem is a paradox, and it is possible to explain how paradoxical statements work, and how this instance functions in a literary tradition where April is familiarly the month of love and spring. And even if Eliot were in the end to be convicted as guilty of having helped to betray his own civilization in time of peril, it would not follow that the shallow indolence and triviality that he depicts in society were not there, or that they are not closely and accurately observed in the poem. On the contrary, it is just because the portrayal is accurate that the charge of betrayal can be made at all. The portrait must first be recognizable if it is to give offence.

Closely allied to the fallacy of the total formalism of poetry is the fallacy of the subjectivism of literary judgements. If poems need not be true, then equally, it has often been held, criticism need not be just. An English philosopher has written in these terms concerning works of art:

> If something is made or done gratuitously, and not in response to a problem posed, there can be no question of preferring one solution to another. . . . A critical judgment is in this sense non-committal and makes no recommendation. . . . One engages in aesthetic discussion for the sake of what one might see on the way, and not for the sake of arriving at a conclusion, a final verdict for or against.*

The entire passage seems to violate in a highly instructive way any ordinary experience of writing and reading literature. Poems are evidently not gratuitous in the intended sense of the word. They may very well be said, with little or no strain upon language, to be written 'in response to a problem', and we may even be capable of explaining with fair accuracy as literary historians what that problem was. And it is a familiar activity of critical discussion to prefer one solution to another. Moreover, critical judgements do commonly make recommendations, and are commonly thought to do so. One is more likely to read a novel or to see a play that has been well reviewed or recommended than one that has not. And aesthetic discussions observably arrive at conclusions, even if those conclusions are not usually as cut-and-dried as 'Guilty' or 'Not Guilty'. The historical situation must be an odd one if it allows intelligent men to deny facts as obvious as these. And yet they are often denied. 'After

---

* Stuart Hampshire in *Aesthetics and Language*, edited by W. Elton (Oxford, 1954), pp. 164–5.

all,' said Leslie Stephen in 1876 with undue humility, 'a criticism is only an expression of individual feeling.' 'There is no argument,' wrote Orwell in 1947, 'by which one can defend a poem.'* It is highly characteristic of subjectivist assertions like these that Orwell's rash remark follows upon an essentially convincing defence of *King Lear* against the strictures of Tolstoy, who despised the play. Those who claim to believe that literary judgements are merely matters of personal taste rarely, if ever, behave as if they believed it. They will sit up into the small hours eagerly contesting the value of novels, plays and poems in arguments that bear every resemblance, mistakes and all, to arguments which in spheres other than the aesthetic would be universally admitted to be rational. And yet the inconsistencies of the subjectivist position rarely seem to impress them on such occasions. Probably the indecisiveness of such arguments in practice puzzle them excessively: in recalling the occasions in which after strenuous debate they have failed to convince their friends of the merits or demerits of a poem, they forget the vast number of literary judgements which are widely accepted – so widely, indeed, that nobody would think them worth arguing about. To argue whether Milton or Dylan Thomas was a great poet is to admit that such cases are in some way genuinely on the borderline and that there are arguments to be advanced on both sides; and in the heat of debate it is often unnoticed how many reputations are beyond dispute. Literature happens for complex reasons to be a disputatious activity, in the sense that its social and journalistic aspects encourage the seeking out of points of difference. The commonest form for a literary conversation to take is for two or more people to move listlessly over a range of questions where they find themselves in apathetic agreement, to pounce at last upon an issue, often a relatively minor one, upon which battle can be waged. And the disputatious temper affects even the academic study of literature, for similar and sufficient reasons: why write a thesis or a treatise on something which everyone is agreed about already? If the contestants were to spend their time differently, and more tediously, than is usual – if they were to total up the matters of literary judgements in which they felt no temptation to disagree – they would find the corpus of common taste, or of what Kant called the common

---

* Leslie Stephen, 'Thoughts on Criticism', in his *Men, Books and Mountains*, edited by S. O. A. Ullmann (Minneapolis, 1956), p. 221; George Orwell, 'Lear, Tolstoy and the Fool', in his *Collected Essays* (London, 1961), p. 417.

sense of mankind, '*gemeiner Menschenverstand*', to be vast beyond imagining. But of course there are excellent social reasons why literary conversation should not be conducted in this way.

And there is another side to the medal. The subjectivist view of literary judgements ('*de gustibus non disputandum*') equally tends to assume that undeniably objective enquiries, as in the physical sciences, move from fixity to fixity, from one laboratory-tested truth to the next. Those who favour a purely textual mode of criticism, supposedly after the manner of A. E. Housman, sometimes argue this case with special enthusiasm. And certainly the history of literary criticism does not offer a prospect of any such accumulated certainty as they demand. But then neither does the history of science, or of textual criticism either. Any department of human knowledge will reveal an entertaining spectacle of experts who have been shown to have been wrong. Those who favour a purely textual ideal of literary criticism on the grounds that it is less subjective and more scientific than literary criticism in general should ask themselves how many of the emendations of Richard Bentley, the greatest classical scholar of his age, have survived, or how much of Malone's Shakespearean scholarship a modern scholar would now accept. To argue like this is not to suggest that Bentley or Malone were wasting their time; only that the massive contributions which they made to human knowledge were subject to the usual and searching tests of posterity. Literary judgements are fallible, it may be admitted: but so are other judgements. And to argue according to the evidence, which is the best one can do in any continent of human knowledge, is not necessarily to arrive at a right answer.

And probably, too, the subjectivist is unreasonably alarmed at what he supposes might be the dictatorial consequences of abandoning the fluidity of his position. If literary judgements can be rationally established, so the nagging suspicion runs, then literary orthodoxies might be enforced with the rigidity once feared of the French Academy or with the severity actually exercized in this century in central and eastern Europe. But alarm of this kind is too clearly irrational to be often voiced. The demand for rationality in literary judgements, after all, is one claim that a dictatorship of literature could never admit, though it might often find it convenient to pretend to admit it. The great Fascist and Socialist tyrannies of Europe, it is true, are officially objectivist: they believe, for example, that defects of Jewish or bourgeois intellectualism are genuinely present in condemned works, and that they can demonstrate them to be there. But this is not to say that they have in fact demonstrated them to be there, or demonstrated them to be defects. And their refusal to allow open debate on these issues is a suspicious circumstance. One principle that dictators could never permit in practice is the principle defended here: that literary debate can be as rational in procedure, and literary judgements as soundly arrived at, as the findings of historians and scientists.

An example may make this claim more acceptable. Consider the following passage:

> He represents in an eminent degree this natural decorum of the English spirit, and represents it all the better that there is not in him a grain of the mawkish or the prudish. He writes, he feels, he judges like a man, talking plainly and frankly about many things, and is by no means destitute of a certain saving grace of coarseness.

The passage is reasonably representative of much in the Western critical tradition, and it hardly matters for the moment who wrote it, or of whom. (It is in fact from Henry James's essay on Trollope, published in 1883.) Its procedures are characteristic of a familiar tradition. It does not advance from fact to opinion, or from historical information to statements of value, but offers an account in which opinion is fact and where statements of value are themselves informative. Is it a fact, after all, or is it James's opinion, that Trollope's style at its most characteristic is 'plain and frank'? Of course it is both. If James is wrong, it is open to anyone to show him to be wrong by rational procedure: by opening the works of Trollope and pointing to passage after passage to which terms like 'plain' or 'frank' could only be misapplied. And if the subjectivist is still obstinate, it would be proper to ask him whether James's account of Trollope's novels could equally serve as an account of Dickens's, and whether he could imagine any sane man writing of Dickens that 'there is not in him a grain of the mawkish or the prudish'.

One last defence, it is true, may seem to remain to the subjectivist: that the language of literary criticism is irredeemably and hopelessly vague. 'Frank', 'mawkish' – how can terms so broad and so flexible be allowed to belong to the world of an academic discipline? One might indeed concede to James that the first epithet was well applied to the novels of Trollope and the second not; but then it is open to the observer to see in such terms, if not anything he pleases, at least a wide variety of possibilities. Why, for that matter, does the critic employ statistics so rarely? Why does he refrain from defining his terms? And why does he habitually allow himself to use terms which in their nature are resistant to definition?

Objections like these are probably familiar enough in their association to be allowed to make a group and to be subjected to a single scrutiny. They form a powerful body of opinion in the last hundred years, when literary studies have felt themselves obliged to measure their own worth against the sciences – or rather, against what many literary men have supposed the sciences to be. Valéry spoke of the need for a great *nettoyage verbal*, or purification of language, and wrote of the 'great day of definitions' that must one day come. Such demands are not in principle peculiar to literary studies, and a convincing answer could hardly confine itself to literary issues alone. Other disciplines are afflicted by the demand for definition of terms, for stated norms, criteria and essences, for the necessary and sufficient conditions why a given claim should be so and not otherwise. And such demands may not in all circumstances be misguided, even if the expectations they arouse are commonly exaggerated. A definition may at times advance an argument, even if it does not have the expected effect of concluding it. If, under certain circumstances, there should be a demand to define the term 'definition' itself, it may be genuinely useful to reply that it is a verbal formula which includes all the cases and excludes all the non-cases. If someone asks about the difference between a simile and a metaphor, he can certainly be told. It would be perverse to deny that such explanations may sometimes help. But 'under certain circumstances' is the operative phrase. The definition of 'definition' just offered is perhaps an adequate one, but it would only advance an argument in which the contestants are more familiar with the sense of terms such as 'verbal', 'formula', 'cases' and 'non-cases' in the given context than with 'definition' itself – an unusual though not impossible situation. Dictionaries depend upon such situations, since they function best in those instances where they explain or define an unfamiliar word in familiar terms. But they are often driven back into unavoidable absurdities, such as the *Oxford English Dictionary* definition of 'goat' as a 'hardy lively wanton strong-smelling usually horned and bearded ruminant quadruped'. This is a moderately good definition, and probably all animals that conform to all its terms are indeed goats, just as almost all that fail to conform, unless for some special reason, are not goats. But it is still unlikely that anybody ever discovered in this way what a goat is, and certain that there are better ways.

It is salutary to recall that most of the realities of literature are far more subtle and less amenable to definition than this. To refuse to define terms such as 'frank' or 'mawkish' is no mere evasion or vacillation, but a recognition of a fact of language which no one engaged in literary study has any business to miss. But to refuse to define is not to refuse to reply. The right reply in such cases is to consider example after example which, in greater or lesser degree, illustrate the contested terms, and to consider what the differences in degree are like.

An example of definition-mania may bring the point closer home. In 1924 Arthur Lovejoy published an influential paper entitled 'On the Discrimination of Romanticisms', in which he argued that 'the word "romantic" has come to mean so many things that, by itself, it means nothing. It has ceased to perform the function of a verbal sign.' Lovejoy described this situation as a 'scandal of literary history and criticism', and proposed in its place 'a plurality of Romanticisms': 'there may be some common denominator to them all; but if so, it has never been clearly exhibited'. A quarter of a century later Professor René Wellek took up the challenge by setting out to demonstrate that 'the major romantic movements form a unity of theories, philosophies and styles, and that these, in turn, form a coherent group of ideas each of which implicates the other'.* He reviewed uses of the term and instances of the movement in a number of European countries, mainly in the eighteenth and nineteenth centuries, emphasizing 'three criteria' which he considered 'particularly convincing': 'imagination for the view of poetry, nature for the view of the world, and symbol and myth for poetic style', and concluded that Lovejoy must be mistaken.

It is only just to concede at the outset that a great deal of value might arise, as in the present instance, in the course of a search for the criteria of romanticism or of any similar literary movement or term. Equally, it is of no concern here who won the

* Arthur O. Lovejoy, *PMLA* 39 (1924), reprinted in his *Essays in the History of Ideas* (Baltimore, 1948); René Wellek, 'The Concept of Romanticism in Literary History' (1949), reprinted in his *Concepts of Criticism* (New Haven, 1963); cf. his 'Romanticism Re-examined', *ibid.*, and 'German and English Romanticism' in his *Confrontations* (Princeton, 1965).

debate. What is above all vulnerable in these opposing positions is not a point of difference between them but rather an assumption they make in common. Both are convinced that the proper understanding of romanticism requires two conditions: first, that a formula of words should be arrived at which includes all the cases of romantic literature and excludes the rest; and second that such a formula, which admittedly need not be brief, should consist of one or more features or elements which, as a group, must be demonstrably present in romantic works and absent from others. Lovejoy rightly argues that there is no such formula, and rashly concludes that the current use of the term is accordingly a 'scandal'. Wellek claims that there is such a formula, albeit a vague and complicated one, and asks that the term should be rehabilitated. The argument shares many of the familiar properties of a Platonic dialogue, where Socrates concludes that, since he and his auditors cannot say what a familiar abstraction such as beauty or justice may mean, it follows that they cannot know what it means.

It is easy and common in such discussions to alternate between equally implausible extremes of scepticism and Procrustean rigidity. Lovejoy, the sceptic, claims not to know what romanticism means: 'by itself, it means nothing. It has ceased to perform the function of a verbal sign.' But he continues to behave as if he understands it very well, distinguishing without difficulty the cases of European poets who were Romantics from those who were not, and both of these from poets who occupy intermediate positions; and distinguishing within such intermediate cases as the 'pre-Romantics' those who were more romantic from those who were less. For one who thinks the term has lost its utility, one is inclined to say, he uses it with remarkable precision. Wellek behaves in an opposite but equally familiar way. Having offered a complicated formula or set of criteria to the number of three, he is bound to admit at times that not all the poets whom he knows to have been Romantics exemplify all the criteria in a simple way. But the evidence only needs to be pushed a little:

Wordsworth, at first sight, is the romantic poet farthest removed from symbolism and mythology. . . . But Wordsworth does stress imagery in his theory and is by no means indifferent to mythology. He plays an important part in the new interest in Greek mythology interpreted in terms of animism. There is the sonnet 'The world is too much with us', and there is a passage in the fourth book of the *Excursion*. . . .

What neither of the contestants can bring himself to admit is that his knowledge of the instances precedes any formula he may devise. It is in no way necessary for knowing what romanticism is to be able to say what it is. What is necessary is to be able to point. And both scholars know perfectly well where and where not to point: to the Schlegels and Wordsworth and Hugo, and away from Voltaire and Dr Johnson.

If one can imagine the demand for definitions, criteria, essences and the rest applied to a literary discussion in which more is at stake than here, its essential futility would become even more obvious. Suppose one were to undertake afresh Orwell's task of demonstrating to Tolstoy that Shakespeare, whom Tolstoy despised, was indeed a great dramatist. The obvious procedure is to meet Tolstoy on his own ground by showing him that the objections which he raised in his pamphlet of 1903 will not stand: that Shakespeare's use of convention is not 'worn-out' but creative, that his 'bombast' and 'obscenities' usually have their dramatic justification, and so on. What no one would do, what even Lovejoy and Wellek would not dream of recommending, would be to set up a norm of excellence for the drama and then measure *King Lear* against it. If *Lear* were to fail in such a test, it would be the norm we should dispense with, not the play. Our knowledge of what great drama is like is not dependent on any account we can offer of what 'greatness' or 'drama' mean, but on what we know of a number of plays which include *Lear*. In the same way, our knowledge of romanticism is not dependent on possessing a norm, still less on being capable of stating what that norm is, but upon our knowledge of the Romantics and their works. But anyone largely ignorant of the subject might none the less be richly if incidentally instructed by an attempt, however ill-conceived, to define the term.

A more difficult test for the objectivity of literary values lies in the claims made for literature as a moral teacher. This is because such claims are often exaggerated; but then they have been exaggerated for a long time. Plato demanded the expulsion of poets from his ideal republic on the grounds that their moral influence was deleterious, and not just as an observable fact of Greek society but as a necessary fact of their profession. Renaissance criticism was fully moralistic, though its morality, like Sir Philip Sidney's, was serene and enchanted, and utterly unlike the killjoy spirit of some Victorian and later critics. Johnson is summarizing a view widely held for two thousand years when he declared in the preface to Shakespeare (1765) that it was 'always a writer's duty to make the world better'. Many people today would probably concede that Johnson, and two thousand years of critics before him, were inclined to be hamfisted in these matters, and that it is common to find some disparity between a reader's own moral views and those implicit in poems which he none the less admires. Some good poems fail to edify; some perhaps even corrupt. It seems idle to deny this, though two large schools of literary influence still continue to deny it: an Anglo-Saxon literary tradition of individual self-improvement initiated by Ruskin, Arnold and their puritan successors such as D. H. Lawrence or the *Scrutiny* school of the 1930s; and the vast totalitarian systems which insist that literature and the other arts exist to make good citizens. 'Art education,' as Adolf Hitler said in 1937, opening the House of German Art in Munich, 'is popular education in the loftiest sense, for it arouses that which is most valuable in man; it makes him say "Yes" to life. It is not by dinning the stuff of learning into our comrades that we improve their social position, but by calling on them to throw their spiritual energies into the struggle.' The passage is fairly representative; it is a notable feature of both schools of moral severity in literature that, austere as they may be in practice, they prefer the heady language of Nietzschean exhortation to anything that smacks of the forbidding. They do not call literature 'edifying' or 'moral', but 'life-enhancing' and 'affirmative'; they speak not of abstention and improvement, but of an 'awareness of life'.

Certain extra-literary objections to literary moralism, whether Victorian or modern, present themselves at once. Literary students, it is sometimes objected, even those who have studied in the approved manner, do not observably behave better than others. And if the object of study is to be considered the moral effect on the student, it is not obvious that literature is the best course of study available: moral philosophy has an obvious claim to be considered here. But neither argument is likely to have much weight with the dedicated moralist. He must know that, regardless whether an approved course has an edifying effect in a general sense, it is still altogether likely to have the effect he wants – broadly speaking, the effect of brainwashing the student in a given dogmatic system. As for moral philosophy as an alternative to literature, it has the double disadvantage of being too sceptical and analytical on the one hand, and too esoteric on

the other. It is natural that the totalitarian should be interested in
literature above every other art or discipline. Its didactic powers
are far superior to those of painting or music, and by the selection of the censor it can be rendered an infinitely subtle mode of
propaganda.

But doubts remain, and not merely anti-totalitarian doubts.
It is not just that every reader knows there are great works
whose moral tendency he is in no way prepared to affirm. Such
cases, after all, tend to be too various in their implications to be
conclusive. It is well known that non-Epicureans may think
Lucretius to be a good poet – indeed, since there are no Epicur-
eans left, it must be so for Lucretius to have maintained his
reputation at all. And it is common form for agnostics to think
the *Divine Comedy* or *Paradise Lost* to be great works. But such
examples are much less decisive than they sound. An agnostic
reading the *Divine Comedy* with admiration may well be admiring features which Dante would reasonably have thought
incidental or even paradoxical, and it would surely be hasty to
exclude the possibility that a Catholic reader is likely to understand the poem better. With works as large as these, too many
possibilities of response arise to be considered in a single argument. Professor Empson, for example, who is an anti-Christian
critic, has explained in his *Milton's God* (1961) that he admires
Paradise Lost not merely for its stylistic properties, but because
he thinks it makes Christianity look vicious and silly: 'the poem
is good not in spite of but especially because of its moral confusions, which ought to be clear in your mind when you are feeling
its power. I think it horrible and wonderful; I regard it like Aztec
or Benin sculpture. . . .'* If Epicureanism were any danger to
our civilization, someone might well argue that the *De rerum
natura* was a great poem because it made the system look obscure,
or wicked, or absurd. But these are all far from being standard
cases of what the moral value of literature is commonly supposed
to be like, and they are mentioned here only to emphasize how
various such cases can be.

Perhaps a more limited example, then, will be allowed to
serve a more direct purpose. Consider the case of a short poem,
Marvell's 'To his Coy Mistress', which is probably accepted by
all who know it as a work excellent in its kind. Such universal
acceptance is an essential premise of the argument, and it can
hardly be argued here. What is notable is that no one, it is surely

* William Empson, *Milton's God* (revised edition, 1965), p. 13.

safe to say, has ever suggested that the poem is edifying, or 'relevant', or 'life-enhancing', or the like. It is simply thought to be good. Nor has anyone ever thought of banning it, though perhaps there have been periods in which it has been avoided as a school text. Of the two extremes, however, it would be more plausible to say that it ought to be banned than that it ought to be read for its moral effects. And this is not because it is a seduc-tion-poem. After all, there are seductions and seductions. It is rather because the form of seduction which the poem re-enacts, in a tradition which stretches back at least as far as the '*Vivamus, mea Lesbia, atque amemus*' of Catullus, is one of such pure carnality that almost no one in a Christian or post-Christian society could be found to defend it as a model of love – not even a libertine, in all probability, since a libertine has more cause than anyone to claim to be something else. And it would equally be over-ingenious to claim that the poem is offered as a caution-ary example or moral warning: indeed what is most impressive about the stance of the poet is his total detachment from the action he describes, which he offers, neither in praise nor blame, as a model of poetic elegance in the form of a dramatic monologue: an advanced and sophisticated example in an ancient and highly competitive tradition of love-poems. If such a man as Marvell's lover were to try to seduce such a woman, one might well feel on reading the poem, he could hardly go about it more expertly than here; but the neutrality of the poem is so finely main-tained, and yet in the face of such challenges and such difficulties, that the reader feels no temptation to commit himself or the poet to one side or the other. The lover begins with some delicately contemptuous ragging of the coy mistress ('Had we but world enough, and time . . .'), a banter which becomes increasingly contemptuous without ever abandoning its poise or descending into abuse, and then moves into a kind of refined intellectual bullying ('The grave's a fine and private place . . .'), concluding with an invitation which is frankly brutal and philandering ('Let us roll all our strength, and all Our sweetness up into one ball . . .'). The sense of the proposal is unmistakable: the tech-nique, almost alarmingly, a model of the adroit.

Probably much in this brief account of the poem sounds prig-gish and beside the point – the point of the poem, that is to say. But then any moral interpretation, whether this or another, is likely to verge upon absurdity in much the same way. The real excellence of the poem lies elsewhere, in the unflagging accomplishment by which a commonplace situation of Latin and Renaissance poetry is revealed anew, pitilessly, accurately and utterly without sentiment, in the historical situation of a mid seventeenth century in which such a literary form was all but exhausted; and to demonstrate the nature of this accomplishment it might be useful to lay the poem beside its analogues in Catullus, Marlowe and others. Anyone who talked of the love-situation here as examplary or cautionary would be talking about something else – a more vital matter, perhaps, but hardly the matter of Marvell's poem.

And yet it is worth admitting that the case is by no means fully representative of literary experience as a whole. It may be common to admire works which teach us little or nothing about how to live, or which try to teach us what we rightly refuse to learn; but it is also clear that other works, which possess what Keats once called 'a palpable design' upon the reader, succeed or fail to a high degree according to their powers of moral persuasion. It is not necessary to accept Tolstoy's idiosyncratic ethical views, or his idea of history, to think *War and Peace* a great novel; but it is observable that almost everyone who reverences the novels of D. H. Lawrence also believes that Lawrence had much of urgent moment to teach his civilization, and Lawrence himself would not have had it otherwise. Studies of Lawrence's technical accomplishment are an extreme rarity, and this points not so much to a failure in criticism as to a fact of the work. And sometimes such emphases shift significantly over the years. Blake and Shelley, for example, are undeniable examples of poets with palpable designs on their readers. But in the twentieth century, for whatever reasons, Blake has continued to exert something like his intended revolutionary influence over his admirers, and Shelley on the whole has not.

Should one conclude, then, that the problem of moral belief in literary studies is insoluble? It is certainly likely that the question in the forms in which it is commonly posed is not answerable in direct and simple terms. Does poetry primarily exist, as Arnold believed, as a 'criticism of life' and in order to answer the question of how to live? Do poems always and necessarily demand moral assent? Those who answer such questions with Yes or No are in equal difficulty. The moralist is at a loss to explain how it is that works he cannot deny to be excellent, like Marvell's poem, can hardly be related to any programme of moral instruction without forcing the evidence. His opponent, who often innocently misapplies Coleridge's remark about 'a willing suspension of disbelief' for his purpose, and who is inclined to employ formulae like 'expressive form', is required to dismiss the moral influence of Blake, Lawrence and many others as exceptional, even perverted instances. Both are pointing to elements in literature which are genuinely there; both are pretending that such elements are all that there are.

The truth is that literature is not homogeneous in the sense required to answer such questions with simple accuracy. It is easy to suppose that, because the word 'literature' is correctly applied to many thousands of works of many ages and in many languages, all such works are alike in respect of the degree of their moral purpose. Put in these blunt terms, it seems surprising that anyone should ever have thought the problem to be soluble in the terms offered. And yet it has been common enough to suppose it. Many critics of the last hundred years, including many of the most influential, have offered Yes or No answers rather than warnings against extravagant generalization. John Stuart Mill put a view widely accepted in his age and far into the twentieth century when, in the last chapter of his *System of Logic* (1843), he confidently claimed that all art is moral, and even that all morality is art: 'The imperative mood is the characteristic of art, as distinguished from science. Whatever speaks in rules, or precepts, not in assertions respecting matters of fact, is art.' Morality, then, is also a matter of art and not of fact. 'Propositions of science assert a matter of fact. . . . The propositions [of art] do not assert that anything is, but enjoin or recommend that something should be. They are a class by themselves.' A more modern critic has repeated the claim: science 'starts with the world as it is', art 'with the world we want to have'.* The answer to such schematic claims lies in looking at the individual cases; and the individual cases do not always permit this to be said of them. In fact literature embraces not a single category, whether Mill's imperative category or anything like it, but rather a vast spectrum stretching at least as far as the distance between Marvell and Blake. And that is a very long way. It is as far as the distance between 'This is the way it can happen, regardless of what one thinks about this sort of thing', and 'This is the way it ought to be, and it is time you realized it'. It sounds a little like the distance that proverbially separates Ought from Is.

And yet probably, if the cases were considered with the care

* Northrop Frye, *The Educational Imagination* (Bloomington, 1964), pp. 23–4.

they deserve, it would appear that the spectrum of literature, though vast, was slightly less vast than this. Is any poem utterly 'pure' in this sense? Marvell's poem admittedly discourages speculation about Ought; but the sheer fact that it is about seduction touches upon the moral sense, however marginally, and it might be argued that any poet who offers such an example in such accomplished terms is, however remotely, encouraging emulation. And, on the other side of the coin, the most morally demanding of Blake's poems, such as 'I wander thro' each charter'd street', is something more than an indictment, though it is emphatically that; it has metrical and other formal properties that are worth discussing. Coleridge once spoke of the 'middle quality' of poetry, of its tendency to hover between a thought and a thing, and certainly it is the intermediacy of literature that impresses if the enquiry concerning its moral status is patiently allowed to go on and on. Those who reply either Yes or No are bound to stop short with their examples, and they are answered by continuing with examples. But even the judicious answer of intermediacy may be inclined to formalize the matter excessively. For if literature tends to hover between the indicative and the imperative (to resort to Mill's terms), it is certainly not distinguished from other forms of discourse by this fact. The same could be said of much and perhaps most human discourse. To emphasize the intermediate status which literature holds in the spectrum is merely to re-emphasize its similarities with other uses to which language is put. And yet none of these considerations need inhibit from pronouncing on individual examples. The spectrum is certainly vast; but a given poem may hold an intelligible position upon it, and it may be a necessary condition of understanding it to know what that position is.

So far the account has been only of literary moralism in the exaggerated form in which it has been commonly and popularly understood in the past hundred years: a doctrine that sees the prime function of literature as teaching men to behave better. But a moral concern with literature might well be far less crude than this. It might readily concede all the arguments that have just been proposed, and still insist that literature deals in moral questions in the sense of embracing large regions of moral knowledge. Whether it characteristically does so, or whether it is necessary for a work to do so in order to qualify as literature, is beside the point; and so is the objection that many who are learned in literature do not behave better than the generality of mankind. Literature may still be said to offer knowledge in such matters, even if we conclude that this is not its chief or only function. And to possess such knowledge, it may equally be argued, is in any case not the same as to act upon it. To have studied and understood *Othello* is to have absorbed information about the moral world; and anyone who has observed with care the steps by which the heroes and heroines of Henry James's novels take or fail to take their decisions could not avoid learning what few men could otherwise know about what a considered decision in all its stages is like. And such limited arguments as these seem incontrovertible. The student of literature may behave better or worse than his fellows; but in either event, his mind will be better furnished than most with knowledge about the nature of moral choices. Such literary moralism as this is too cautious to found a school, and it is not the view of Plato or Sidney or Johnson or Arnold or Marx. They, and their disciples, would certainly have thought it pale and uninteresting. All it attempts to do is to fit the observable facts of literary study in a mild and uncontroversial way, and to leave it at that.

3
THE LANGUAGE OF
VERSE AND PROSE

It seems prudent, then, to distrust absolute statements which assume literature to represent a single character of utterance with a single purpose, and to insist upon its diversity and its range – a diversity not infinite, certainly, since there are writings to which we deny the name of literature without hesitation, but still too wide to admit easy delimitation. One way of emphasizing this diversity is to consider literature as a vast spectrum stretching almost all the way from pure form to pure statement – the distance, for example, between the poem of Marvell and the poem of Blake. In this chapter I shall remain at one end of the spectrum and consider some of the more pressing and immediate problems of verbal formality.

It is often said, and even believed, that form and content in literature cannot be separated; and yet nothing is so common in literary discussion as to hear them discussed apart. And it is natural not be intimidated by those who claim the two to be inseparable. Of course it is obvious that in any given poem no other set of words could mean exactly the same thing; and of course no translation is utterly exact. But it hardly follows that it is always improper to discuss the formal properties of a work in isolation, or to ask what a poem is about, or to use a translation as a way of approach to some great original. There may be many good reasons why, in the process of analysis, a single and even a minor aspect may justify special attention. A complaint would lie against a critic who offered a single aspect in exchange for the whole work; and it is now a familiar charge against certain Shakespeare critics of the 1930s, who offered moral banalities in exchange for *Othello* or *Lear*, that they offended in just this way. But equally, there might be situations in which a moral banality, or a crude indication of a formal property, could be the most useful contribution to be made. 'Has anyone here ever been in love? . . .' 'After all, the book *is* a novel . . .' – calls-to-order like these might be exactly what a critical discussion most required, and it would be no objection to call them crude. There are situations, after all, in which crudity is useful, even indispensable. A signpost which reads 'LONDON, 100 MILES' announces two facts with utter crudity; and if you know the neighbourhood well, you may think the signpost to be something of a banality too. But for the motorist who is looking for London all this would be a clear advantage, and he would not complain that the sign told him nothing about the varied and interesting scenery on the way. Critical statements are often like this: they predict and answer questions to which answers are genuinely sought in a given, and often impermanent, situation. It need be no objection to say that they fail to mention what is, in an absolute sense, the most important thing in the poem. The most important thing may be too obvious in itself to be worth mentioning; or it may have been mentioned so often as to be unworthy of further emphasis. To assert the essentially social function of literary criticism is to insist that it exists not as a form of self-expression in a void, but in order to tell certain people what they need to know for a given purpose. That is one reason why the criticism of the past is so rich in evidence of the history of literature itself. It is evidence, both positive and negative, of what in a given historical situation was known, of what was unknown, and of what was thought to be needed.

The most familiar of all formal distinctions in literature is the distinction between verse and prose; and it is also among the most ancient, being widely explored before the Christian era. Provided that the modern confusion between 'verse' and 'poetry' is excluded, it remains fully viable in itself, and might even prove a growing-point in literary discovery. In the following discussion, in speaking of prose, I shall always mean literary prose: what is involved here is not the language that men speak, unless in the way of the most formal oratory, but the language which they write for literary purposes in unmetrical forms. Such language is certainly a formal construct, and it would be almost as alien to conversation as verse itself. If anyone doubts this, let him record his own conversation and see it reduced to typescript or print: the startling informality of spoken language will be instantly apparent. It remains natural, if a little misleading, that the liberty of prose should be stressed as a contrast to the supreme formality of verse. When Cicero calls prose an *oratio soluta*, or free speech, he surely means no more than this – that prose, artificial as it is, is at least free of the constraint of metre. When the Arabs call verse an 'ordering' and prose a 'scattering'. they are presumably making a similar point. But none of these views necessarily denies the formality of prose: in the *De oratore*, indeed, Cicero offers the public speaker a range of artifice of stupefying deliberation and complexity. Dryden echoes the point in a memorable way when he calls prose 'the other harmony'; and Coleridge even thought there was a case for calling prose the more sophisticated form of the two; in its origins, he once wrote, 'prose must have struck men with greater admiration than poetry. . . . To hear an evolving roll, or a succession of leaves, talk continually the language of deliberate reason in a form of continual preconception, of a Z already possessed when A was being uttered – this must have appeared godlike.'

VERSE

Metre, whether composed by classical quantity, or alliteration, or the stress-system characteristic of the modern Germanic and Slavonic languages such as English and Russian, or the syllabic system characteristic of the Romance, such as French, always represents an audible pattern imposed upon language for the special purpose of intensifying its formality. A formality so imposed may have two objects: to dignify the matter of the work, or at least to match it in dignity; and to render the work more memorable; but there are further and more complex possibilities, especially when metre is used for comic or ironic effects, as in Byron's *Don Juan*. The pattern is audible in the sense that it is there to be heard, regardless of whether in fact it is uttered or not. Most reading in Western countries in this century is silent, but this is something of a novelty, and perhaps arises from the wide increase in reading habits ultimately consequent upon the invention of printing in the fifteenth century. Augustine in his *Confessions* (V.3) noticed on a visit to Milan in A.D. 384, as a matter for surprise, that Ambrose the Bishop read silently and with closed lips ('*vox autem et lingua quiescebant*'); but by the nineteenth century, if not earlier, Ambrose's manner of reading was common form. Nietzsche even complained that Germans in the 1880s were capable of reading only with their eyes, and that German books were torture to those who possessed 'a third ear'; but he is presumably referring to prose. Every reader of verse, at least, needs three ears. And the pattern which metre imposes, whether it be internal to the line or, like rime, a matter of the relations between lines, amounts like other patterns to a principle of recurrence. An audible motif is repeated, with or without variation, and this repetition is the metre.

Two doubts arise over the principle of recurrence, and it may be useful to lay them to rest at once. The first objection is extremely *a priori*. Since no two lines are phonetically identical, it has been suggested,★ and since in any case even the same line may, mistakes apart, be differently pronounced by two readers, metre cannot be an audible property of verse or be subject to phonetic analysis, and the pattern it creates cannot exist for the ear. This revealing mistake about the nature of metre is based on an excessively absolute view of phonetic analysis. Such analysis may be broad or narrow according to its purpose: broad, for example, if we wish to represent the pronunciation of an utterance for the guidance of foreigners and others; narrow if the purpose is one of minute description. Divergences between good readers of verse remain facts which are genuinely awkward to the student of metre, but they are none the less facts which are subject to analysis and intelligent disputation. If two readers disagree, for example, as to whether the first line of *Paradise Lost*,

Of man's first disobedience, and the fruit,

contains four stresses or five, the argument need not stop short with a mere agreement to differ: Milton's undisputed handling of blank verse in other and less controversial lines, and certain known facts concerning the state of the language in the seventeenth century, can be put to use here. And many of the minute divergences of pronunciation that exist between individuals can be demonstrated to have no metrical value. In claiming that metre is a phonetic fact, no one commits himself to the view that all phonetic facts in a given reading are metrically relevant. Readers of many diverse dialects and speech-habits in English, for instance, are usually capable of recognizing the main metrical

★ Cf. C. S. Lewis, 'Metre', *Review of English Literature* I (1960).

types of English verse for what they are; and English blank verse does not cease to be such when it is read aloud by a Scot or a North American.

The second doubt concerning the principle of recurrence is more particular than the first, and relates to the rise of 'free verse' in the past hundred years in French and English poetry. It is sometimes thought that the 'freedom' of Walt Whitman, Mallarmé or Eliot breaches the principle of recurrence in a radical sense. Sixteenth-century Englishmen may have felt similar fears over the contemporary invention of blank verse. Such fears are usually exaggerated, and it is common for successor-generations to be puzzled at the alarm and hostility that such mild metrical innovations incurred. The 'sprung' rhythm of Gerard Manley Hopkins, which once seemed a highly radical device, is now clearly seen for what it was: the intensification of a possibility present in English poetry for over a thousand years. The free verse of the late nineteenth century and after amounts to little more than the freedom to intermix at intervals lines of varying but still familiar metrical quality. The metrical variety of Eliot's *Waste Land* may once have puzzled at first reading, but there is not a line in it which is not readily analysable in familiar terms. (Much of it, ironically enough, is in Miltonic blank verse.) It should be clear that terms such as 'free' or 'blank' are paradoxical as metrical descriptions, and that they serve only to emphasize certain features. If verse were totally free or blank, it would cease to be verse altogether.

Since metre is a matter of recurrence, it seems natural to regard it as a conservative principle within verse, a kind of fixative. But this is not so. The mistake arises from the natural assumption that form and content are inseparable. One approaches the problem of metre with a false expectation of decorum; as if, as Pope put it,

> . . . *The sound must seem an echo to the sense.*

Pope goes on in illustration:

> *Soft is the strain when Zephyr gently blows,*
> *And the smooth stream in smoother numbers flows;*
> *But when loud surges lash the sounding shore,*
> *The hoarse, rough verse should like the torrent roar . . .*

But it is worth noticing at once how unusual in his own practice this crude principle of re-enactment is: the simple illustrative function of this passage from the *Essay on Criticism* (ll. 365–9) is hardly to be paralleled elsewhere in Pope – not even elsewhere in the *Essay*. If Pope's 'numbers' merely echoed his sense, we should probably think him a very minor poet. It is much more characteristic of great verse that its metre should defy its substance, a 'salutary antagonism' (as Coleridge called it)* which Pope's own verse abundantly illustrates. In the fourth book of *The Dunciad*, where the young fop sets out upon his continental Grand Tour, Pope's ironic imitation of epic style and metre comes perilously close to resembling the reality of a great heroic poem, and it is a sense of the precarious, of an irony that almost forgets itself in the creative act, that affords to his verse its subtlety and excitement:

> ... *To where the Seine, obsequious as she runs,*
> *Pours at great Bourbon's feet her silken sons;*
> *Or Tiber, now no longer Roman, rolls,*
> *Vain of Italian arts, Italian souls:*
> *To happy convents, bosomed deep in vines,*
> *Where slumber abbots, purple as their wines:*
> *To isles of fragrance, lily-silvered vales,*
> *Diffusing languor in the panting gales:*
> *To lands of singing, or of dancing slaves* ...
>
> (ll. 297–305)

The example may seem too sophisticated to be representative; but there are good reasons, on reflection, for considering the triumphs of metre to be more often those of antagonism than of decorum. Is it ever the case, in memorable examples, that metre merely echoes the sense? Rime might be considered a clinching argument for the theory of antagonism here, since it hardly ever possesses a logical function of a direct kind: the fact that two words end with the same set of sounds in the same order is commonly a fact that lies outside their meaning altogether. Rime is a happy accident, as far as significance is concerned, and it is its purely accidental quality that makes it the felicitous device it often is. It is pleasant that the English should for centuries have possessed the proverbial phrase 'neither rime nor reason': there is indeed nothing reasonable about rime. But what is true of rime, in this unusually precise and obvious way, is probably true in a subtler sense of metrical properties in general. They are often at their best when they do not altogether fit, and

* *Biographia Literaria* (1817), ch. xviii.

when they succeed in drawing attention to their own existence. The verse of a Racine play might be considered an instance: its extreme and unvarying regularity, which is not at all the same as uniformity, is imposed upon a world in which unregulated human passions and instincts count for almost everything. The massive and varied formality of Milton's grand style is imposed upon a religious epic where the theological programme of justifying God is felt by poet and reader to be problematical, even intractable. The heady concentration of some of Shakespeare's sonnets arrests and startles the reader: it is not to be anticipated that fourteen lines should naturally encompass so much argument. Coleridge's *Ancient Mariner* and Byron's *Don Juan*, in the metrical forms of the medieval ballad and Italian epic, defy the natural expectations to which such metres give rise; and so on. Metre at its best is not decorous. On the contrary, it often has a lively and disturbing vitality of its own.

Why do poets write in verse? Coleridge offered a starting-point to an answer when he replied bluntly: 'I write in metre because I am about to use a language different from that of prose.' Metre announces a formality which is about to occur. The pattern in the spoken voice, or the appearance of the poem on the page, warns the listener or the reader against assuming that the utterance he is about to receive is a commonplace one. On the other hand, it is less certain that Coleridge is right when he suggests that the language of verse is necessarily different from that of prose. It may often be so, and there may be cases where it must be so; but to suggest that no other possibility exists is surely to underrate the formality of prose itself. Some poets, such as Wordsworth, employ a prose so formal, even in their private letters, that it is hard to see that the language of their verse needs be formalized in any way – a fact to be borne in mind in considering the preface to *Lyrical Ballads* (1800), where Wordsworth's notion of what constitutes 'the real language of men' is avowedly very different from any ordinary one. A private letter of April 1808, and a poem written at the same time, both describing a dawn walk up Ludgate Hill, may help to confirm the point:

... beyond, towering above it, was the huge and majestic form of St Paul's, solemnised by a thin veil of falling snow. I cannot say how much I was affected at this unthought-of sight in such a place, and what a blessing I felt there is in habits of exalted imagination. My sorrow was controlled ...

and beyond
And high above this winding length of street,
This moveless and unpeopled avenue,
Pure, silent, solemn, beautiful, was seen
The huge majestic temple of St Paul
In awful sequestration, through a veil,
Through its own sacred veil of falling snow.

It remains uncertain whether Wordsworth, in a private letter, would have allowed himself to use such a term as 'awful sequestration'. But if he was prepared in the letter to use phrases as literary as 'solemnised by a thin veil' or 'habits of exalted imagination', then it seems just possible that 'awful sequestration' might have been admissible in his prose as well, and that its presence in the poem alone is an example of an afterthought. At all events, it is not at all clear that the language of the poem is radically more formal than that of the prose. But then the poem is more formal than the letter simply because it is a poem. The fact of metre attracts attention to itself, and demands of the reader that it should be viewed in a more formal way. Even if the language were identical, it would none the less seem different in verse; which is as much as to say that it would in fact be different. It is in this absolute, and perhaps unintended sense, that Coleridge was after all in the right: 'I write in metre because I am about to use a language different from that of prose.' It is just because it is the expectation of our civilization that the language of verse is different from that of prose that it can, at times, allow itself to be the same.

The formality of verse also makes it the more durable of the two forms: not just in the obvious sense that it makes it easier to get by heart – a fast declining tradition in the present century – but in the more important sense that its formality lends a toughness and a clarity to language. The verse of past ages is often easier to understand than its prose. Shakespeare in the theatre, played before audiences lacking any special instruction in Renaissance English, often seems more lucid in his verse passages than elsewhere. The reasons for this phenomenon are not merely accidental. If Shakespeare, for the most part, prefers verse for his court scenes and prose for the yokels, with the natural consequence that his prose is the more regional, allusive and topical, there are after all good reasons why he should do so: it is not merely a matter of obeying an existing convention. When he violates this natural order, as in *As You Like It*, the inversion is itself a formal property of the play, a rather daring example of the principle of salutary antagonism. What appears to be the intense linguistic naturalism of Hamlet's soliloquy 'To be or not to be', a dramatically convincing example of a reflective intelligence working itself through an untidy argument within the gentle formality of blank verse, is a more subtle example of the same poetic art. There must be many exceptions: but the general tendency of verse is surely to toughen and clarify the texture of language, regardless of whether we choose to learn it by heart or not. Consider a parallel in Donne, which is probably fortuitous. In a letter of September 1608, in characteristic vein, he wrote to a friend:

Therefore I would fain do something; but that I cannot tell what, is no wonder. For to choose, is to do: but to be no part of any body, is to be nothing.

Some fifteen years earlier, perhaps, in his third satire he had already written:

> Yet strive so, that before age, death's twilight,
> Thy soul rest, for none can work in that night.
> To will implies delay, therefore now do.
> Hard deeds, the body's pains; hard knowledge too
> The mind's endeavours reach, and mysteries
> Are like the sun – dazzling, yet plain to all eyes.

The two cases are by no means parallel throughout; but at the point where they do run parallel, it is notable that the verse has weathered better than the prose. Formality tends to work as a preservative against time, and verse often endures better than prose. The ordinary language of the past, if it had survived, would surely have dated still more damagingly than the language of literature.

PROSE

Prose is now widely regarded as more workaday than verse – so widely that it must represent a real fact in the conventions which currently determine the use of language. Verse, at its most characteristic, is often felt to be conscious of the texture of its language in a way that prose is not. 'Verse is a pedestrian taking you over the ground,' as T. E. Hulme once put it, while prose is 'a train which delivers you at a destination'. Sartre makes the same point still more succinctly when he calls poets 'men who refuse to *use* language'.* Epithets like 'poetical' and 'prosaic' confirm this view: they may be used to describe the tone of a work irrespective of its form. But nobody wishes to regard the distinction as definitive. A poem which happened to be prosaic in tone would still be a poem, and might not be less of a poem if it somehow contrived to put its prosaic tone to some special use, like Lear's 'Pray you, undo this button. Thank you, sir.' The poetic intensity of such a line leaves little to be said for the traditional view of decorum expounded at length by Cicero in the *De oratore* and widely accepted by Europeans for some two thousand years. This view proposed three prose styles, high, middle and low, and described their features. But since the Romantics, at least, decorum has rightly seemed a more relative matter than this, and literary language can now be seen to operate by simultaneously observing and defying the conventions within which it moves. Such discoveries as this relate to literary language in general, and not only to prose. But this is an unavoidable fact of exposition here. If verse is characterized by metre, and only by the fact of metre and its consequences, then it follows that a discussion of prose must be a discussion of the nature of literary language itself without the special problems that metre presents.

It is significant that histories of prose are rare and largely unsuccessful. To write a history of English prose, for instance – a task no one has attempted at length since the First World War – would require a single and yet decisive feature, or group of features, to be observed in operation in hundreds or even thousands of texts. And it is not yet clear what such a feature would be. The content of prose would not do, since it would represent something approaching the whole activity of the intellectual energy of the English peoples. Form is more promising than content here, but the form of prose is not an easy concept. Its linguistic features, such as imagery, it shares with verse. If prose is merely what is left of literature when metre is taken out, then it seems a hopelessly residual concept. But in practice prose has often evolved syntactical conventions peculiar to itself, and probably a history of prose would have to centre upon a history of its syntax. English prose in the sixteenth century, outside the drama, is widely believed to have adopted two contrasting syntactical patterns, the convoluted Ciceronian and the curt

* Hulme, *Speculations* (London, 1924), p. 135; Sartre, *Qu'est-ce que la littérature* (Paris, 1948), p. 17.

Senecan – though these terms are crudely traditional, and do an injustice to the variety of Cicero's own prescriptions, and still more to the variety of Renaissance prose itself. The scientific revolution in English prose in the 1660s and after is equally a fact of syntax, as a study of Dryden's revision of his essay *Of Dramatick Poesie* between 1668 and 1684 would show; and the elaboration by Johnson, Burke and Gibbon of Restoration and Augustan prose into a more formal and complex tool, at once more dignified and more ironic than Dryden's, is a subtler example of the same phenomenon. Syntax may not be the most important fact of prose style in many individual instances; but it is probably the fact that holds out the best hope of a traceable evolution in a field of enquiry as vast and as various as this. And yet such a study would certainly call for sharper critical instruments for describing the facts of syntax than are yet current in Western literary discussion.

The analysis of individual prose works may seem a more promising beginning, but the difficulties remain large. It is not at all clear what constitutes the individuality of a prose style. Word-frequency is one possibility, but it is one that remains to be demonstrated. Baudelaire once claimed that if we could identify the words an author used most often, then we should have discovered his obsession; but this is a remark which cannot be regarded literally. The commonest word in the novels of Dickens is almost certainly 'the'; but this tells us nothing about Dickens's obsession, if he had one, though it may be a fact of some interest about the English language. Frequency is only a significant factor in style to the extent that it is exceptional; and to recognize the exceptional, one must first recognize the norm. And the norm for the whole of literary language would hardly serve, even if it could be obtained: we should need a norm that operated in its place, time and circumstances. The language of a novel poses the complexity of the problem in its full force. It most naturally invites comparison with other novels; but then the novel is a literary *genus* of a multiple kind, and may vary widely in accordance with the audience for whom it is designed. And it may demand comparison with the styles and usages of quite other forms, as the language of Fielding demands comparison not only with Richardson's, which it sometimes parodies, but equally with the language of the historian and the epic poet, to which it claims at times to belong. It is usual to discover in such enquiries that we do not really know with much precision what is normal and what exceptional. It remains perfectly true that an informed reader can recognize the exceptional when he sees it, which is perhaps all that Baudelaire meant. Concordances, especially, can perform a clear and limited function in confirming the significant oddities that come to light. But the hope that the essence of a prose style could be isolated in this purely mechanical way seems remote.

In any case, the meaning of words, in an absolute sense, is established only in context, so that there is a clear sense in which the 'same' word even in the same author is not the same thing. This is not offered as an occult literary observation: in fact it may apply even more strongly to non-literary language such as ordinary conversation, where the human context of a visible auditor is often more powerfully determinant than that of an invisible poet. If I say 'Good morning' to someone, the significance of what I say – which has very little to do with the separate meanings of either 'good' or 'morning' – is powerfully determined by the immediate human context. If I address such words to an acquaintance seen that morning for the first time, then the remark is an expected formula. If I have already seen him, the remark is likely to be facetious or absent-minded. If we have just quarrelled, then the remark may have powerful diplomatic significance; and if the interlocutor is in fact a total stranger, it is significant in a wholly different way, as a manner of initiating a new acquaintanceship. And there are numerous other possibilities of a conflicting kind. Yet nobody thinks of 'Good morning' as an ambiguous expression: if it means many things, it is none the less nearly always clear in context what it does mean. And literature is commonly thought of as being more complex than ordinary conversation. This indeed it is, even in its simplest form, and independently of the fact that it is commonly more ambitious than conversation, and concerned to organize knowledge of greater range and complexity. The verbal patterns of speech, after all, include devices which are lost on the page, such as intonation. To compose a sentence on the page, for just this reason, is a far more conscious and difficult operation than speech. By his special skills, an author offers compensation and more for something which, since the decay of the oral tradition in literature, has now been largely lost.

But it is still true that literature is essentially a social activity. Books are published in order to be read, and those who write them ordinarily hope that they will be read. The communication effected by literature is painfully indirect, it is true, being mediated through the slow processes of the setting of type and the correction of proofs; but it is still there, and in most aspects it is likely to share with ordinary spoken language the common properties of comprehension. But what, after all, is it like to understand language? and how, more specifically, does literary prose shape itself for the purpose of making itself readily understood?

It is now familiar in linguistic study that verbal communication is a parallel process by which the hearer or reader, from the beginning of the utterance, provisionally forms a silent sentence which, so far as he is able, resembles the sentence he hears or reads. Each successive detail in a sentence affects, usually by diminution, the probabilities that remain. Comprehension is completed when the silent sentence conforms to that which is spoken or written, and when the parallel between the two, hitherto irregular, has been made exact. Many of the familiar difficulties of discussing literary style, though they cannot perhaps be resolved by this view, can certainly be posed in a clearer way. A parallel which is present and perfect from the start would certainly render the work tedious: and conversely, a case where the reader cannot attempt a silent sentence at all represents a case of total obscurity. Literature in its social aspect aims at some condition between these two extremes of hopelessness, the extremes of the banal and the unintelligible. And yet this view only re-affirms the difficulties of stylistics as a literary discipline, since it adds to the variety of literary convention itself a new and still more variable element: that of the variety of readers themselves. The degree to which the readers of literature understand the literary conventions that operate seems likely to be a matter of vast diversity; and the most natural conclusion to the argument seems to be one of total scepticism.

But to argue like this is to neglect the large and important sense in which literary conventions are themselves verifiable. Some readers, it is true, understand the conventions of literature better than others. But these conventions surely exist whether they happen to be understood or not. A reader who complained that a twentieth-century thriller lacked in depth of characterization could certainly be shown, by reference to other thrillers, that the supposed deficiency was in fact a necessary element in the work. Again and again historical criticism has recorded triumphs by demonstrating the literary kind to which the work belongs, and in what degree it conforms to its kind. Probably such considerations as these leave the problem of prose intact, in all its baffling diversity. But they serve at least to render the outlines of the problem clearer. Prose exists and flourishes in relation to a vast mass of existing knowledge concerning the given state of the language and of its literary conventions. And this relationship is deliberately inexact, in the sense that the author meant it to be so. He attracts the silent sentence of the informed reader, and then repels it. He conforms and rebels. And to say all this is to re-emphasize the difficulty of realizing a history of prose. Certainly the extreme relativity of its values seems to render any absolute statement unsure. The same device of syntax may convey different implications in different ages and even, according to context, in the same age. Words change their significance not just in the lexical sense, but in the sense that they grow through literary employment, are expelled, and later re-enter in new contexts. A vital prose tradition is infinitely sensitive in the exploitation of such effects. It is no use demanding, like the French Academy, that a state of perfection should be achieved and then maintained. The art of literature licenses an abuse of language which is understandably the despair of lexicographers, but in this unequal struggle it must be the good grace of the lexicographer to submit.

METAPHOR

Metaphor is only one of many kinds of imagery, or of analogy considered as a rhetorical device, and much that is true of metaphor is equally true of such other kinds as simile, conceit and extended illustration. But metaphor poses the problem of analogy in language in a peculiarly acute way, since it occurs by displacement, entering the language without the explicitness of such warning terms as 'as' or 'like'; and once entered, it may choose not to leave, so that any given language is likely to be full of dead or dying metaphors which may never be ejected from its system. And there are many degrees of vitality. Some dead metaphors, such as the English verb 'to understand', have been dead for so long that even philologists cannot explain them. Others, like 'to comprehend' or, in a similar sense, 'to grasp', are dead and yet readily explicable. Others again, like 'a wildcat strike', are in process of rapid decay, so that it is possible to talk of 'a wildcat', or even to use the verb 'to wildcat', meaning to strike without warning. Others again, for the moment, are in their full vigour; though it may be true of all metaphors, as of all human beings, that their end is predictable in their beginning, and that all their lives they 'grow towards death'.

Professional analysts of imagery, such as Aristotle in the *Rhetoric* or sixteenth-century rhetoricians such as Puttenham, have tended to ignore these considerations and to write as if figures of speech were stable in language rather than subject to rapid obsolescence. More seriously still, perhaps, they have tended to assume that in a logical sense literal language is normal and figurative language exceptional – parasitic upon literal language, usually for some ornamental purpose. But the analogical properties of language are much more far-reaching than this traditional account allows. Indeed it is the concept of the literal in language that is now rightly questioned. The British Empiricists, among many others, tended to assume in a familiar way that literal language was the norm of usage. More than that, they often claimed that it was in some sense truer, or more reliable, than figurative language. And most characteristically of all, they claimed it to be more appropriate to discursive, especially scientific prose. In the same traditional view, poetry might use what figures it pleases, being not so much a mode of truth as a delightful hocus-pocus, a way of moving or entertaining. In the Empiricists all these mistakes are commonly drawn into one, and expressed historically: language was held to have begun as something literal, and to have developed the abuses of the figurative in the Middle Ages as a late corruption, to be rescued from the sins of metaphor and the rest by Bacon, Newton and the Royal Society. Hume, who was himself a devoted and often acute reader of poetry, puts this historically implausible view in these terms in his *History of England* (1762):

On the origin of letters among the Greeks, the genius of poets and orators, as might naturally be expected, was distinguished by an amiable simplicity which, whatever rudeness may sometimes attend it, is so fitted to express the genuine movements of nature and passion. . . . The glaring figures of discourse, the pointed antithesis, the unnatural conceit, the jingle of words: such false ornaments were not employed by early writers; not because they were rejected, but because they scarce ever occurred to them.   'James I', appendix

Hume's fantasy, which represents the view of many generations of Europeans, is no doubt based upon the natural though mistaken expectation that early forms tend to be simple and late forms complex ('as might naturally be expected'), though a study of Homer or of *Beowulf* would hardly support this view. It was equally easy to suppose with Locke that language would become more truthful by becoming more literal:

If we would speak of things as they are, we must allow that all the art of rhetoric, besides order and clearness, all the artificial and figurative application of words eloquence hath invented, are for nothing else but to insinuate wrong ideas, move the passions, and thereby mislead the judgment; and so indeed are perfect cheats.

Essay concerning Human Understanding (1690) 3.10.34

The readiest way to refute the false scientism of these views is to indicate how much of the 'artificial and figurative' has entered such studiously literal language as Locke's by the back door: 'insinuate', 'move', 'mislead'. A man does not write literally by deciding to do so. If it is objected, as it often is, that 'it is impossible ... to handle a scientific subject in metaphorical terms',★ it is right to ask in reply what other terms there are. In an absolute sense, all language is analogical. The earliest literary documents that survive employ figures of speech abundantly; there is no certain evidence that language has grown more figurative with the centuries; and scientific terms are as metaphorical as any other, being coined, usually from classical roots, with a view to recording helpful resemblances, as 'molecule' derives from the Latin '*moles*' and signifies 'a little heap' of atoms. It is true that the metaphorical value of such scientific coinages is quickly lost, and that the physicist's understanding of the term is in no way dependent upon his knowing or remembering the analogy which gave it birth. But then the same is true of the dead or dying metaphors of literary language. This is to emphasize yet again the community of character that unites literary language with language in general. Indeed, if we consider those difficult and borderline examples of the literal or the figurative, such as 'the wing of an aeroplane' or 'the leg of a table', where the status of 'wing' and 'leg' are doubtful not because of any historical process that has overtaken them but simply in themselves, then the essential complexity of metaphor begins to assume the proportions of the complexity of language itself. Even the line between the literal and the analogical cannot

★ C. K. Ogden and I. A. Richards, *The Meaning of Meaning* (London, 1923), p. 4.

be drawn with precision; and this, not because the line has not yet been discovered, but rather because it is not there. Any line would necessarily falsify the facts, that is to say, since the language we commonly call literal is already analogical in a high degree.

But to argue like this is perhaps to suggest that our confusion is greater than it is. If all language is in some absolute sense analogical, it does not follow that it is all analogical in the same sense or to the same extent. It is certainly possible to attribute a clear meaning to such remarks as 'I don't wish to be taken literally' or, like Oscar Wilde's embarrassed clergyman in *The Importance of Being Earnest*, 'I was speaking metaphorically. My metaphor was drawn from bees.' Differences between the literal and the metaphorical are often clearly recognizable – and not less so because such clear cases are interconnected by intermediate examples which are by no means clear. In a developed and highly self-conscious poetic tradition, such as Latin poetry of the Augustan age, or twentieth-century English, such intermediate cases may become a large element in poetic language, and such questions as 'Is this imagery or literal speech?' come to look crude in their assumptions.

> *Begin, ephebe, by perceiving the idea*
> *Of this invention, this invented world,*
> *The inconceivable idea of the sun.*
>
> *You must become an ignorant man again*
> *And see the sun again with an ignorant eye*
> *And see it clearly in the idea of it.*
>
> *Never suppose an inventing mind as source*
> *Of this idea nor for that mind compose*
> *A voluminous master folded in his fire . . .*

Wallace Stevens, 'Notes toward a Supreme Fiction' (1942)

It would be absurd to ask of most of this passage whether it is literal or figurative. Imagery is, so to speak, held at arm's length by the poet. The poem is something like a warning against imagery, indeed: a paradoxical demand that the poem should dispense with language as it is commonly known and enter into the object – 'not ideas about the thing but the thing itself'. It is only because the figurative possibilities of the subject, such as the classical gods, are a secret joke shared by poet and reader ('A voluminous master folded in his fire') that they can be admitted into the poem on special tolerance, like children at a tea-party, while the pretence of literal language is elegantly maintained:

> *How clean the sun when seen in its idea,*
> *Washed in the remotest cleanliness of a heaven*
> *That has expelled us and our images . . .*

The argument concerning literary imagery may be carried a stage further than this, though at the risk of growing more than ever tentative. It has been suggested that metaphor is of two kinds, and that this contrast reflects something characteristic about literary language itself. 'On the one hand,' it has been said, 'there is the metaphor which we invent to teach by; on the other, the metaphor from which we learn. They might be called the Master's metaphor and the Pupil's metaphor. The first is freely chosen; it is one among many modes of expression; it does not at all hinder, and only very slightly helps, the thought of its maker. The second is not chosen at all; it is the unique expression of a meaning that we cannot have on any other terms.'* Perhaps the second kind of metaphor, the pupillary, helps to explain such cases as romantic symbol, like Blake's tiger or the albatross in Coleridge's *Ancient Mariner*, where explanations may characteristically help to show what is there, and yet cannot hope to show everything that is there. The poet himself, one may suspect, could do no better, since the symbol is 'the unique expression of a meaning' that he cannot have on other terms. And it would surely be odd for discursive prose, such as the scientist's, to admit such a device. Scientific terms are often metaphors, and there may be occasional cases such as 'sound-waves' where the metaphor may even assist in further research. But such metaphors are not 'unique expressions of a meaning'; so little, indeed, that the scientist does not even need to understand their metaphorical function (just as many scientists are doubtless ignorant of the defunct metaphor in 'molecule') in order to understand them. It may be that the principle of the pupillary image is of far wider application than the romantic symbol, which is still less than two hundred years old. Great poems of any period may be said, in a sense only a little removed from this discussion, to represent 'unique expressions'. They tend to resist explanation in a total sense – which is not to say that explanation is pointless, but only that it is necessarily incomplete. The meaning of *Othello* is not

* C. S. Lewis, 'Bluspels and Flalansferes', in his *Rehabilitations* (Oxford, 1939), pp. 140–41.

the same as anything we can truthfully say of it, or even the total sum of such sayings. Those who speak of poetry as that which cannot be translated are putting a view parallel to this; and the point against translation, which is often made in an excessively sceptical and absolute way, needs to be qualified in much the same sense. The virtue of a translation, like that of a good critical explanation, may lie precisely in the fact that it does not tell the whole truth about a great original. It draws attention to an element to which attention needs to be drawn, and triumphs by its very partiality. After all, if it is the original we want, we have no business, except provisionally, to have dealings with anything else.

4

THE LITERARY PAST

Few arts in the English-speaking world today look so thriving and yet so unpretentious as the art of literary history. It is thriving in the plain sense that there is a great deal of it. Discoveries are certainly being made about the literary past, and at great speed. Literary history is demanded, commissioned, published and reprinted as never before. Its lack of pretension, which hardly amounts to a merit, lies in the contrasting circumstance that, in a serious intellectual sense, no one actively concerned with literary studies expects much of it. To expect today, as a European might reasonably have done a century ago, that a great intellectual discovery should be announced in a history of literature is plainly unlikely.

The sharp descent of literary history from the status of a great intellectual discipline to that of a convenient act of popularization can reasonably be dated to the years following the First World War. It is remarkable how suddenly, in the 1920s and after, the critical essay replaced the narrative form of literary history as the staple of literary study. The most influential arbiter of literary judgement in the English-speaking world in this century, T. S. Eliot, effected his revolution almost entirely through the mode of the brief essay, never writing a literary history of anything, mocking delicately at those who did, and willingly abandoning to lesser men the task of making connected sense of his own striking historical intuitions, such as the celebrated 'dissociation of sensibility' among English poets in the seventeenth century. I. A. Richards, who moved two generations to active literary controversy in the wake of Eliot, has chosen to write treatises rather than histories. Other decisive works like William Empson's *Seven Types of Ambiguity* (1930) or his *Structure of Complex Words* (1951) tend to be articulated series of essays rather than continuous narrative studies; and though history does not need to be narrative, it certainly presupposes an active concern with the priorities within the events it describes. *The Oxford History of English Literature*, which began to appear in 1945 as an ambitious attempt to recreate the achievement of the *Cambridge History* (1907–16), clearly suffers from the sudden lack of confidence that had overtaken literary history in the intervening decades; in an attempt to compromise with a sense of uncertainty, perhaps, it has adopted the practice of reducing biographical information on individual authors to footnotes, as if aware that the case for such information can no longer be assumed. And in 1947 an American journal published an article 'The Intentional Fallacy' by W. K. Wimsatt and Monroe C. Beardsley which formidably summarized the objections of a generation of New Critics, arguing that 'the design or intention of the author is neither available nor desirable as a standard for judging'. The question whether literary history remained a possibility if the study of the author's intention had to be abandoned remained, during the brief heyday of the New Criticism in the 1940s and 1950s, a matter for confused debate. But nobody doubted that the doctrine was somehow or other radically subversive of literary history in the traditional sense.

In this chapter I shall consider whether it could ever be possible, in the light of such familiar objections, to recover the tradition of a confident historiography of literature. Can one ever again write literary history, in the extended sense, that is not demonstrably wrong, in the sense that it is not contradicted by the present state of our knowledge of political and social history, of language, and of literature itself? And if so, could such literary history ever be more than trite, or could it ever again aspire to large and original contributions to human knowledge? Such questions may sound demoralizing. But they are meant at this point of the argument merely to sum up, with some mild exaggeration, the difference between the intellectual climates of the twentieth and the nineteenth centuries, when the composition of intellectual history – Ruskin on modern painters, Sainte-Beuve on the Pléiade and Port-Royal, Burckhardt on the Italian Renaissance, Buckle on the history of civilization, Nietzsche on the origins of tragedy, Frazer in the *Golden Bough* – could without affectation be numbered among the larger achievements of the human mind.

This chapter will take the form of summarizing and refuting

some of the principal objections levelled against literary history, not always explicitly, in the present century.

CAN LITERARY HISTORY BE ORIGINAL?

Nineteenth-century literary history served the unexceptionable function of showing what was there to be read, and at a period when the great modern literatures were becoming educational subjects on a large scale for the first time. Nobody, it may be supposed, would wish to question that function even now, and it is likely that extended histories of English literature, for instance, will continue to be written and published. But equally, nobody would normally attribute to that function anything greater than an elementary interest. It may be the task of the schoolboy to find out what there is to be read, but it is the task of maturity to read it, so that a history of a literature conceived in these terms can at the best only map a familiar terrain as a guide to the beginner.

This is a comprehensible and familiar view of what literary history can do, but it is based upon a highly exaggerated notion of the degree to which the great modern literatures are known territories. It is perilously easy to suppose that the main tasks of literary history have now been performed. The triviality of many subjects accepted by universities for literary research, and even by publishers as books, is often adduced as evidence here. It is natural to suppose all this to be symptomatic of a subject nearing the point of exhaustion, and common to find scholars engaged in literary research who are ready to sell the pass by claiming to think just that. In a similar way, it is said, the study of physics in the late nineteenth century was thought by many physicists to be nearing completion, with a few loose ends to be accounted for by the end of the century: but the loose ends proved more interesting than anybody could then imagine. And it is possible that literary history today is in a similar condition. Nobody engaged in the serious teaching of English, certainly, could suppose on a full examination of the evidence that all the best subjects have been 'done'; though equally, the teacher may often feel that the questions he finds unanswered are too momentous to be confided to a beginner. There is still no history either of Old or of Middle English which consolidates the achievement of W. P. Ker in the 1890s and after in demonstrating a wide grasp of the intellectual issues involved in the texts and an awareness of their place in a European setting. If English Renaissance drama is amply discussed, its prose is not. It is notable, indeed, that there is no satisfactory history of English prose in any age. The relations between the novel and society have been well, if incompletely, discussed: but novels tell stories, and there is no good study of what it is to tell a story. There is no convincing study of Restoration drama, none of Dryden and his contemporaries as poets, and no connected study of the English eighteenth century which clarifies the relation between its greatest authors and the European Enlightenment. There are good individual studies of the intellectual debts and preoccupations of certain of the English Romantic poets, but no connected history of English romanticism that makes full use of these discoveries. The Victorian novel has received most rewarding attention since the 1940s, but the controversial prose of the Victorians far less; and there is still no work of the first interest on the totality of Victorian poetry. These deficiencies in English literary history are not mentioned here in order to provoke offers of help. Anyone with the capacity to do work like this has the capacity to see without prompting that it needs to be done. But they certainly suggest that English literary history is a study still little advanced beyond the pioneer stage.

The question at issue here is the prospect of a continuing and original study of literary history rather than particular answers to particular questions. If large questions are unanswered, then a prospect of long and vital activity is clearly in view: actually to answer them would be to defeat the argument. And to assert that they need to be answered is not meant to imply that in the present state of knowledge they can be answered. There may be convincing reasons, for the moment, why they cannot. It is easy and even convincing to argue, for example, that the time for a definitive study of Victorian poetry has not yet come: but then it is precisely because it has not yet come that the future of literary history seems in principle to be so well assured. The loss of confidence in the discipline in the first half of the twentieth century, at least in the English-speaking world, may soon come to look like a mere eddy in a flood that no fashion like the New Criticism can stem. It is not credible, after all, that societies as advanced and as leisured as the West should ever lose curiosity about the processes by which their civilizations were formed. And the homeland of a great world literature, such as England, is in no position to set a limit to the interest the world may choose to take in what has now become its lingua franca. If the English do not write English literary history, in a word, then somebody else will.

ARE POEMS HISTORICAL ACTS?

But the nagging doubt about literary history in the present century does, after all, have more than the semblance of an objection of principle and is something more than a mere intellectual fashion. It is based upon a persuasive scepticism about the status of a poem as an historical act. This scepticism needs to be seen in perspective. Nobody has ever doubted that poems were written in the past. But it does not plainly follow that a poem is an historical document in the sense that it derives its chief interest and value from the personality and purpose of its author in the historical conditions under which he wrote. The debate surrounding the 'intentional fallacy' has been concerned with this larger issue – an issue in which 'the poet's intention' is only one of the problems involved. To speak of the intentional fallacy at all was to react against an historical view of literature which, by the 1940s, had been dominant in the West for over a hundred years. And to accept it as a fallacy was to offer a view deeply subversive to literary history, as it was meant to be, since the literary historian is bound to assume a correspondence of some kind between what the poet and his age might reasonably be thought to have in mind, on the one hand, and the true meaning of the poem on the other. When the historian investigates the question whether the figure of Shylock in *The Merchant of Venice* represents an anti-Semitic view, for instance, he regards the question as hardly distinguishable from a question about what Shakespeare and his first audience would have thought of Shylock. If the literary historian is to be told that the play now exists independently of its creator, and that the modern reader or actor is entitled to make what sense he can of it, then he had better gather up his writing materials and go elsewhere. Such an atmosphere is not for him.

In the following discussion, which is offered among other things as a refutation of the claim that intentionalism is a fallacy, I shall deliberately widen the scope of the argument to include issues beyond the intention of the poet himself. This procedure is justifiable to the extent that the issue involved in contemporary controversy is genuinely wider than the protagonists have always fully realized. What is involved here, at its widest extent, is the momentous issue whether literature is primarily to be studied as a purposive activity or not. It was among the greatest achievements of nineteenth-century historiography to emphasize, perhaps even to exaggerate, the sense of purpose out of which a great poem is born. If this process is to be put into reverse, and if literature is now to be regarded as the first audiences for the Homeric poems perhaps regarded the *Iliad*, or as those who listen to pop-songs today regard what they hear – experiences involving curiosity about the performers, it may be supposed, rather than about the creators – then powerful reasons would be needed for supposing that such a reversal would represent a gain to civilized values. For most men who have valued the literary experience in the past century and more, literature is by contrast the supremely purposive activity: 'an objective, a projected result,' as Henry James once called it emphatically, adding sententiously: 'it is life that is the unconscious, the agitated, the struggling, floundering cause'.★

It was the Victorians themselves who raised the first protests against the prevailing obsession of their age with the pastness of the past. Robert Browning, who was perhaps the first Englishman to consider the issue in print, argued in a preface of 1852 on Shelley that, in the case of 'objective' poets at least, biography may be dispensed with as 'no more necessary to an understanding or enjoyment ... than is a model or anatomy of some tropical tree to the right tasting of the fruit we are familiar with on the market-stall'. Saintsbury sometimes claimed to believe – in his study of *Dryden* (1881), for example – that only the verbal analysis of poems can be defended in principle, though he practised many other sorts himself. Matthew Arnold spent half a lifetime emphasizing the essential timelessness of great poetry. Oscar Wilde spoke of the work of art as having 'an independent life of its own' which may 'deliver a message far other than that which was put in its lips to say'. Quiller-Couch, in his Cambridge lectures *On the Art of Writing* (1916), held that the greatest literature is always

> *seraphically free*
> *From taint of personality.*

★ 'The Lesson of Balzac' (1905), reprinted in *The House of Fiction*, edited by Leon Edel (London, 1957), p. 64.

E. M. Forster, in an essay of 1925 entitled 'Anonymity', argued that 'a poem is absolute', and that 'all literature tends towards a condition of anonymity. . . . It wants not to be signed.' Like so many campaigns against the Victorians, the campaign against literary history is itself Victorian in its origins. But the real reason for rehearsing these objections, which if placed beside the manifestoes of French '*l'art pour l'art*' and Proust's *Contre Sainte-Beuve* would make a massive dossier, is to emphasize the scope and variety of the campaign rather than its antiquity. And many of these issues are rightly associated, various as they are. If in the following account I attempt to refute the case point by point, it is rather in the hope of marshalling a lucid argument in favour of a new tradition of literary history than out of any inclination to convict others of muddle or equivocation.

First, there is the issue of evaluation by intention. I mention this here only for the sake of completeness, since no one, it may be supposed, has ever seriously held that a poem is good because its author intended it to be so. To deny, against Wimsatt and Beardsley, that an author's intention is properly 'a standard for judging . . . success' is to consider a phrase that opens many issues: but so far as this one is concerned, it would be better to suppose that it had never existed.

The appeal to fulfilled intention, however, is a more serious matter, in the sense that it is a fallacy which is plausible enough to be believed. It is often suggested that a poet has done enough if he fully performs what he set out to do, and often objected that it is improper to demand of the author that he should have written a different book. But it is notable that good critics often demand of an author, and with good reason, that he should have written a different book. And it is not at all obvious that in principle they should not. When Dr Johnson, in his Life of Dryden, complained of *Absalom and Achitophel* that

> the original structure of the poem was defective; allegories drawn to great length will always break; Charles could not run continually parallel with David,

he is certainly regretting that Dryden had not written a radically different poem, and to object that he should accept the poem for what it is amounts to a demand that he should abdicate his function altogether. But then to fulfil an intention, in literature as in life, is not necessarily to behave as one should. If a man sets out to shoot his mother-in-law, and does so, one may applaud his marksmanship but not the deed itself.

If these were the only uses to which the determination of authorial intention were put by critics, it would be easy to agree that intentionalism is a fallacy. But they are not. After all, there is the wide and distinct issue of the distribution of literature: not just in the way of mechanical improvements like the invention of printing, but in matters which affect the literary experience at its deepest roots. It is of much less than decisive importance that Chaucer did not intend his poems to be printed, for instance; though the fact that he probably intended his poems to be heard rather than silently perused is a fact of real interest. To print is to multiply copies, and the world is evidently right to assume that Chaucer's intentions in the matter are of little concern now. But a new form of distribution might represent a more radical change of emphasis than this. Milton is unlikely to have intended *Samson Agonistes* for the stage; Shakespeare designed his plays altogether for performance, and is unlikely to have taken much interest in their publication. Again, nobody supposes such intentions to be decisive upon posterity; but equally, the probability that *Samson* was written for the study rather than for the stage is a major fact about *Samson*. Anyone who supposed that Milton was attempting a theatrical rival to Dryden's *Conquest of Granada*, for example, would probably prove an unreceptive reader of Milton's play. It is said that Tibetan tea, which is partly composed of rancid butter, is revolting to Western tastes if considered as tea but acceptable if considered as soup. When we ask of a poem questions of the order of 'What did the poet intend it for?' – whether stage or study, whether court audience or popular – the answer seems in principle likely to be useful to the extent that it is accurate. This is surely a good question to ask, and anybody who objects at this point that the search for the author's intention is necessarily a fallacy should be sent about his business.

It seems likely, too, that the purposive property of literature is under unnecessary attack at this point. To concede, for instance, that a good stage-play could be written by someone who is not trying to write a stage-play at all is not only to concede something vastly improbable in itself. It is also to humiliate the status of literature as a human act. As Wordsworth put it, a poet is a man speaking to men. On the whole, we listen to those who address us in order to discover what they mean. It is also true that, in rare and memorable instances, people say remarkable things without meaning them. But anybody who conducted his social life on the principle that conversation is worth listening to only or mainly for the sake of such instances would be guilty of continuous discourtesy and, still more important, would find himself much the worse for the bargain. Freaks in creation exist: Musset, for example, is said to have written his plays with no thought for the stage, though in fact they succeed there. But freaks are exactly what such cases are.

A further support for the doctrine of the poem as an historical act seems to arise from the study of the literary kinds. This is an extension of the preceding argument concerning the distribution of literature, and one to be distinguished from it only with difficulty. Nobody, in all probability, has ever denied that on the whole a novel is a novel, or an elegy an elegy, because its author intended it to be so. But in the anti-historical atmosphere of the early twentieth century it was possible to protest that, since works usually bear the evidence of the kind to which they belong on their faces, the historical critic had little to contribute by 'going outside the poem'. This view is certainly mistaken. When a reader recognizes a novel to be such, or chooses it because it is such, he is certainly using evidence from outside the work as well as evidence from within. He is recognizing features in the novel he holds in his hand which resemble those in other novels he has read. The uncertainty that overhangs early and unestablished literary forms, such as the novel in early eighteenth-century England, and the hesitating attempts to confer dignity and status upon such forms, as in Fielding's formula of the 'comic epic in prose', are examples of the problems that ignorance or uncertainty concerning the literary kinds can raise. And when the literary historian identifies the lineage of poems whose pedigrees have fallen into oblivion – when he identifies one of *The Canterbury Tales* as a beast-fable, for instance, and another as a romance of courtly love – he is restoring to the consciousness of the reader knowledge of an indispensable kind. But then the achievements of genre-identification seem among the most massive and incontestable triumphs of historical criticism over the past two hundred years. To demonstrate the complex relation between Spenser's *Faerie Queene*, for instance, and the Italian epics which in the sixteenth century dominated the mode of romantic epic throughout Europe, is to restore to the English poem the status and interest of a masterpiece and rescue it from the imputation of a work that might otherwise barely survive as a loose collection of occasional beauties.

If the wider problem of language is considered in the same light, the historical status of literature grows steadily and inescapably clearer. It was sometimes objected of historical criticism that it encouraged a chaos of romantic individualism on the part of poets in their use of language, whereas the fashionable demand in the earlier years of the century was for continuity, order and 'the tradition'. Words, it was emphasized by the New Critics and others, need to be disciplined to fit the norms of language, so that the poem itself might ideally exist in a void of space or time, a formal object or 'well wrought urn'. 'The work after being produced must continue to exist independently of the author's intentions or thoughts about it. The idiosyncrasies of the author must not be repugnant to the norm.'* But certain celebrated literary effects, after all, *are* repugnant to the norms of language as established in their age. The obscenities of Swift are repugnant to the norms of polite language in the Augustan age, as they were meant to be, and it is just their repugnancy – in this case, their power to shock – that makes them tell. Some English poets are well known to have used linguistic devices – Milton's syntax, Dylan Thomas's diction – which deviate from any known use of language in their age, and the reader is meant to sense that a deviation or perversion of usage is happening. It is admittedly tempting to suppose that there must be some limit to the degree of repugnancy that is admissible in literature; and certainly there is a point beyond which language can only turn into nonsense. But then nonsense can be literature too, and sometimes is – a warning that, if there is a limit to be placed, it may be worth insisting that it should be placed at some remote point.

In any case, to speak of norms of language is to concede, however unwittingly, the case for an historical discipline. The poem itself is not the norm, after all, and in itself it cannot reveal what the norm is. In order to demonstrate the idiosyncrasies of Milton's syntax in *Paradise Lost*, it is of no use to confine the discussion to the poem itself: one must look at other documents by Milton and by his contemporaries. The oddities of Thomas's diction exist only in relation to mid-twentieth-century usages outside his poems. If we are anxious to pretend that poems could ever 'exist independently of the author's intentions', we had

* Wimsatt and Beardsley, in *Dictionary of World Literature*, edited by Joseph T. Shipley (New York, 1942), p. 327.

better banish all idea of the norm. And in banishing that, it is easy to see, a great deal of significance must go too. A reader content to suppose that Milton's language was the ordinary language of his age would certainly miss much of the significance of *Paradise Lost*. To evade in all circumstances the study of the author's intentions, in fact, is at times to evade the meaning of the poem itself.

What does it mean to speak usefully of an author's intentions in his poem? I emphasize 'usefully', since it is right to concede at once that such discussions need not be useful at all; and doctrines like 'the intentional fallacy' probably represent an exaggerated reaction to this realization, obvious as it is. But then the historian, whether of literature or of anything else, is in no way committed to the view that everything about the past is of equal interest: in fact it is precisely the historian who is expected to show the greatest skill and experience in sorting the important evidence from the insignificant. That is his trade. When we have shown that much skilful and informed speculation about the poets' intention does not help in reading his poems – a charge sometimes levelled against J. L. Lowes's study of Coleridge, *The Road to Xanadu*, for example – nothing decisive has been said or shown against the nature of such enquiries in general. If it sometimes helps, it does not follow that it always helps. Equally, the historical critic need not allow himself to be held committed to the view that his enquiry is utterly limited to the question of what the poet intended. It is notorious that Shakespeare would not understand much modern Shakespearean criticism. But then that, in itself, is hardly an objection to what the critics are doing. Newton, equally, would presumably not understand modern physics. It seems likely that one or the other, if he could return to life, might be trained in understanding and would prove an unusually apt pupil; but to demand of the historical critic that he should in all circumstances limit himself to seeing in a Shakespeare play only as much as the dramatist himself might have seen and in something like the very terms in which he would have seen it is to ask, in large measure, that literary studies should be stopped.

On the other hand, the historical criticism of literature imposes a limit of another and more reasonable kind than this. If it does not forbid elucidation beyond the point where the poet himself might cease to follow the argument, it commonly forbids explanations that run counter to what the poet could have thought or felt. The enlargement of 'intended' to 'thought or felt' is a safety-device in this argument, but an allowable one if it is conceded how much wider than the conscious and articulate intention of the poet the scope of the modern argument about the poet's intention has proved. To set out to show that Shakespeare was something like a Marxist, or that he had a horror of autocracy and the police-state, is to attempt to prove something that runs counter not only to the texts of the plays but, short of the remotest freak of intellectual history, counter to anything an Elizabethan could have believed. When one exclaims 'But Shakespeare *can't* have thought that', the curtain that drops upon the line of argument is a curtain that has good reason to be there.

'SUBCONSCIOUS' INTENTION

In studying the poet's intention in his poem, is there a useful distinction to be drawn between intentions that are conscious and those that are not? Could there, for that matter, be any question of preferring conscious to subconscious intention, or *vice versa*, on grounds of authenticity? It seems unlikely that there could ever be a single and simple answer to questions of such complexity as these; but in saying that, and in showing that, doctrines of a rasher and more absolute kind would at least have been rendered more difficult to sustain. Literature is not a single substance with a single set of properties: it represents countless systems of language at their greatest extent and diversity. It is far more diverse than ordinary conversation, for example; and yet no one would seriously expect a single and simple answer to the question whether, in listening to the conversation of a friend or acquaintance, one should attribute greater importance to what he consciously means to say, on the one hand, or to what one guesses from his word or gesture to be the secret and unsuspected springs of his behaviour. It would depend upon the friend, one would reply, and upon the context of the conversation. An answer as dull and as accurate as this would at least have the merit of dismissing the notion that there is a single correct way in which to interpret language.

It is certainly clear that in literature, as in other uses of language, both concerns are normal. There is nothing exceptional or remote about the activity of psycho-analysing an author as one reads him, or a friend as one listens: though the term 'psycho-analysis' suggests a more formal and regulated activity than any that is commonly involved here. To ask, in reading Byron's *Don Juan*, whether Byron's exhibitionism of style and moral licence does not subconsciously reveal a sense of tragic despair is not in itself to offend against any reasonable canon of judgement. It is an appropriate question, just as it may be appropriate to wonder of an acquaintance who boasts of his sexual prowess whether it is more than a boast. Much intelligent comment on *Wuthering Heights* and *Jane Eyre* plausibly attributes to the novels an interest in feminine sexuality which the Brontë sisters themselves would have been shocked to learn of. Or consider this interpretation of 'Sohrab and Rustum', which exploits the fact that Matthew Arnold's father was a famous headmaster:

However dangerous may be the practice of unraveling unconscious literary symbolism, it is almost impossible not to find throughout 'Sohrab and Rustum' at least a shadowy personal significance. The strong son is slain by the mightier father; and in the end Sohrab draws his father's spear from his own side to let out his life and end the anguish. We watch Arnold in his later youth and we must wonder if he is not, in a psychical sense, doing the same thing.*

The example is an unusually pure case of imputing a subconscious intention to a poet, since there is no external evidence that Arnold consciously disliked or resented his father. He would almost certainly have been shocked and repelled by this interpretation. In itself, one need not consider that a decisive objection: indeed there have been extremes of psycho-analytical criticism which would have considered it confirmatory evidence. But in this controversy, fortunately, there seems to be no point in the critic taking sides. If the intentions of the poet are none the less that for being subconscious, there is no obvious advantage in insisting that subconscious intention is exceptionally significant. The very phrase 'subconscious intention' is paradoxical enough without exaggerating the paradox to the point of absurdity.

But equally, it seems clear that conscious and subconscious intentions differ strikingly in their evidences and are usefully, even inevitably, distinguishable. We might choose to accept, for instance, with the several careful qualifications offered, the view that in 'Sohrab and Rustum' Arnold was subconsciously working out a sense of a fear or hostility of which he was himself unaware. Such a view makes good sense of the epilogue of the poem, what

* Lionel Trilling, *Matthew Arnold* (New York, 1939), pp. 134–5.

is more – 'But the majestic river floated on . . .' – and in a way that no other view can easily do, since the gradual frustration of the great river in its march to the sea fits nothing in the story of the Persian tragedy of father against son, but could momentously record Arnold's own sense of personal failure and inadequacy. But this view, helpful as it is, depends heavily upon understanding the difference between conscious intentions and other kinds. To suggest that Arnold was knowingly exploiting in this poem a hostility towards his father of which he was fully aware would be to offer a distinct, even a radically opposed, view to the first. That would amount to a very different poem indeed. It seems clear, in fact, that the critic commonly investigates both conscious and subconscious intentions in literature, and that when he performs his function well he tends to be sharply aware of the difference between them.

IS INTENTION PRIOR TO CREATION?

It is a matter of common experience to anyone who writes that a work rarely, if ever, merely represents the fulfilment of an original intention. A poem is a progressive act. It may arise out of an itch to write a poem. The Trinity manuscript of Milton, for instance, suggests that the young Milton had decided to write an epic before he had settled upon a biblical subject: the ambition to compose a poem of heroic dimensions preceded the ambition to justify the ways of God. It is often observable that the ambition to be a novelist precedes the choice of a subject or plot for any specific novel; and even in those cases where the idea for the novel was genuinely the impulse that set the novelist writing, it is hardly conceivable that the idea should fail to grow and to change under his hand. The fact seems so universal as to be worth elevating into a law. Kleist once spoke of the act of writing as a 'gradual fabrication'; and R. G. Collingwood, in his *Principles of Art* (1938), raised the point to the level of a major distinction between art and mere craft, while admitting that some works of art partake of some of the properties of craft as well:

The artist has no idea what the experience is which demands expression until he has expressed it. What he wants to say is not present to him as an end towards which means have to be devised; it becomes clear to him only as the poem takes shape in his mind, or the clay in his fingers.

(p. 29)

The principle may have been overstated by Collingwood: to suggest that the artist has no idea of what he means until he has said it is perhaps best regarded as a truth exaggerated for rhetorical effect. But creation can be usefully interpreted in this way if Collingwood's terms are moderated and refined beyond the point to which he felt it necessary to go. Composition is not, after all, confined to the period in which the poet holds pen in hand. The process of 'gradual fabrication' has begun long before, perhaps years before; and the finished poem is more likely to represent a point of abandonment than an end of the journey foreseen from the start. But then there is nothing destructive to historical criticism in the view that the poet's intentions are subject to continuing change and revision. Rather the contrary: many poems may be best interpreted by an historical study of a progressive intention. Milton's *Lycidas* is perhaps a classic example, since it begins and ends as pastoral elegy but incongruously includes much else besides. It invites an informed and disciplined speculation about Milton's private ambitions as a poet ('Fame is the spur . . .'), about his view of the condition of the clergy in the 1630s, and about his own religious sensibility and hopes of after-life. It is entirely plausible to suggest that Milton only discovered the totality of what he meant by *Lycidas* in the act of writing it. But the poem is in no way less Miltonic for that reason. Because a man alters his intention in the course of action, it can hardly be said of him that he is acting other than according to intention.

SCHOOLS AND INFLUENCES

The tradition of nineteenth-century literary history, then, may be considered in better repair than is commonly supposed: it is rather the confident arguments of its opponents in the last century and in this that are in urgent need of help. But even when the arguments for history have been carefully reviewed, and when it has been admitted anew that poems are best studied as human actions in the contexts of their time and place, it is often objected that the tools of traditional literary history are no longer in working use. The study of the great vernacular literatures such as French and English took their rise, almost inevitably, from the formal study of classical texts in the Renaissance, where the task of establishing historical priorities within literary traditions which had already ceased to exist for a millennium and more, or of grouping poets into schools of literature and of tracing literary debts and influences, was already well advanced by the seventeenth century. In England Bacon, in his *Advancement of Learning* (1605), proposed as a task for others an intellectual history of modern civilization in which poetry would play its part; and by the end of the century Rymer had written the first clear example of the history of a literary kind in English, *A Short View of Tragedy* (1693); to be followed almost at once by Dryden's long histories of satire and of epic (1693–7) in the form of extended prefaces to his poetic versions of Juvenal and Virgil. By the mid eighteenth century literary history might be considered an established form in England. It had grown out of two kindred disciplines of the preceding age, criticism and literary antiquarianism; so that by the time Johnson and the Warton brothers came upon the scene it had fully digested the implications of Dryden's remarks in his preface to the *Fables* (1700) half a century before:

Milton was the poetical son of Spenser, and Mr Waller of Fairfax; for we have our lineal descents and clans as well as other families: Spenser more than once insinuates that the soul of Chaucer was transfused into his body; and that he was begotten by him two hundred years after his decease. Milton has acknowledged to me that Spenser was his original . . .

The remark parallels the numerous classical discussions of literary debts and literary traditions in ancient literature based upon the principle of *imitatio veterum*, or the conscious imitation of a poetic forerunner. By the 1750s it is a familiar principle of modern criticism. Thomas Warton's study of the *Faerie Queene* (1754), which included a study of Spenser's literary sources, and Johnson's *Dictionary* of the following year, which based itself heavily upon quotations from the best English authors, show how firmly established the discipline already was. William Warburton, in his edition of Pope (1751), spoke proudly of 'the rise and progress of the several branches of literary science' as being 'one of the most curious parts of the history of the human mind', adding that it was an achievement as such still unrecorded among Englishmen.

These are all studies in similarities. The more sophisticated doctrine of literary history as a species of reaction or counter-influence is more difficult to trace. It is certainly part of the practice of antiquity, if not part of its theory. The relation of

Virgil to Homer, or of Lucan to Virgil, is not merely one of learning and imitating: it is also a relationship of repulsion, marked by a determination to *'faire autre chose'*,* to avoid or invert characters, incidents or turns of style which have exhausted themselves in the existing tradition through mere familiarity. The doctrine of imitation as doing something different, whether radically or subtly so, lies at the root of much literary history and is a necessary assumption of any advanced example of the narration of a tradition such as the history of a literary kind: advanced, since any history content merely to describe one work after another without seeking causal relations between them would be lacking in an essential historical property. It is a familiar truth that we do not know enough about the past fully to explain why it was that what happened actually happened: but it does not follow from this that causal enquiries should not be attempted at all. When theories of imitation as counter-influence, of 'doing something different', were adopted into the discipline of literary history in the late eighteenth century and after, they introduced a new consciousness of the principle of literary causality which has hardly been explored even in outline. How far, it may be asked, can the principle of counter-influence extend before the relationship as a whole ceases to count as significant? To do something different is not to ignore the tradition, after all: on the contrary, it is to take stock of its potentialities with a cool, or hostile, or perhaps appreciative eye. When Fielding in *Joseph Andrews* resolved to write a novel as little like Richardson's *Pamela* as he could (if one may so exaggerate and simplify his purposes) he none the less wanted and needed to maintain a resemblance clear enough to make his points against Richardson tell. Sterne's parody of many narrative styles shortly afterwards in *Tristram Shandy* presupposes an intimate recollection of the narratives he is parodying. The principle is familiar, and examples could be paralleled many times over. It helps to suggest the range and unexplored possibilities that the practice of literary history, once thought to be a dying art, may still have to offer. Certainly the study of the literary past is in no way limited, as is often assumed, merely to recounting what happened, to showing what is there to be read, to grouping in 'schools' and abstract categories such as romanticism. Such categories, it has often been objected, may

* Ferdinand Brunetière, *Manuel de l'histoire de la littérature française* (Paris, 1898), p. iii.

The Literary Past 83

harden rapidly into easy formulae for the avoidance of thoughtful and disciplined response. But if literary history has its vulgarities, it has its classic achievements too. The greatest original intelligences of Europe, including Dryden, Voltaire, Johnson, Coleridge and Nietzsche, have at times not disdained to practise it. The objections raised against it in the last hundred years, it is true, have been numerous, fashionable and widely believed, but they cannot be called powerfully argued or easily sustained under critical examination. And there seems to be no good reason to suppose that the study is in the remotest sense an exhausted one. The world has surely been right, in defiance of intellectual fashion, to continue to read literary history and to ask for more. It has writers and readers, tasks to perform and good reasons for performing them. What it strangely seems to lack, in spite of all this, is a sense of its own importance and a will to assert it.

5

THE THEORY OF KINDS

There are three grand systems of classification to which the whole of literature has at times been subjected, one ancient and two modern. The first, the theory of literary kinds such as epic, drama and the lyric, is so ancient that its source cannot be fixed; but it was inherited by Aristotle in the *Rhetoric* and the *Poetics*, restated three hundred years later for Latin usage by Cicero and by the Horace of the *Ars poetica*, among others, and universally accepted in one form or another by Renaissance critics. It is a doctrine by which literature is classified according to its formal properties, though the ancient doctrine of decorum linked such properties powerfully with issues of substance, and it forms the subject of this chapter. The other two systems or orders of system, of which the ancient world was ignorant, must be dealt with more briefly here.

The first is the doctrine of historical descent, of literary schools and influences and of abstractions such as realism and romanticism, of Dryden's 'lineal descents' of poets. This system of descent is only as ancient as literary history itself, and in England at least possesses no very active life before the eighteenth century. The other is more difficult to isolate, being more various and elusive, and is almost entirely a twentieth-century phenomenon: the notion that the whole of literature can be categorized according to its archetypal modes, and that such modes can be related to the total history of man. Literature in terms of this third and most modern system is seen as a late reflection of ancient religion and ritual, a system of displaced myth with a surviving relationship to ritual practices, and it may conveniently be dubbed anthropological criticism. Its chief impulses have been the *Golden Bough* of J. G. Frazer and C. G. Jung's studies of the collective unconscious. It is true that anthropological criticism has so far proved too wayward and too uncontrolled to amount to a school or to have founded a traditional procedure in the way that the ancient doctrine of kinds or the modern doctrine of literary history have clearly done; but it deserves to be mentioned here as a recent and clamorous newcomer in the field of literary classification. Its own history is uncertain, and it would be difficult to demonstrate a continuity between the classical studies of Jane Harrison and Gilbert Murray, on the one hand, and such diverse works as Maud Bodkin's *Archetypal Patterns in Poetry* (1934), Erich Auerbach's *Mimesis* (1946), which is a study of the 'representation of reality' in European literature from Homer to Virginia Woolf, or Northrop Frye's *Anatomy of Criticism* (1957) on the other. Auerbach's book is a tentative exploration of individual texts where the intelligence of the critic himself is allowed to count for more than the conceptual framework of the whole design: Frye's *Anatomy*, by contrast, is an imposing attempt to revive the grand principle of recurrence in literature viewed across many centuries and throughout the Western world. But here the archetype, such as Quixote or the Byronic hero, is studied as an observable fact of recurrence rather than as a matter of causation: the patterns are held to be there independently of whether they came to be there through literary influence or not. Speculation licensed in these terms can afford to be uncontrolled; and when the ancient myth of the rebirth of the earth-goddess is instanced by Pope's Belinda in *The Rape of the Lock* and by Richardson's Pamela, it is easy to see how independent such procedures are of any anthropological support. At times such spirited anatomy as this must seem independent, indeed, of any verification whatever.

The theory of kinds, however, is both ancient and accepted. Nobody denies that it is worth something. A novel is a novel, and a farce a farce, whether we choose to attach supreme importance to the fact or not. It is the great strength of the Aristotelian system that, though it may be shown in detail to be mistaken or incomplete, it can never be shown to be worthless. And yet, though the theory has been widely accepted, it can hardly be said to have flourished as a total theory for long at any period in the modern age. It is perhaps significant that the English language lacks any precise equivalent to the French *genre;* but the term *kind* can be made to serve. Dryden, who was perhaps the first Englishman to speak of the literary kinds, investigated in something like Aristotelian language the constituent parts of his plays and poems in the 1660s and 1670s, and ended his life with histories of the satire and of the epic. But the early prefaces of Dryden lack the impartiality of Aristotle, being defences of his own works; and the later essays are somewhat too diffuse and derivative to achieve classic status. Johnson assumes a theory of kinds in his *Lives of the Poets* (1779–81), and there are points in his argument where the theory becomes the vital principle of his argument, as in his discussions concerning the pastoral as a living or a defunct poetic form. But much eighteenth-century English criticism, including Johnson's, was frustrated in its attempt to achieve a grand taxonomy of literature by the embarrassing disparity between Augustan theory and practice. If the epic is 'the greatest work which the soul of man is capable to perform', as Dryden and his Augustan successors confidently believed, how is the failure of the English to produce such a work after Milton to be explained without national disgrace? Why are the English of the neo-classical age so weak in tragedy, which was held to be the literary kind that stood second only to the epic in dignity? And could the clear achievements of the age, such as *The Dunciad* or *Tom Jones*, be justified by Aristotelian theory without forcing the evidence? Eighteenth-century Englishmen were vexed by questions as radical as these when they came to consider the classification of literature, and they were not questions that submitted easily to an answer.

The nineteenth century did not succeed much better, though it is an error to suppose that it did not try, or to imagine that the Romantics were indifferent to questions relating to the formal properties of poetry or the problem of poetic category. Words-worth in his 1815 preface speaks unequivocally of the 'materials of poetry' being 'cast, by means of various moulds, into divers forms', and enumerates seven such moulds: the narrative, the dramatic, the lyrical, the 'idyllium' (like Milton's *L'Allegro* and *Il Penseroso*, or Thomson's *Seasons*), the didactic, the satirical and, finally, a 'composite order' constructed out of the last three, such as Cowper's *Task*. Keats puzzled over the intricate question of which mode of imitation to employ, shifting from Spenser to Milton to the Pindaric ode; and Coleridge and Tennyson studied and experimented in varieties of metrical forms in a century that saw the formal species of literature grow wider and wider. But when Brunetière, near the end of the century, tried to make modern sense of the theory of kinds in his *L'évolution des genres dans l'histoire de la littérature* (1890), he none the less found the question in a state of total uncertainty, and ambitiously attempted to re-classify the literary kinds on the analogy of the natural sciences and in the spirit of Darwin. And in the 1930s and 1940s, when the Chicago Aristotelians attempted to revive the formal analysis of literature in the context of the American New Criticism of that age, they found opportunities, in their brief life as a school, for little more than a handful of essays on isolated works. As a total theory the doctrine has failed to flourish since the seventeenth century.

If the existence of certain kinds is widely accepted, then, it must also be clear that the theory as such has little active life in literary controversy. It would almost be just to speak of the neglect of Aristotle's *Poetics*. One approaches the work with the assumption that, as the foundation-stone of European criticism, it is unlikely to have any surprises to offer; one leaves it with the sense of a freshly original and startling intuition by which the whole of literature might plausibly be re-organized. It is not even remotely true that its substance has been absorbed into the Western literary tradition. On the contrary, its doctrines are radically alien to most of what the modern critic has to offer. The introduction, for example, offers a programme for considering not only the whole range of the literary kinds, but also 'the types of plot-structure that are required if a work is to succeed' – and it is easy to imagine the blank look that would appear on the face of any twentieth-century critic if he were challenged to enumerate what in the present age are the plot-structures of Western literature. Again, Aristotle proposes in his opening to name and describe 'the number and nature of the constituent parts' of a poem: and it would be difficult to think of a single living critic who would so much as attempt to answer such a question. And the fresh and alien quality of the *Poetics* is not merely a fact of general interest: it is equally an aspect of the difference between Aristotle's critical language and our own. Aristotle uses a battery of technical terms, such as 'prologue' and 'episode', in describing what the parts of a poem are. But if a modern critic were rash enough to attempt an Aristotelian analysis of a modern play, he would be obliged on the whole to invent such terms for himself. Anyone bent upon reviving the classical theory of kinds and the forms of analysis that have traditionally accompanied it, in fact, would in no sense find himself inheriting a critical system in full working order. The decision would involve a radical change not only in method but in equipment too.

Why is the theory of kinds so nearly extinct? It cannot be that the twentieth century is ignorant of the matter, since the *Poetics* has been subjected to more detailed analysis in this age than at any time since the sixteenth century. It cannot be that we find it utterly implausible, since we continue to use certain elementary terms drawn from the system, such as 'tragedy' and 'the epic'. And it cannot be a lack of curiosity about the formal properties of literature, since this century has been characterized by an intense concern for analysing and reinterpreting its literary past. I suggest two reasons for scepticism: first, that the novel, which has dominated the literary traditions of the West for the past two centuries, has so mastered the other literary forms and drawn so many of them within its orbit that no neat classification of kinds now seems possible; and second, that since the nineteenth century, at least, our view of the literary past has been so enriched and complicated by historical considerations such as issues of priority, influence and intention that it is no longer easy to see any literature in boldly analytical terms, as Aristotle seems to have done, or as a single substance subject to a single if complex system of classification. Literature no longer looks like a body ready for dissection; and any system of classification demands that the body should lie still for long enough to be taken apart. This helps to explain the fashion for anthropological criticism, which characteristically sees literature as an historical system, an evolution rather than a corpus. Now it is true that Aristotle and his classical successors were themselves in some degree concerned with the genetic properties of literary forms. The fourth chapter of the *Poetics*, for instance, treats of the origins and development of poetry, and amounts to a brief exercise in literary history: 'Both tragedy and comedy had their first beginnings in improvisation. Tragedy originated with those who led the dithyramb; comedy with the leaders of phallic songs. . . . Little by little tragedy developed, each new element being developed as it came into use. . . .' This is evidently a potted version of what an historical critic of the last hundred years might have written if he had known what Aristotle knew about the rise of Greek drama. But Aristotle continues with a remark which renders his method utterly alien to anything one can now readily understand or accept: '. . . until after many changes tragedy attained its natural form and came to a stop'. Aristotle's certainty that tragedy could only represent what it already was in his own time seems all the odder when one observes that he goes on to recount how Aeschylus increased the number of actors from one to two, and Sophocles from two to three. He does not seem interested in the notion that the process of expansion might continue – as in the event it did. Perhaps he believed that there was some powerful *a priori* reason why there could not be more than three; but if he did believe anything like this, he does not say what that reason might be.

The idea that literature could simply achieve perfection, should 'come to a stop', understandably and rightly repels the modern mind. How can any sane man agree in advance that what has been done can never be improved upon? It is a conclusion both implausible in itself and destructive to any creative conviction. If Dryden had seriously believed, as he once claimed, that 'all came wasted to us' from the Ancients, or Pope that Homer and Virgil stood 'above the reach of sacrilegious hands', they could hardly have approached the poetic craft with any sort of reasonable confidence, or written, as they did, works which have no warrant in classical precept or practice. Johnson tried to solve the dilemma by liberalizing the sense in which the modern poet should regard classical precedent as authoritative; but his attempt at a solution draws intelligent attention to the problem rather than offering a clear settlement: 'Every new genius', he argued expansively in the 125th *Rambler* (May 1751), 'produces some innovation which, when invented and approved, subverts the rules which the practice of foregoing authors had established'. This is something like the modern and sensible view of the matter: that when a poet imitates an ancient source, he attempts not to equal but to surpass it; and that in surpassing it he enlarges, even transforms, the possibilities that it seemed to offer. We can eagerly accept that the poet needs in some sense to be a literary historian and to know his precedents – 'Why should I prefer to remain ignorant rather than learn my craft?' as Horace put it in the *Ars poetica* after reviewing the sources in Greek poetry open to him (l.100). But the conclusion he draws now looks too rigid to convince: 'A comic subject is not susceptible of treatment in a tragic style, and the banquet of Thyestes cannot be fitly described in the strains of everyday life or in comic terms. Let each style keep to its proper purpose.' On the contrary, it is now clear that no such line is to be easily drawn, or is perhaps to be drawn at all.

In the following discussion I propose to neglect the first of the two reasons I have tentatively offered to explain why no theory of kinds is today in full working order: the advent of the novel as the dominant form in Western literature. The fact is in itself overwhelming in its consequences in the particular instance of Western literature in the past two centuries. But it is surely not decisive enough to daunt an Aristotle, who would in all probability have known how to distinguish the cases and sub-cases within the vast phenomenon of the modern novel much as he distinguished the characteristic features in the forms of classical Greek literature. Faced with such a problem, by the way, he would surely not have committed Fielding's error in his prefaces to *Joseph Andrews* and *Tom Jones* – the error of supposing that the novel can be accommodated as a 'comic epic in prose' within the ancient and classical system of kinds. On the contrary, it is the classical system of kinds which is now largely accommodated within the novel, and it remains for some future systematizer to show how prose fiction over the past two centuries has ceased to function as a single literary kind, if indeed it ever was such, and has become almost as wide as literary activity itself. The difficulties of any future Aristotle here might be considerable in detail, but they are not for the most part difficulties of principle. And a difficulty of principle is just what is involved in the second instance.

I have already argued that any system of classification demands a static property, and that the historical sense has rendered it difficult or impossible for modern man to see literature as a given object in the sense that must have seemed natural to Aristotle and Horace. The difficulty is particularly vivid in respect of the doctrine of decorum. Decorum is the link-doctrine in the system of the kinds, since it holds that each kind possesses a style that is proper to itself: 'A comic subject,' as Horace put it, 'is not susceptible of treatment in a tragic style.' Each kind is accordingly like a molecule consisting of two atoms: a tragedy is a play about a tragic subject composed in a tragic style, and so on. Plautus, in the prologue to his *Amphitryon*, makes Mercury alternate dizzyingly between the tragic and comic modes of dramatic Latin verse, first announcing a tragedy, then offering to change it through his divine power into a comedy, and concluding that the play which is about to be performed must be a mixture of the two, on the grounds that its substance is mixed:

It would never do for me to make it simply a comedy, with kings and
gods on the stage. What *shall* I do, then? Well, since there are parts in it
for slaves, I shall do just what I said and make a tragi-comedy out of it.

(60-3)

The argument as a whole is knowingly trivial, since the audience
knows as well as Plautus that the *Amphitryon* is radically a
comedy and nothing else; but the full joke depends on recognizing that an accepted critical precept, such as the view that kings
and gods belong to tragedy, is being quoted in an absurd context. Nobody would now use the argument in that form, so
that the force of Plautus's joke needs in some degree to be
explained to a modern reader; and yet it still seems to be widely
believed that the difference between tragedy and comedy is a
difference of subject. 'Certain events and responses are tragic,'
it has been suggested in a recent study of tragedy, 'and others are
not.'* It is often felt that there is something painfully academic
in denying anything like this, and especially in insisting
that tragedy is after all a literary form which might in principle
be about almost anything; and certainly this popular insistence
upon 'events' draws terms like 'comedy' and 'tragedy' closer
to non-literary usages, in the direction of common phrases such
as 'There is something comic about him', or 'He has had a
tragic life'. More than that, to speak of 'events and responses'
rather than merely 'events' helps to make the argument look
less vulnerable than it is. At least it is not open to the sort of
easy refutation that seems to be offered by the classical view that
Plautus parodied, where it was suggested that it is a difference
of subject alone – kings and gods on the one hand, as against
slaves on the other – that makes all the difference. But 'response'
is probably a trap rather than a safety-net, none the less. After
all, there are tragedies that are funny, in the plain sense that they
are meant to make an audience laugh. Much of Marlowe's
Jew of Malta, much of *Hamlet*, and much of *Waiting for Godot*,
seem clearly designed to amuse the audience, and in good
performances of these plays there is plenty of laughter to be
heard. The proponents of 'tragic response' (assuming that they
accept such plays as being rightly described as tragedies) are
forced back upon one of two expedients when confronted with
awkward evidence of this sort. Either they may argue that the
parts of these plays that make the audience laugh are not the

* Raymond Williams, *Modern Tragedy* (London, 1966), p. 14.

tragic parts, in which case they are faced with some uncomfortable surgery which anybody would rather not perform; or else, rather hurriedly, they are obliged to invent some hasty concept such as 'tragic laughter'. In both cases one has the impression of arguing with people who would prefer not to be forced into using such arguments at all.

It would generally be admitted that the difference between tragedy and comedy, whatever it is, is likely to be among the simpler distinctions that separate one literary kind from another; so that the complexity which this argument is beginning to unravel should be viewed with all the greater sense of significance. The plain fact is that, two thousand and more years after Aristotle, we still cannot say with any justifiable certainty what the difference between comedy and tragedy is. 'Cannot say' is not the same as 'do not know'; in fact we evidently know the difference pretty accurately, since there is wide agreement on the vast majority of cases, and wide recognition about certain delicately intermediate categories such as the *comédie noire* or Peter Weiss's *Marat/Sade*. It is astonishing how rarely modern Western man, who has had little or no formal instruction in any theory of the literary kinds, is prone to disagree with his fellows on the kinds to which the books that he reads and the plays that he sees belong. But he tends to become over-assertive when asked to explain why it is that he thinks what he does. It is certainly not at all clear, as he often supposes, that we use terms like 'tragic' and 'comic' in identical senses in art and in life. But the similarities may still be worth considering. To speak, in everyday language, of someone's tragic life, or to read a headline like TRAGEDY IN PICCADILLY, is certainly to understand that events of a gravely regrettable kind, such as sudden bereavement or an unusually serious traffic accident, have occurred; and to suggest this is already to suggest a similarity with *Hamlet* or *Godot*. It is undeniably to be regretted, and in the gravest sense, that a Prince should die young, or that two men should wait as upon an only hope for something or someone that does not come. But the notion of what is and is not worth regretting is even more elusive in art than in life. It is certainly rash to suggest in advance which subjects are fit for tragedy and which are not. If nobody now supposes that tragedy needs to be about gods and kings, we need not slip into assumptions as indefensible, in the long run, as those of ancient or neo-classical poetics. The error was once made of supposing that only the fate of great men could be a grave matter, and Ibsen demonstrated with finality that this was wrong. But if we continue to suppose that there is indeed some limit to what may be considered a comic or a tragic subject, and that the only difficulty is the purely accidental one of discovering what that limit is, then the error is in principle just as absurd. It neglects to notice that tragedy, being a literary form, is practised in making us see events in a tragic light which may not previously have been regarded as such; and that comedy, in its most radical examples, may show as comic what may previously have passed unnoticed altogether, or unnoticed as comedy. There seems no sure way of imposing a limit in advance upon what poets may reveal about what is laughable or grave; it is not even possible to demonstrate such limits in the literature that already exists. And if this is so, it seems implausible to suggest that the difference between tragedy and comedy is a difference of subject.

To fall back upon the familiar expedient, however, and describe the difference as one of 'treatment', is an altogether more promising beginning. If it begs the question, at least it begs the right one. Tragedy is indeed a manner of treatment. It has often been noticed that only a hairline divides it from its polar opposite of comedy. The same events, it is often said, if handled differently, produce a generically distinct effect; so that when assertions are made about what is comic and what is not, they commonly appear as statements about the current of taste in a given age rather than assertions that can be shown to be true in an absolute sense. To say that a fat and well-dressed man slipping on a banana-skin is funny whereas a cripple is not, for example, is to make an important observation about the quality of twentieth-century life; but it tells us little enough about the difference between comedy and tragedy, especially when one reflects on the spectacles of blood and lunacy that were once thought of as subjects for entertainment. What turns the gladiatorial victim or the madman from a figure of fun into a figure of tragedy is a way of seeing: what he is remains a constant in the equation.

Much of this discussion now seems to point back to the classical solution of decorum, and certainly what I have loosely called 'treatment' is a deliberately vague and extended term that includes decorum and much besides. Horace's notion – or rather the notion of ancient criticism itself – that each style should 'keep to its proper purpose', and that each kind should preserve its own proper style, is a tight, austere version of the wider concept of 'ways of seeing' and 'ways of treating'. It seems likely that it was felt to be too tight a doctrine even by the Ancients. Even Horace is anxious to show that the doctrine is not a straitjacket. The dramatist must 'follow the beaten track, or else invent something consistent within itself', which sounds austere enough: 'See to it that Medea is fierce and indomitable, Ino tearful, Ixion faithless . . .' But he also speaks, in an obscure passage, of the poet 'making a familiar theme his own' and avoiding hackneyed treatment (*vilem patulumque*), and he is against 'slavish' imitations (ll.123f.). The balance of the argument is delicate: a good poem is best composed on an old theme, but should be handled in a new way – new, but not too new. A good poem is the same and yet different. . . . The doctrine helps to explain so much in literary evolution that no one could wish it away. It is almost painfully obvious, in fact, that a poet inherits his tools, that among these tools are the literary kinds themselves, that a system of kinds is in some complex way essential to the act of comprehension, and that if the poet supposes he can create a new form *ex nihilo* he must have misunderstood the larger problem of literature in its social relations. A poem is there to be used; and if the poet is 'before his time', he must still be concerned that his time should some day come. There is evidently a kind of necessity in the classical view that the poet is a man in a literary situation which he has not himself created, that he is a man who can alter that situation but not totally transform it. Exaggerations may be allowed for effect, and we may find ourselves speaking of literary revolutions in cataclysmic terms; but we still know that in the strictest sense there is no such thing, just as we know that an anti-novel is really a kind of novel and an anti-play a kind of play.

And yet the classical doctrine of decorum, hedged about with sensible qualifications as it was even in the ancient world, still looks too tight to serve. And its grand defect lies in its failure to notice that the relationship between a kind and its style need not be 'proper' or decorous at all. It may be a reverse relationship: and no version of the doctrine of decorum, however liberal, can accommodate a principle as disturbing as this. It is true that classical and neo-classical criticism knew that at least one kind of reverse relationship, the parody, existed. Aristotle in the fourth chapter of the *Poetics*, for instance, speaks of the lost comic epic of Homer, the *Margites*, as 'bearing the same relationship to our comedies as the *Iliad* and *Odyssey* bear to our tragedies'. It seems natural to assume that the *Margites* was a parody of an epic, or a mock-epic; and certainly parody was recognized by the Ancients as a comic form with its own function and status. Since comic parody is a form with a continuous life of its own, the notion raises no difficulties: one can match the *Margites* of Homer with Ben Jonson's little mock-heroic poem 'The Voyage' and Pope's *Dunciad*, or Catullus's elegy on the death of a sparrow with Gray's 'Ode on the Death of a Favourite Cat drowned in a Tub of Gold Fishes'. What seems rarely to have been noticed before the nineteenth century is that parodic forms such as the mock-heroic are highly simplified instances of relationships which may in practice be vastly more subtle. If the style of the *Iliad* offers a model of decorum for the epic, and the *Margites* (it may be supposed) a model for the mock-epic, what is one to say of intermediate instances such as the language of the *Aeneid* or of *Paradise Lost*? Virgil and Milton are attempting something inconceivable without the model of the Homeric poems; but equally, they are not simply trying to copy the language of Homer or of Hesiod. Nor, at the polar extreme of the spectrum, are they writing mock-heroics, though there are occasional elements in both poems that smack of the parodic. The Turnus of Virgil has been ingeniously held to be in some measure a ridiculing view of the Achilles of the *Iliad*, for instance; and Milton's war in heaven, in his sixth book, mocks the rebel host of angels by letting them play an horrific version of epic battle in language that echoes the *Theogony* of Hesiod – but in a battle against Omnipotence itself:

> *The rest in imitation to like arms*
> *Betook them, and the neighbouring hills uptore;*
> *So hills amid the air encountered hills*
> *Hurled to and fro with jaculation dire,*
> *That under ground they fought in dismal shade:*
> *Infernal noise; war seemed a civil game*
> *To this uproar.*   (vi. 662–8)

The mock-heroic elements in the *Aeneid* and *Paradise Lost* are of course out on the margin of both poems. But how is one best to describe the workings of a device which classical critics such as Horace would presumably have recognized and approved: the classic device of *alter et idem*, of performing something similar but not the same? The openings of the three epics furnish an obvious example. The *Iliad*, in Pope's version, begins:

> *The wrath of Peleus' son, the direful spring*
> *Of all the Grecian woes, O Goddess, sing!...*

And the *Aeneid* (following Dryden):

> *Arms and the man I sing, who, forced by Fate,*
> *And haughty Juno's unrelenting hate,*
> *Expelled and exiled, left the Trojan shore...*

The Miltonic echo of both openings is subtly orchestral and difficult to analyse, and yet some facts about it are clear. The vast suspension by which the first six lines of *Paradise Lost* are organized ('Of man's first disobedience ... Sing') is improbably continued as a *tour de force* through varying syntactical devices until the sixteenth line, where an enormous sentence finally comes to rest upon an echo from Ariosto's *Orlando Furioso*: 'Things unattempted yet in prose or rhyme'. Miltonic commentators have already shown that the opening of *Paradise Lost* is a fusion of Milton's models in Homer and Virgil, a device by which Milton proudly side-steps the Renaissance controversy concerning which of the two should be considered the greater poet by demanding that his own Christian epic should be compared with both, and in the loftiest terms: 'That with no middle flight intends to soar.' Homer in his invocation had asked of the Muse that she should herself tell the story; Virgil had sought the aid of the Muse to inspire him to sing. Milton combines the two by demanding of the Muse that she should herself sing and also inspire his song, and then adds a component unthinkable in the pagan epics, an appeal to the Holy Ghost which openly renounces rivalry with the Ancients:

> *And chiefly thou, O Spirit, that dost prefer*
> *Before all temples the upright heart and pure*
> *Instruct me, for Thou know'st; Thou from the first*
> *Wast present...*

This is a relatively clear instance of the sort of evidence that a developed theory of kinds would have to learn to accept and explain – clear in the sense that any comparison between the *Iliad*, the *Aeneid* and *Paradise Lost* amounts to an unravelling of sources which Virgil and Milton surely wished the reader to notice for himself. The comparisons and echoes now helpfully documented by modern scholarship are directly visible in clues by which the poets themselves have helped us to recognize both similarities and differences. In this instance the poets are like conversationalists who mimic the speech and gestures of an absent friend. If all the instances of literary kinship were as simple as this, it would be sufficient to return to the views of Horace and others and to leave it at that. But beyond such cases as this, and yet closely related to them, are instances of what I have called 'reverse relationship', whereby the kinship between a kind and its style is the contrary of decorous and yet in no way provided for by the simple category of parody. These are the difficult and yet rewarding instances of literary kinship, where relations are reverse and yet other than comic. And any fully plausible theory of kinds would have to take account of them.

Many examples of reverse kinship may be provided from seventeenth-century English poetry, that most varied and problematical of ages stretching from Donne to Dryden which often works in forms unwarranted by classical precedent, and in modes often mysterious, it may be supposed, even to the age itself. The period (which strictly begins in the 1590s) opens with collections of love-poems such as Shakespeare's sonnets and Donne's *Songs and Sonnets*, poems which undeniably illustrate the classical principle of *imitatio veterum*. They depend upon a memory of the literary past, that is to say, having absorbed not only the metrical forms but even the doctrines of earlier European love-poetry, and notably three: the 'Platonic' tradition of asexual love, the Latin or Ovidian tradition of carnality, and the medieval or Petrarchan tradition of a love purely spiritual and forever unfulfilled. And yet nobody would wish to say of Donne or Shakespeare as love-poets that, in their most characteristic poems, they merely imitate in the classical sense, 'keeping each style to its proper purpose'; nor conversely that they are writing parodies of Plato, Ovid or Petrarch. Poetry is no longer as simple as that: perhaps it never was. Admittedly the issue is far more speculative than the relation between Homer and Virgil, where the Roman can be shown to practise upon Greek literary models certain principles fully familiar to his own civilization. English poetry in the Renaissance and after is not like that, unless in certain self-conscious instances such as the poetry of Ben Jonson. When we speak of the Metaphysical poets, following a phrase adapted from Dr Johnson's Life of Cowley (1779), we use a term that Donne, Cleveland, Herbert and Marvell would not have understood. More than that, there seems no reason to suppose that the seventeenth-century English conceived of the 'Metaphysical style' as constituting a special literary kind, still less that as a kind it possessed its own rules of stylistic decorum. There is in any case almost no surviving contemporary criticism of Metaphysical poetry. Even that most characteristic of all figures of the school, the extended metaphor or Metaphysical conceit, is rarely discussed at length by Elizabethans and Jacobeans, so that one is confronted with the oddity that the most fertile of all poetic languages in the English Renaissance, at least in the short poem, may not have been observed to exist even by those who practised it. The style seems to have been convincingly demonstrated for the first time, at least in print, only as late as the Restoration, and then by those anxious only to expel it from the system of permitted forms. Dryden in his dialogue *Of Dramatick Poesie* (1668) writes derisively of those poets who 'perpetually pay us with clenches upon words, and a certain clownish kind of raillery . . . wresting and torturing a word into another meaning', and he goes on to mock at the poet who is forever

reaching at some thin conceit, the ghost of a jest, and that too flies before him, never to be caught; these swallows which we see before us on the Thames are the just resemblance of his wit: you may observe how near the water they stoop, how many proffers they make to dip, and yet how seldom they touch it; and when they do, 'tis but the surface; they skim over it but to catch a gnat, and then mount into the air and leave it.

The passage is itself an example of a Metaphysical conceit, so that Dryden is demonstrating the very language he derides, and he is a knowing enough writer to make one suspect that the trick is deliberate. It is a much subtler trick than Swift's, some forty years later, parodying the Metaphysical style in *A Meditation upon a Broomstick*:

When I beheld this I sighed, and said within myself: 'Surely man is a broomstick! Nature sent him into the world strong and lusty, in a thriving condition, wearing his own hair on his head, the proper branches of this reasoning vegetable, till the axe of intemperance has lopped off his green boughs, and left him a withered trunk . . .'

Swift's is an easy case of parody, of a reverse relationship at its boldest and clearest, and the resemblances between the *Meditation* and the language of a highly figurative tradition of Puritan preaching that Swift despised is like a simple mirror-reflection here: at once utterly accurate, and pointed exactly to the extent that it is accurate. Dryden's passage is quite different. One would not readily call it parody at all. For one thing, it is a success in its own terms, and evidently offered as such – part of the fascinating vestige of the Metaphysical mode in which Dryden had begun as a young poet in the 1650s and which clung to him all his life. And just because it is a success in its own terms, it lacks the accuracy essential to parody. If the minor Metaphysicals whom Dryden is deriding here had written like *this*, one would be inclined to say, there could be no reason to deride them. Besides, it is perceptive in a way that Swift's parody is not: perceptive even to the point where perception begins to look like sympathy. When Dryden calls the conceit 'the ghost of a jest' he is making a point of major critical interest: that the conceit has the structure of a certain kind of joke (a pun, for instance, or what Dryden calls a 'clench') in which the pleasure derives from the coincidence that a single word in its designed context is suddenly seen to have a double sense; except that in its minor examples, so Dryden argues, the joke or 'raillery' is only of 'a certain clownish kind', and the coincidence is not happy but rather a matter of 'wresting and torturing a word into another meaning'. Anybody who can see all this in the Metaphysical conceit is not in any simple sense of the word its enemy. And the point is confirmed in the 'just resemblance' between conceits of this kind and the swallows on the Thames: they almost touch the water, but not quite, just as the later Metaphysicals seem in this view to be constantly on the point of intelligent discourse without ever quite achieving it; and if like the swallows they catch something in the end, it is only a gnat.

To turn from Dryden's subtly affectionate pastiche of a Metaphysical poem, oddly embedded in a prose dialogue, and back to the monumental examples of the Metaphysical mode itself in its flourishing state, is to turn to examples which are at least as complex as these. Donne's 'Relic' may serve here as a prime example of literary kinship at the apex of complexity. Short as it is, it is not a poem with a single source, and the question whether it is a parody or pastiche of a previous work or class of works does not arise. On the other hand it is decidedly a poem with a past. If it does not itself belong to a kind, in any simple sense, it contains elements which are richly if elusively echoic of theological controversies and of Renaissance Platonic speculations about an ideal of love beyond and above the merely physical. Examples of such highly complex relations as this poem represents are surely too numerous and too important in Western literature to be simply dismissed by anyone in search of a coherent doctrine of the literary kinds: it would hardly be good enough, that is to say, to suggest that any theory is bound to neglect certain oddities of which this is one. There are too many such instances; and in any case the poem, simply because it is richly echoic, clearly possesses some sort of relationship with its literary past and asks to be brought into an intelligent relationship with it. One may also guess that it is a poem more anxious to defy that relationship than to conform to it, and that it must always have seemed a subversive (if only a playfully subversive) work. The provocative little jibe against women in the opening:

> *(For graves have learned that woman-head*
> *To be to more than one a bed),*

and the flirtations with blasphemy at a further point:

> *Thou shalt be a Mary Magdalen, and I*
> *A something else thereby,*

are among many hints that the literary and theological sources of the poem are lightly regarded within its total pattern. This is a love-poem, after all: but it makes mocking fun of women. It mocks at religion, too: and yet it is not the poem of an unbeliever. The 'miracle' of love is a miracle of lovers who do not touch, beyond an occasional kiss: but the poem is no more a serious defence of the possibility of continence than is Shakespeare's *Love's Labour's Lost.* It is among the profoundest facts of literary history as it is now practised that there is no language in which to describe relationships as complex as these. The poem is not a parody, like Swift's *Meditation,* since it has no single target and is too subtle and too glancing in its techniques to sustain a single mode of kinship. It is not pastiche, since it does not clearly have even a whole class of past models, like the Metaphysical style in Dryden's essay, as a point of reference. And it is not (at the other extreme) an imitation, even in the remote and varied sense in which the *Aeneid* is an imitation of the Homeric epics. The poem is a shimmering object, and it takes many lights and many colours at many points in its three-and-thirty lines. The human situation which a reading best resembles is perhaps that of listening to a highly intelligent man of practised social attainments talking gaily in a circle of friends where many learned allusions are enjoyed in common. He is capable of far more sustained and serious discourse, and the evidence is there in what he is saying, though what he is saying is neither sustained nor serious. One can guess at what most deeply concerns him, though it is only a guess; but there is no doubt whatever that far deeper concerns are within the usual range of his intelligence. If challenged by some ignorant and enquiring reader with a sensible question concerning the kind to which 'The Relic' belongs, there are many more or less accurate answers to be offered in ascending order of sophistication: that it is a love-poem; that it comprehends many strands in that tradition, both an ancient tradition broadly called Platonic and the medieval tradition of love-worship with its many analogies between the mistress as Virgin and the lover as a saint at her shrine. And yet when it is all said, there is only one thing, in the absolute sense, that is like this poem, and that is itself.

But then the great strength of any developed theory of the literary kinds would surely lie in helping one to conclude just there. To identify the relations between a work and its analogues is also to identify the uniqueness of the work itself, and in the end this is surely the only sort of uniqueness that counts. One might begin by saying, of a literary work, perhaps out of ignorance, that one has never seen anything like it before; but having looked at the cases that are more or less like it, one might echo one's first innocent remark with a new sense of weight and force. Of course, in the end, there is nothing like it: but now one has earned something like the right to say so. And certainly this leaves the doctrine of kinds credited, as is its due, with the value of helping one to see what a complex relation or set of relations might be like. It is also unfortunately true that this very complexity is damaging to some of the ancient certainties concerning the classification of kinds. Literature is not like botany, and any attempt to divide and subdivide it with finality is predoomed to failure. Its relationships are evolutionary, and a new factor may change the appearance of all the rest. But the triumph of historical method should be seen as fertilizing a doctrine which in the hands of the neo-classicals, after all, had shown little enough vitality of its own. What it can now be made to do is to demonstrate the subtle movements of similarity and divergence within an evolutionary process, and the manifold ways in which one poem may contain and exploit a recollection of others.

6

COMPARATIVE LITERATURE

At first glance there may seem little to distinguish the study of literary works composed in more languages than one. If any special talent in the reader is involved beyond a knowledge of the languages themselves, that is to say, then it is not at all clear what that talent is. And yet it is equally evident that the nineteenth and twentieth centuries have developed a consciousness utterly unknown to previous ages that 'comparative literature' is an activity subject to special conditions and procedures. There are chairs and degrees which are so entitled, and demands for more. And this sort of consciousness is unlikely to be without a foundation in fact. My task in the present chapter is first to examine the nature of this consciousness, now only about a century and a half old, and to ask how it differs from classical and neo-classical procedures; and secondly to enquire how such a consciousness, if it is well founded, might be advanced and refined.

The concept of comparative literature as such is an early nineteenth-century one. Sainte-Beuve, in an article on J.-J. Ampère in the *Revue des Deux Mondes* (1 September 1868), is explicit on the matter, and his information is characteristically full and accurate:

The branch of study known as comparative literature dates in France only from the beginning of this century. Indeed one could hardly include under this title the successive fashions and the invasions of foreign literatures, Italian or Spanish, which marked the second half of the sixteenth century and the first half of the seventeenth. Authors from beyond the Alps and the Pyrenees were read, imitated and copied with greater or lesser discernment, and sometimes appositely quoted; but nobody made a critical analysis or comparison of them.

Nouveaux Lundis vol. xiii (1870), p.184

And he goes on to recount the prehistory of the subject, such as Voltaire on the English, and the pioneer activities of Mme de Staël and Benjamin Constant. What characterizes the new school, in his view, is its 'purely intellectual curiosity', as opposed to the more interested activities of a polemicist such as Voltaire, who took possession of English ideas and 'used them like a weapon in battle, like an instrument for philosophical inoculation, instead of seeking matter for an impartial and critical comparison'. There is evidently something to be said for the contrast, with whatever scepticism one may choose to regard Sainte-Beuve's view of criticism as an impartial activity: and certainly his profound conviction that it could be impartial, and his resolution to make it so, are among the qualities that preserve for the *Lundis* their classic status. The conviction helps to explain how it could be that nineteenth-century critics felt themselves to be pioneers even while remaining aware of the centuries of activity before them in which works from different literatures had been critically juxtaposed. One reads with a sense of amazement, for example, the remark of the ageing Goethe to Eckermann in January 1827 that 'national literature is now rather an unmeaning term; the epoch of world-literature is at hand, and everyone must strive to hasten its approach' – a remark which seems to bear no relation to the previous century of German criticism, where the subjection of German letters to French and English models had been almost total. If Goethe's remark refers to the outbreak of national consciousness in German culture during and after the Napoleonic Wars, as no doubt it does, then it reflects a stage in the long civil war within German culture in the nineteenth and early twentieth centuries between nationalists and internationalists; and certainly Goethe's heroic stand against nationalism, and his refusal even under foreign occupation to allow himself to be anti-French, are among the most memorable acts of his mind. But if challenged with the international interests of Lessing and Kant, he might have replied in terms something like Sainte-Beuve's: that Lessing's interest in Shakespeare, or Kant's in Milton and other English poets, are on much the same level as Voltaire's interest in the English earlier in the same century. Their concern, that is to say, was not properly disinterested: they sought for allies in a struggle and weapons in battle.

A glance at ancient and neo-classical precedents tends only to confirm the confidence of nineteenth-century critics in the novelty of their procedures. In Greek criticism from Plato to the Alexandrians the issue of comparatism does not arise, since the Greeks recognized the existence of no literature but their own: the purest example of what Goethe called a 'national literature', perhaps, that the West has to offer. The startling and solitary exception of a single remark made by Longinus is all that needs to be offered in qualification here. After quoting three passages on Poseidon from the *Iliad*, in the ninth chapter of *On the Sublime*, as supreme examples of the description of divinity, Longinus adds an unexpected comparison with Moses:

> So too the lawgiver of the Jews, no ordinary person, having formed a high conception of the power of divinity, expressed it at the beginning of his Laws, where he wrote: 'God said' – what? – 'Let there be light, and there was light; let there be land, and there was land.'

The Roman situation was the precise reverse of Greek self-sufficiency. Whereas the Greeks saw their literature as unique, Roman critics such as Cicero, Horace and Quintilian saw their literature as existing almost wholly as a poor relation to Greek. Nearly all Roman criticism is in some sense comparative. Cicero sees the task of the orator as that of measuring himself against Greek models; Horace in the *Ars poetica* offers a programme for imitating in Latin the Greek poetic models both in their formal properties and in substance: 'The Socratic writings will supply you with material' (l.310), and Greek civilization is in any case superior as a whole to the Roman: 'The Muses gave the Greeks native wit and the faculty of turning phrases, and they longed for nothing more than fame: we Romans as schoolboys learn how to divide weights. . .' (ll.323–5). Quintilian regards Roman independence in the field of satire as a matter for surprised comment, an almost unique exception in a record of cultural dependence. If Greek criticism is never comparative, the Roman is rarely anything else. But a Sainte-Beuve might have noticed two severe limitations upon its activities. First, it never worked in more than two factors, Greek and Latin, whereas the modern comparatist thinks it natural to operate through the whole of Western literature and perhaps beyond. And second, it is not disinterested. If the Roman critics were concerned with Greek literature for its own sake, they seldom write as if they were. They treat it as a series of models for Latin imitation.

With the Renaissance the two factors become three or more: Greek, Latin and one at least of the modern vernaculars; and some of the great literary debates of the sixteenth century, such as the controversies concerning what Aristotle meant, how his views in the *Poetics* should be applied to the composition of modern tragedy, or whether Homer or Virgil should be regarded as the best model for the modern epic poet, are comparative in the limited sense that Roman criticism had been so. But the first stirrings of what the modern mind would recognize as comparatism are perhaps to be found here. When Dryden, in the middle section of the essay *Of Dramatick Poesie* (1668), compares the merits and weaknesses of French and English drama, or compares Homer, Ovid, Chaucer and Boccaccio in his preface to the *Fables* (1700), he is admittedly using foreign examples as what Sainte-Beuve would have called 'weapons in a battle'; but he is also behaving as a pioneer in free and uninhibited critical analysis. The neo-classical mind was, after all, radically hospitable to comparative studies; and if it did not practise them much in a manner that would satisfy the comparatist of today, it seems more likely that this represents a limit placed upon the total activity of critical analysis rather than any reason that Sainte-Beuve might have condemned as mere partiality. Certainly the neo-classic had no special commitment to the notion of a 'national literature'. He never supposed the literature of his own people to exist in isolation, or supposed that it ought so to exist. Dryden's programme for English poets is that they should learn to imitate the Ancients more intelligently, and hence less rigidly, than the French had usually done; but he does not deny that seventeenth-century French is the measure of success in a vernacular, however overrated a success; and he does not doubt that modern literature must always exist under the shadow of the ancient, even if he is anxious to emphasize that the shadow should not and need not depress or constrain. The programme is fiercely patriotic, indeed, but it is not insular. Voltaire, again, in the *Lettres philosophiques* (1734), though he does not seriously doubt the French superiority over the English in literature, thinks it useful to translate passages from Rochester, Waller, and Pope (letters 21–2) as examples of the un-French vigour of the best English poetry, '*la licence impétueuse du style anglais*', which is creatively opposed to the constraints of French metre and the 'delicate proprieties of our language'. Johnson took a still bolder and firmer view of the universality of poetry. He seems at times to have held the classic doctrine of human nature as a common property of all nations and all ages with an unusual rigour and consistency. It is the proper business of poetry, in this view, to mirror accurately those properties which are common to the nature of all intelligent men, to express (as he puts it of Gray's Elegy) 'images which find a mirror in every mind' and 'sentiments to which every bosom returns an echo'. But equally, the doctrine does not justify puerility: 'Eton College' as a poem is the worse for the fact that the view 'suggests nothing to Gray which every beholder does not equally think and feel'. It is always clear that the perspective in Johnson's *Lives of the Poets* is humanity rather than the English, so that Johnson is scarcely open to Goethe's stricture about 'national literature' either. In fact the extremity of Johnson's humanism may be seen in its most startling form in his comments on Denham's *Cooper's Hill* (1642), where he makes a point well in advance of modern comparatism as it is now commonly understood. After quoting the most celebrated passage in the poem,

> *O could I flow like thee, and make thy stream*
> *My great example, as it is my theme!*
> *Though deep, yet clear; though gentle, yet not dull;*
> *Strong without rage, without o'erflowing full,*

Johnson goes on to object that the passage is imperfect, since

> most of the words thus artfully opposed are to be understood simply [i.e. literally] on one side of the comparison, and metaphorically on the other; and if there be any language which does not express intellectual operations by material images, into that language they cannot be translated.

This is to suggest that for Johnson poetry was excellent, or at least of the highest excellence, only if it could be translated entire and without loss into other languages: a view worlds away from the received view of nineteenth-century criticism, where it is more commonly held that poetry is precisely 'that which is untranslatable'. Johnson's view in the Life of Denham is not his only view of the matter; several years before, in a conversation reported by Boswell (11 April 1776), he had spoken in other terms of poetry as contrasted with science and history in that it 'cannot be translated; and therefore it is the poets that preserve languages; for we would not be at the trouble to learn a language, if we could have all that is written in it just as well in a transla- tion'. It is only by a species of misplaced ingenuity that such contrasting views can be reconciled. But the more bracing and unfamiliar view in favour of translation seems to rise directly out of Johnson's humanism, a humanism held in so extreme a form that even a minor seventeenth-century poet like Denham is seen to have written for mankind rather than for Englishmen. Whatever the objections to be levelled against this imposing doctrine of poetry as universally available, a narrow-minded nationalism is clearly not one of them.

The neo-classical view of the relations between literatures is to be studied in its most constructive and detailed form in seventeenth- and eighteenth-century theories of literary transla- tion, and it is remarkable how firm was the confidence upon which the translators of the great age based their faith in the importance and dignity of what they were doing. Translators such as Dryden and Pope often complain of the niggling difficulties presented by the English language in the task of translating Juvenal, Virgil or Homer; but their emphasis is commonly in favour of correcting a merely accidental fault in an undeveloped modern vernacular. There is rarely any suspicion that some poetic essence inheres in the original poems simply by virtue of the languages in which they are composed. A modern translator would be very unlikely to possess this sort of confidence: he commonly begins his preface with a disclaimer to the effect that the translation of poetry is well known to be impossible anyhow. Pope's preface to his version of the *Iliad*, by contrast, boldly proposes that 'it is the first grand duty of an interpreter to give his author entire and unmaimed', and he goes on to declare his independence of Dryden's theory of 'paraphrase', or moderately free translation, by putting a more strenuous case for 'a version almost literal':

I know no liberties one ought to take but those which are necessary for transfusing the spirit of the original, and supporting the poetical style of the translation: and I will venture to say, there have not been more men misled in former times by a servile dull adherence to the letter, than have been deluded in ours by a chimerical insolent hope of raising and im- proving their author. . . . It is a great secret in writing to know when to be plain, and when poetical and figurative.

The evident difficulty in relating confidence like this to what modern literary studies know as comparative literature is the plain fact that Pope is so little aware of any question of difference. Comparison involves some sense of separation: but for Pope, Homer is simply the fountainhead of European poetry, and he evidently regards himself as in due line of succession. If he later modestly confesses himself 'utterly incapable of doing justice to Homer', he nowhere seems ready to allow that the task itself might in an absolute sense be an impossible one. When he draws attention to a genuine linguistic difference which stands in the way of accurate translation, namely Homer's use of compound epithets, he seems to regard the difficulty as a merely accidental one – to be resolved, perhaps, by some further enrichment of English to accommodate such possibilities:

Many . . . cannot be done literally into English without destroying the purity of our language. I believe such should be retained as slide easily of themselves into an English compound, without violence to the ear or to the received rules of composition: as well as those which have received a sanction from the authority of our best poets, and are become familiar through their use of them . . .

To Sainte-Beuve's point in favour of the critical disinterestedness that characterized his own age, a second point may then be added, and one which may have stood too close to Sainte-Beuve to be visible to him: the sheer consciousness of literary nationality, whether nationalistic or not, which characterizes the nineteenth century for the first time in the modern age. In the past hundred years and more critics have chosen to compare one literature with another rather because of their sense of nationhood than in spite of it. It is the rise of national consciousness, pre-eminently among other causes, that has made the comparative study of literature look like a cause rather than a ready and natural assumption.

Another factor which Sainte-Beuve failed to mention is the pressing analogy of the natural sciences. There is little doubt that this analogy underlies the term 'comparative literature', and perhaps some of the assumptions it involves as well. Nineteenth-century uses of the term suggest that humane studies in that age were under pressure, as they still are, to imitate what are popularly supposed to be the more stable and positive procedures of the natural sciences. 'You must have comparative theology as you have comparative anatomy,' as somebody says in Oliver Wendell Holmes's *Poet at the Breakfast-Table* (1872). And you must have comparative literature, so it is often felt, much as you have comparative theology and anatomy. It is remarkable how quickly the new literary nationalism of the last century was felt to be insufficient. And some comparative literature over the past hundred years has affected the hard, 'scientific' air of those who seek for certainty in the causes of things and who insist that literature arises directly out of the social and political conditions in which it is born. 'In the literature of France,' wrote H. M. Posnett in 1886, in a work actually entitled *Comparative Literature*, 'since the firm establishment of centralized monarchy in the seventeenth century, we everywhere feel the presence of that centralizing spirit which in the Académie Française found a local habitation and a name' (p.343). The passage is unfortunately characteristic, though the shallow determinism that seeks in literature a national character, and the sources of national character in history and climate, is evidently no worse than a passing excess which the discipline as a whole is in principle well able to avoid.

The real triumphs of comparative literature in the present century, since the foundation in 1921 of the first journal devoted to the subject, the *Revue de Littérature Comparée*, have lain in the sphere of intellectual history, and especially in the tracing of influences and correspondences across linguistic frontiers. Courtly love, Petrarchanism, Machiavellianism, the characters of Faustus and Don Juan, the Cervantic spirit in the French and English novel, the Byronic hero in nineteenth-century Europe – these are the species of subject that appear most readily assured of success. Success here seems the more natural when one reflects that ideas are often more exportable than literature itself. It took more than a century for the plays of Shakespeare to begin to have a major influence upon the literatures of France and Germany, and Racine seems to have failed almost totally to take literary effect in England; but the ideas of certain seventeenth-century Englishmen such as Locke rapidly became the foundations of the European Enlightenment, and the ideas of Rousseau and of the French *philosophes* were scattered fast over Europe and America. If comparative literature is a study of influences across frontiers, then it is natural that it should be closely linked to the history of ideas. Ideas, plots, character-types can easily be handed on. But can a language? It is surely here, in the debate that rages around the difficulties of literary translation and the defiant genius which a great literary language is often felt to possess, that the comparative spirit must always confront its gravest test.

Perhaps the problem can be posed in its most lucid form by setting up, in opposition to each other, two groups of Western critics who have debated the problem of the relations that are possible between literary languages. In the first place, there are those who have believed, like Horace, Pope, and Johnson, that poetry is essentially imitable or translatable in other languages. To speak like this is to group various instances with a view to emphasizing what they have in common. Horace believes that the Roman poet has a duty to imitate both the metrical form and the substance of some of the greatest of the ancient Greek poets, even though he is presumably aware that the phonetic structure of Latin is different from that of Greek; and if he does not make it sound easy, at least he makes the difficulties sound testing and fruitful. Pope believes that the right way to translate Homer is to stay as close to the Greek as may be, provided only that 'the spirit of the original' is not lost and the 'poetical style' of the English not impaired; and he even suggests that a 'servile dull adherence to the letter' of the Greek is among the least dangerous and delusive of faults in a translator. Johnson, in his discussion of Denham, even goes so far as to suggest that the status of a poem is reduced if it can be shown to resist translation by following the grain of its own language so closely that it depends upon features which other languages do not share: 'if there be any language which does not express intellectual operations by material images, into that language they cannot be translated'. Poetry, in this view (to pervert a well-known saying), is precisely that which is translatable.

In opposition, there are those who consider that it is part of the essential property of poetry to resist translation. Dante, in the *Convivio*, speaks as if the view were widely accepted in his time:

> But everybody knows that nothing which is harmonized by means of artistic organization (*legame musaico*) can be converted from its own tongue into another without destroying all its sweetness and harmony. And this is why Homer cannot be translated from Greek into Latin, like other Greek authors. And this is why the verses of the Psalmist [in Latin] are without sweetness, music and harmony.   (I. vii)

Dryden in his preface to Juvenal (1693), talks as if looseness were a desperate and yet imperative duty upon the translator, and fidelity to the original a plain impossibility:

> The common way which we have taken is not a literal translation, but a kind of paraphrase; or somewhat which is yet more loose, betwixt a paraphrase and imitation. It was not possible for us, or any men, to have

made it pleasant any other way. If rendering the exact sense of these authors, almost line for line, had been our business, Barten Holyday had done it already to our hands: and by the help of his learned notes and illustrations, not only of Juvenal and Persius but, what is yet more obscure, his own verses, might be understood.

Voltaire, in the twenty-first of his *Lettres philosophiques*, speaks of his own 'free translations of the English poets', which he justifies by an appeal to the differing qualities of the two languages; 'the constraint of our metre and the delicate properties of our language cannot render the equivalent of the impetuous licence of the English style'; and later, in an admiring account of Pope, he speaks despairingly of the 'harsh piping of the English trumpet' which Pope had succeeded in reducing to the sound of a flute. But the great age of the doctrine of poetry as essentially un-translatable is of course the late nineteenth century; and in this age, and especially among the French *symbolistes*, language-consciousness achieves its most extreme expression. Language by now is held to be an activity almost totally self-regarding and self-justifying, and it exists to defy reality rather than to represent it. 'Sonnets are not made with ideas,' as Mallarmé once told Degas, 'but with words'; and elsewhere he tells how 'the Word, in its vowels and diphthongs, presents a sort of flesh; and in its consonants something like a bone-structure'. Poetry in this view is an incantation rather than a message: it deliberately breaches the conventions of known speech in order to achieve something approaching the purity of an abstraction. In extreme versions of the doctrine, as in the poetry and criticism of Wallace Stevens, language may even be granted the status of a mystical religion in a world in which reality is mediated through the imagination of the poet; so that the measure of a poet is 'the measure of his power to abstract himself, and to withdraw with him into his abstraction the reality on which the lovers of truth insist'.* The doctrine stops short of solipsism, but so little short that it is hard to say how. In his 'Notes toward a Supreme Fiction' Stevens seems at first glance to put a view of extreme, even visionary objectivity:

> You must become an ignorant man again
> And see the sun again with an ignorant eye
> And see it clearly in the idea of it.
>
> Never suppose an inventing mind as source
> Of this idea . . .

* Wallace Stevens, *The Necessary Angel* (New York, 1951), p. vii.

But the rejection of what one inventing mind has seen in the sun is merely a demand for another and more modern impression; and the new mythology is a blank confrontation between reality and the fables that the poet makes anew for his own age:

> *The freshness of transformation is*
>
> *The freshness of a world. It is our own,*
> *It is ourselves, the freshness of ourselves,*
> *And that necessity and that presentation*
>
> *Are rubbings of a glass in which we peer.*

The poet offers new mythologies for old: but in the new, made for a world incapable of faith, mythologies are much like linguistic play where language finds its reason for existence largely in its own inner exuberance and form.

Irreconcilably opposed as they are, neither of these views of poetry is plainly absurd, at least in any of its more moderate forms, and it seems likely that the course of truth is to steer perilously between them. It is common knowledge that poetry is in some absolute sense untranslatable; and yet translations exist and are used. To widen the issue beyond translation, contiguous literary civilizations like the English, the French and the Italian have often been noticed to learn surprisingly little from each other, and then in a haphazard or accidental way – even, at times, through sheer misunderstanding, as in the widespread horror of what the Renaissance English supposed to be the doctrines of Machiavelli. But equally, no one doubts that literary relations between languages exist. To scrutinize the two extremes of the question represented by Johnson and Mallarmé, however, is to observe a paradoxical relation between them. Johnson appears to believe that the difficulties of a comparative relation are merely accidental; that the poet, what is more, has something like a duty to avoid them – a duty to make his poem translatable. But nothing in Johnson resembles for long anything that a modern man would normally dub the study of comparative literature, and it is hard to see how such a doctrine could lend itself to such a study. It is too international to be comparative: since it neglects or underestimates the differences between literary languages, it denies the conditions under which comparison can flourish. The *symboliste* view, by contrast, exaggerated as it may be, is exaggerating features to which the modern comparatist is naturally drawn: those which genuinely exist

between what one literary language will allow and what another
will not.

This is the most challenging prospect for the future of comparative literature, and it may be as well to see what it involves.
First, there is the matter of the sound that characterizes any
given language, and the unique way in which a poem may exploit
that sound. The past hundred years, at least in France and
England, since the manifestoes of the French *symbolistes*, of
Pater, Ezra Pound and Robert Frost, have seen an immense
expansion in interest in the musical properties of poetic language.
Frost, in his introduction to his *Collected Poems* (1951), even called
sound 'the gold in the ore', and spoke of sense as a secondary
feature of poetry required by the poet essentially to institute
artistic variations in the flow of sound. But whether it is regarded
as of primary or secondary importance, it is obvious that sound
constitutes an absolute and irreducible fact of poetry, and one
which ultimately resists conversion into another form. No
version of Shakespeare into French, German or Russian, however
skilful, will ever sound like Shakespeare on an English stage, and
the loss cannot in the end be regarded as a tolerable one. No
one, it seems fair to guess, will ever translate some of the finest
of Goethe's short poems in a manner that could fitly represent
their uniquely dynamic energy and quick, lucid vitality, where
the weight of a heavily accentual language is masterfully rendered
in witty rather than in laborious terms; so that the embarrassment
of explaining to someone who knows no German why Goethe
should be considered a great poet remains forever an embarrassment. As for a translation of Mallarmé, it might serve usefully
as a crib, but it is hard to see how it could serve as anything
else.

And yet the almost total absence of convincing comparative
studies concerned with the differing sound-systems of literary
languages must be significant of something more than an
ignorance of phonetics itself. Ignorance of phonetics, after all, is
purely a matter of choice. Any literary historian, if he wishes,
may acquaint himself with the technique by which the major
literary languages are analysed and described in their properties
of sound; and though there is a wide margin of doubt concerning the sound of Shakespeare's English, or Chaucer's, this doubt
is not likely to be the reason why literary studies have so far
failed to prosper in that direction. If it were so, there would be a

difference to be observed between success in the modern field and failure in the study of the remoter past. But in practice no such difference is observable. In fact it is difficult, even impossible, to talk intelligently for long about the sound of a poem. The fact may be a temporary one, in the sense that future discoveries may make it possible to excel where it is not yet possible: but it is not less a fact for that. The gold in the ore resists any attempt to be distinguished and discussed in critical terms. To speak of euphony, vowel-music, alliteration, cadence or the beauties of style is in existing circumstances only to equivocate. 'To read histories of literature,' as C. S. Lewis once wrote scornfully, 'one would suppose that the great authors of the past were a sort of chorus of melodious idiots who said, in beautifully cadenced language, that black was white and that two and two made five.'*

The real question is whether the future of comparative literature offers anything better. But it is important in the first instance to understand what 'something better' might be like. It would not involve knowing more about the individual sounds in a given language, and the science of phonetics, as it is at present understood, has nothing to offer here. Critics who understand phonetics do not in practice find it any easier to talk usefully about the sound of a poem than those who do not. To identify the phonemes in a given line of verse may be more accurate than to speak of its vowel-music, but in literary terms it is hardly more helpful. The reason for this is the evident truth that the sound of a poem is not an isolated phenomenon, and the more it is isolated the less significant it is likely to appear. A poem might be transliterated to a phonetic script of a most refined kind, for instance; but though this exercise might be of great use to a phonetician, it is hard to see how it could ever be useful to the literary historian. He is presumably well beyond the point of needing to be told what the poem sounds like: what concerns him is rather some subtler question such as whether the poem has any good reason to sound as it does.

The solution to the dilemma is in principle very easy, and in practice just as difficult as the art of reading itself. It is to insist the issues of sound should be related to sense or else not considered at all. The reason why the study of formal properties in general – including features of euphony and metre – is as unfashionable

* *Letters*, edited by W. H. Lewis (London, 1966), pp. 145–6 (22 November 1931).

as it is probably lies in a very proper suspicion that in themselves formal properties amount to very little. To say that in a given passage a poet is practising alliteration or onomatopoeia is to provide a label or a set of labels which, in itself, may easily serve no literary end at all. Any recognition by the reader of a fact so obvious is not, in itself, advanced by having a label placed upon it. Indeed it is possible to recognize the features without knowing the terminology at all, and the sense in which it helps to know the terms seems, on the face of it, a rather artificial one. The same observation applies to more original and ambitious enquiries than the identification of alliteration. A. C. Bradley in his *Miscellany* (1929) has demonstrated in an essay on 'Monosyllabic Lines and Words in English Verse and Prose' that the well-known monosyllabic quality of English is a quantifiable fact, and that lines like Hamlet's

And in this harsh world draw thy breath in pain

can be paralleled, in varying percentages, in other English poets from Spenser to Robert Bridges. More than that, he shows that though this fact repeats itself in German in some degree, in certain plays by Lessing, Goethe and Schiller, it is almost unknown in the Greek, Latin and Italian texts which he examined for the purpose, and rare in Corneille, Racine and Molière. But it is one thing to show all this, and another to demonstrate the significance of such a discovery in literary terms. Bradley takes us close to the brink of literary significance when he observes that 'the Shakespeare percentages are not reached or nearly approached again till we come to Byron', partly because the monosyllabic line is a feature of dramatic verse; and he adds that, for no apparent reason, the percentages suddenly rise sharply again with Tennyson and Browning. The discussion hovers upon the line, or frontier region, at which a study of formal properties becomes a study of literature itself. It demonstrates how the one might contribute to the other; but equally, it must be confessed, how the one is not the same as the other.

The literary significance of the metres which characterize the great literary languages poses a similar problem in a starker form: though here it cannot be said, as it could be said of phonetics, that enough is known to show how little knowledge alone can help. Ignorant as we are, it is conceivable that if metre could be described more exactly, it might then be possible to make more literary significance of the facts of national contrast than can now be attempted. But this is uncertain and even unlikely. The significance of metre in a given poem, after all, is not an isolable fact any more than its euphony. It is often assumed that a metre has a character of its own; but when claims for the importance of metre are made in these naïve terms, the argument takes care to confine itself to certain relatively simple cases such as the sonnet in the European Renaissance. There, admittedly, and especially in the sixteenth century, the comparatist can offer an undeniable example of an international form governed throughout Europe by a similar set of conventions deriving from a medieval inheritance of love-poetry. The phenomenon is so genuinely international, indeed, that nobody could prudently attempt one aspect of the subject, such as the sonnets of Ronsard or Shakespeare, without being in some degree versed in the rest. But a case of a broadly contemporary school of poets who happen to be international is unrepresentatively easy. A more characteristic problem concerns the ancestry of a great metre such as Italian *terza rima* or English blank verse. And here the comparative principle which the historian studies is a principle of the poems themselves, in the sense that the poet himself asks us to compare. Indeed it is in this way that metre ceases to be isolable and takes its place, among other features of the poem, in the vast memory-system of language itself. It is all but impossible to write a poem in *terza rima* without challenging comparison and contrast with Dante's *Divine Comedy* or, as in the case of Shelley's *Triumph of Life*, with the *Trionfi* of Petrarch. It is difficult to write in English blank verse without risking a recollection of Shakespeare and Milton – a fact which has understandably tended to relegate the metre, at least in its more familiar forms, to the class of abandoned possibilities. And a genuinely original metre is not exempted from the operation of the memory-system. Originality, of course, is only a relative term here, and signifies some case like the 'free verse' of the late nineteenth and early twentieth centuries where the derivative features are less obtrusive than the rest. But here too the sense of originality and of freedom from set forms depends upon a memory of what those forms were like.

It should be clear, then, that comparative literature has a promising future only if it is viewed as subject to the laws of historical enquiry. This appears to be true whether it is viewed as a species of international literary history or as a study of formal properties such as sound and metre. It is a kind of literary history, not an alternative to it. It is not a matter of substituting an analysis that is spatial for one that is temporal, but rather a way of conceiving temporal relations without the trammels of a single language and the single set of assumptions that one culture may damagingly impose. It helps the historian of literature to stand outside and see. But it is sobering to recall that this truth is not a necessary one. It is the accidental fact that Western civilization is polyglot, and has been so for centuries, that makes the case for comparative literature convincing, and not any inescapable fact about the study of literature itself. Anyone who disputes this has the example of ancient Greece to contend with: a culture that provides, once for all, the supreme example of combining insularity with excellence.

And after all, the decisive case for holding that comparative studies are obligatory upon no one is the argument from language itself. Everyone can now see that the case for calling poetry untranslatable is in some ultimate sense unanswerable. The interest of the reverse position, as represented by Pope or Johnson, is not cancelled by admitting this: that interest remains when it is clearly seen that there are many situations in which the aims of translation are properly less than ultimate. But if one were to take the modern and exacting view of translation seriously and literally enough, the case for confining literary study to a single language could plausibly rest upon the practical foundation that a lifetime is not enough in which to learn the totality of a great language and its literature. The same argument could be further refined, and it seems to grow more convincing with every step. It is not only that (outside certain rare and fortunate situations such as the bilingual) one cannot hope to learn another language to the level that literary study dictates: it is also a question of seeing that to know one's own literature to its depths is a process that takes it out of comparison altogether. It is no accident that even the most ambitious comparative studies often look thin and unrealized at the point where they touch upon something that one knows. Even Auerbach's *Mimesis* suffers in this way: if Shakespeareans admire it, it is not usually for its chapter on *Hamlet*. There is every justification for this. No one expects a large-scale map to be as detailed or as accurate as one in small-scale. But equally, nobody would describe a movement from the making of detailed maps to the making of broad diagrams as one of progress or sophistication. Some of the claims for comparatism may seem exaggerated on this score.

The study of literature advances beyond the point where

comparison can help at the point where it is most intimately allied to points of language. A work like Empson's *Seven Types of Ambiguity* (1930) is a case in point: there is no reason why precisely these techniques of interpreting poetic ambiguities should work for any language other than English, though they might happen to do so; and there is no reason to suppose that Empson's own procedures would have been more refined if they had been more comparatist. At this level of extreme detail, every language is unique; so that the case for comparative literature is the case for saying that this is not the only level. The fact of uniqueness is most striking in the vast range of instances that stretches all the way from the relative simplicity of the pun, through increasingly complex instances of verbal equivocation, and on into the large indeterminate area where one is content to speak of 'verbal associations'. The pun is by its very nature unlikely to be related to anything in any other language. The equivocation, where two or more senses are associated more intimately than by a mere coincidence of sound, is commonly outside comparison too. If a recent speculation about the best known poem in Herbert's *Temple* (1633), 'Love bade me welcome', is accepted as correct, then the missing title of the poem is 'The Host', and the little story of a guest refusing, as one who is unworthy, to be seated at table and waited upon would become an emblem of Holy Communion and a play upon the two senses of the missing title.* Since the two senses of 'host' are derived from unconnected words in Latin – *hospes* (a host or guest) and *hostia* (a sacrificial victim) – the coincidence of the domestic and the liturgical senses happens to be a peculiarity of English alone. If the title is not quite a pun, it is because many native speakers of English are probably unaware of the fact of separate derivation and associate the two words more intimately than as two distinct homophones.

The case for linguistic uniqueness grows even stronger and more complex than this when one enters the shadowy realm of word-association and multiple meaning. What is involved here is genuinely a fact of language and not of wilful or idiosyncratic attribution – associations which are shared by a whole society, in fact, where a foreigner may find himself forever a stranger. Boswell recounts a story (9 April 1778) of how Johnson once corrected Goldsmith in company concerning the proper meaning of the first line of his *Traveller* (1765):

* M. M. Mahood, *Shakespeare's Wordplay* (1957), pp. 24–5.

Remote, unfriended, melancholy, slow . . .

Goldsmith had been asked whether by 'slow' he had meant 'tardiness of locomotion', and had over-hastily agreed. Johnson confidently corrected him: 'No, Sir; you do not mean tardiness of locomotion; you mean, that sluggishness of mind which comes upon a man in solitude'; and a bystander mistakenly concluded that this was evidence for Johnson's suspected collaboration in Goldsmith's poem. In fact it was merely evidence that the two men, among many others, could after due consideration interpret a word accurately in context from among the range of senses that it might lexically possess. In this instance the critic showed that he could do it more promptly than the poet himself.

At the most minute level of interpretation, then, and outside the sphere of translation itself, comparative literature may often have little to offer. It is most characteristically the technique of the large-scale map. And the value of such maps derives from the need to see whole continents at once. It is as if one were to decide to travel by jet rather than by donkey: one may choose, and often for good reason, to study whole movements of forms and ideas rather than the texture of individual works. But there is evidently no absolute need to choose one rather than the other, and nobody need feel a sense of omission for having chosen to study a single literature rather than several. And equally, no one has yet shown that the rules of analysis are different or the procedures utterly distinct. Both disciplines are historical; and the process of tracing a tradition across linguistic frontiers is in all its major features like that of tracing one within a single language. The one activity is a model for the other. To observe the understandings and misunderstandings, the moments of interest and of influence contrasted with periods of indifference, which characterize the relations between languages is to observe the characteristic processes of literary tradition itself.

7

THE EDITORIAL ART

Henry James once spoke of criticism as having for its object a need 'to appreciate, to appropriate, to take intellectual possession', and the phrase aptly describes the editorial art. It is still a common mistake to suppose that there is some opposition between the editorial and critical functions. But to edit a literary text is to take intelligent possession of it: it is one way of performing the critical task, and among the most exacting. What has regrettably proved damaging to literary studies, and inevitably to the quality of editorship itself, has been an easy assumption that the characteristic virtues of the editor are accuracy and perseverance. The mistake is a double one, moreover; to write a critical essay requires accuracy and perseverance, among other virtues; and equally, any editor who supposes that these virtues will alone sustain him to the end of his task is bound to discover, or to have it discovered for him, that a delicate literary sense is indispensable too.

No one has seriously denied for long that it is useful to edit literary texts, and in the present century the importance of bibliographical techniques to literary scholarship has been widely urged and accepted. But two misunderstandings are still common even among those who have urged to most effect. The first is to suppose that editorship is somehow a more objective activity than literary criticism: to put it in a familiar form, that editors are concerned with facts whereas critics merely have opinions. The notion that facts are more objective than opinions – that to establish the text of a Shakespearean play, for instance, is somehow a procedure on a higher level of the verifiable than to hold a considered view about its significance and value – is a misconception which has influenced assumptions about literary study far beyond the range of textual criticism, and it is more fully

discussed in my second chapter. The other fallacy is a refinement
of the first. It holds that editorship is not only more objective in
itself than other functions of the literary critic, but that its
internal organization as a subject possesses the characteristics
commonly thought proper to an exact science, notably a common
set of assumptions which critics are supposed to lack. 'In contrast
to the general uniformity among textual critics about ends and
means, literary critics – as we might expect – hold diverse opinions
about the operation of their discipline.'★ 'As we might expect' is
a revealing aside here: it suggests a sceptical prejudice about
critical procedures rather than a considered view about how
literary arguments work in practice, about how they are demonstrated to be right or wrong, or in some degree right or wrong,
or about how agreement in such arguments is achieved. And the
phrase 'general uniformity among textual critics about ends and
means' is equally revealing, and especially so in the mouth of a
bibliographer who has himself contributed with distinction to the
controversies that rage among bibliographers in this century about
the ends and means of textual criticism. Such disagreements, it
may be argued, bitter as they sometimes are – such as the disagreement about the case for old-spelling or modernized texts –
do not disturb the 'general' uniformity of ends and means
which textual critics are supposed to enjoy. But if 'general
uniformity' means a uniformity above every particular controversy, then it may safely be said that the literary critic enjoys
such uniformity too. It is hardly to be doubted that the critic,
like the editor, is concerned with what the work is, and that his
view of the work may be wrong as well as right; and that, being
in some degree one or the other, he may in favourable conditions,
like the textual critic, be shown to be so. The continuities and
discontinuities in the history of textual criticism are not in this
sense distinct from those of literary criticism in the wider sense.
The history of both present examples of agreements, disagreements and agreements to differ among experts, and tell a similar
story of how the procedures and discoveries established in one
age may later find themselves sustained, revised or discredited in
the next.

Whatever the difference between the editorial function and
others, then, it is unlikely to resemble the difference between the
certain and the speculative. Editing can be a speculative activity
too. More than that, it is an activity rather than an end. As the old

★ Fredson Bowers, *Textual & Literary Criticism* (Cambridge, 1959), p. 1.

certainties dissolve and the complexities of textual problems are seen in a clearer light, it becomes increasingly likely that solutions to the grand problematical issues such as the text of Shakespeare are never likely to be more than tentative. And that property, too, the editorial function shares with the critical.

To edit a work, in the full sense of the term, is to establish a text and to write a commentary upon it. The first of these procedures has been weightily discussed in all the great literary languages; the second, and more significant, has scarcely been discussed at all. In this chapter I shall attempt to restore something approaching a balance between the two, though the problem of textual criticism will involve longer discussion by reason of the fact that it has traditionally proved by far the more contentious of the two.

THE TEXT

Modern textual criticism has only a doubtful and interrupted debt to ancient and Renaissance practices, and derives as a continuous process from eighteenth-century classical scholarship and the refinement of these techniques by Lachmann and others in the early nineteenth century, when the principles of ancestry in manuscript texts were formalized in the process of editing Old and Middle High German poetry and classical texts. Such techniques were designed primarily for cases of transmission by manuscript; and since the fifteenth century, when printing replaced manuscript as the principal mode of transmission for most literary forms other than certain examples of coterie literature, the problem of textual criticism has tended, for modern vernaculars at least, to merge with the study of bibliography. By bibliography may be understood the study of books as physical objects, and the associated problems of printing and distributing them. Textual problems in the modern vernaculars, with which I am mainly concerned here, have inevitably widened the scope of what students of classical literature would normally consider textual criticism. It is almost inevitable that vernacular editing should be less minute than the classical: which is not to say that it is less concerned with detail, but rather that it is concerned with details over a far wider area, and is accordingly less likely, out of sheer necessity, to attribute importance to a single crux. A. E. Housman, for instance, in his lecture 'The Application of Thought to Textual Criticism' (1921), called textual criticism 'the science of discovering error in texts and the art of removing it'; but one can hardly imagine a Shakespearean editor conceiving of his duty in just these minute and rigorous terms. The editor of a classical Latin text, for instance, works on the assumption that certain standards of spelling and syntax are all but absolute. But whatever the truth about classical Latin may be, it is certain that Elizabethan English was not like this. The demand that Renaissance editors should operate as rigorously as classical editors, freely as it is often made, is for these reasons ill-judged. Again, Housman's remark about the textual critic being rather like 'a dog hunting for fleas' strikes no chord in the editor of medieval and modern texts. The difficulty is that one can imagine a dog with no fleas, and one can imagine a classical text with no corruptions. Perhaps examples of both actually exist. But bibliography has taught scholars both respect and scepticism about sixteenth- and seventeenth-century printed texts. If we do not now 'improve' as carelessly as Bentley improved *Paradise Lost*, we are also properly more doubtful about the probability of achieving exactitude with the materials that have survived.

The first achievement of modern bibliography, which in English studies may be said to begin with R. B. McKerrow's edition of Thomas Nashe (1904–10), and to continue through the first half of the twentieth century in the works of successors such as W. W. Greg and R. W. Chapman, has been to impress as never before with a sense of the radical imperfection of all printed texts. 'Every book, every newspaper,' as Chapman wrote in *Two Centuries of Johnsonian Scholarship* (1945), whether before or after 1700, 'reminds us of human fallibility' (p. 29). The point has been brought home to modern readers and publishers by dint of reiteration, and examples of literary historians and others who have exposed themselves to ridicule by quoting words their authors never wrote, or did not write at the specified date, and basing airy theories upon such foundations, have succeeded in making most students of literature feel justifiably nervous. Even the classic English novel since Richardson, which with rare exceptions such as Chapman's pioneer edition of Jane Austen (1923–54) had been allowed to collect textual corruptions from reprint to reprint, is now encouraged to appear in purified texts supported by textual and explanatory commentaries.

This useful process finds itself under attack from two extremes of absurdity. On the one hand, there are the anti-pedants who demand to know in advance why any given text is worth editing and why the existing text will not do; and they are not always impressed with the answer that until the edition has been undertaken it is not possible to venture an opinion. The other extreme is perhaps more dangerous, being backed by an air of expert knowledge. It holds that until a text has been edited in some absolute sense, no one is entitled to put a critical view of any but the most tentative kind concerning it.

Before a critic can attempt a definitive evaluation of the contents of any book, he must be in possession of every fact which has any bearing on the history of its text. He must have sorted out for him the various editions with their dates, and the relations between these editions . . .*

Warnings against 'definitive evaluations' are never amiss; but this warning smacks of empire-building. One is tempted to ask whether A. C. Bradley was in possession of every fact concerning the history of the text of *Hamlet* before he wrote *Shakespearean Tragedy* (1904), and whether it would have been sensible of him to wait until he became so before committing himself in print. There cannot be much doubt that the answer to both questions is No. In fact the answer needs to be No, since no human being is ever likely to find himself in possession of every fact that has any bearing on the history of the text of *Hamlet*. Many such facts are forever unknown; and it is difficult to believe that the mind of any one man could hold all those that are already known. The extreme bibliographical demand here is evidently a demand for nothing more nor less than silence. And when it is considered how much good criticism the plays of Shakespeare have provoked from critics with too much sense to be intimidated by the more extravagant claims of bibliography, it is matter for congratulation that the demand has been so rarely heeded.

But it is hardly beyond the wit of the student of literature to steer a course between these absurdities. He may be grateful for what textual criticism has done and expectant of what still remains for it to do, and yet refuse to believe that he is required to down tools and wait till all is done. Literary studies are rarely a matter of knowing all the facts before venturing upon a view: to examine the processes by which textual studies inform and enrich criticism is to realize that such processes are necessarily

* Bowers, *Principles of Bibliographical Description* (Princeton, 1949), p. 9.

more informal and irregular than this simple diagram would suggest. The oddity of the extreme bibliographical view that I have quoted is that it is offered as being identical with the sanity of Greg's dictum of 1939, where a moderate case is convincingly argued:

The use of bibliography arises largely from the fact that a book seldom supplies us with all that should be known about itself. The transference of an author's words into print gives opportunity for various accidents, the title is often incomplete or misleading, while the circumstances and fortunes of books before, at, and after publication, vary enormously. . . . Bibliography attempts to straighten out the tangles in the history of the book, by giving accurate descriptions, and by distinguishing editions . . .*

This is an unexceptionable summary of the case. The duty of the literary historian, in practical terms, is not the visionary duty of trying to know everything, but the more ordinary duty of taking due precautions. When he quotes, he should know, for instance, that ordinary reprints of most eighteenth- and nine-teenth-century novels, useful as they are, are seriously corrupt, and he should verify what he sees there against an original text of some authority. He should know that many modern reprints use radically abbreviated titles and omit mottoes and other features from the original title-page as a matter of modern printing convenience, so that an original edition may offer him clues unavailable elsewhere; that chapters are sometimes printed in the wrong order, as the chapters of Henry James's *Ambassadors* were for half a century of reprints; and that misprints are not occasional facts in ordinary reprints, but may number dozens or scores per page. He cannot be omniscient, and the wealth of modern editing and bibliographical scholarship makes it less and less important that he should pretend to be so. But he need not invite disaster by supposing that a bad text is much the same as a good one.

For the editor, the problem of choice is naturally more com-plex, and the state of the subject no longer looks as reassuring as once it did. Fundamental to orthodox notions of the subject in this century has been the concept of what McKerrow called the 'copy-text', or the text adopted by the editor after due delibera-tion as the basis of his edition. In editing a text of the past five centuries, since the introduction of printing into the West, the

---

* W. W. Greg, *Proceedings of Oxford Bibliographical Society* v (1939), p. v; quoted by Bowers, *Principles*, p. 9 n.

choice may be an embarrassingly wide one. Manuscripts may survive, authorial or other; and in addition there may survive a printer's copy (such as the manuscript of Herbert's *Temple* now preserved in the Bodleian Library at Oxford), reported speech (such as notes of Coleridge's lectures made by members of his audience), marked proofs, and a variety of revised editions – and even a variety of states and issues within editions, since early printed books were especially subject to correction during the period when they were in the press, and tend to differ from copy to copy. The cases differ enormously. On the one hand there is the simplicity of Coleridge's *Biographia Literaria* (1817), where there is no surviving manuscript or proof and no edition in the author's lifetime other than the first. And on the other there is the unending complication of the text of some of Dickens's novels, where manuscripts, proofs, serial publication, first book edition and later revisions must all ideally be taken into account.

Which should the editor choose? The century began with a successful campaign by McKerrow and others against 'mere eclecticism', or the easy doctrine (as it was held to be) that the editor should adopt one reading from one source, and another from another, according to his own taste. McKerrow's early doctrine of the supremacy of a single copy-text was devised to combat a policy of mere individual preference. But it was soon found that the doctrine was tyrannous. Authors who revise their own work in later editions are unlikely to proof-read more than the revisions themselves, so that, as McKerrow put it in his *Prolegomena for the Oxford Shakespeare* (1939), a 'later edition will (except for the corrections) deviate more widely than the earliest print from the author's original manuscript'. And he concluded that the nearest approach to an ideal procedure might best be 'produced by using the earliest "good" print as copy-text and inserting into it, from the first edition which contains them, such corrections as appear to us to be derived from the author' (p. 18). Greg, in his paper delivered ten years later on 'The Rationale of Copy-Text', critically restated the established view in terms of a distinction between mere accidentals, such as insignificant variations in spelling and punctuation, and substantive readings. The copy-text, in this increasingly more liberal view of the editor's duty, 'may not by any means be the one that supplies most substantive readings in cases of variation', and he went on in still bolder terms:

The failure to make this distinction and to apply this principle has naturally led to too close and too general a reliance upon the text chosen as basis for an edition, and there has arisen what may be called the tyranny of the copy-text, a tyranny that has, in my opinion, vitiated much of the best editorial work of the past generation.*

Unfortunately the orthodox view, even as intelligently liberalized by Greg in the last years of a long life devoted to English bibliography, remains even in its most prudent form open to grave objections. In the first place, it assumes that the author himself took an intelligent and consistent interest in the accidentals of the first edition. But this is far from normal. Heminge and Condell, in their preface to the First Folio (1623), regret that Shakespeare did not live 'to have set forth and overseen his own writings'. But in what may be the only connected instance that survives of Shakespeare's hand, in the play *Sir Thomas More*, there is probable evidence that the dramatist was indifferent to variations of spelling; and the evidence of his surviving signatures is that he did not even care about the spelling of his own name. The early editions of Dryden's texts suggest that Dryden paid only slight attention to accidentals, though he could be irritated by gross errors of substance, and once protested in a private letter about the absurdity of misprints like 'Ariosto' for 'Aristotle' in his Virgil of 1697. Certain twentieth-century authors, such as Scott Fitzgerald, never learned to punctuate or even to spell; and where an author is in general capable of both, it does not follow that he is capable in every single instance where he is reading his proofs. It is admittedly true that there are contrary instances. Ben Jonson was perhaps the most assiduous proof-reader among English Renaissance authors, especially in his 1616 folio, where 700 authorial corrections have been reported; and Pope can be shown to have taken active interest in such details as capitalization and italic in successive editions of his poems. Where such an interest can be shown to have existed, an editor will naturally wish to preserve accidentals as significant. But there is no reason to suppose that most cases are like this. A poet may be a bad editor of his own works. Greg, in his *Editorial Problem in Shakespeare* (1939), was rash enough to assert that

* Greg, *Collected Papers*, edited by J. C. Maxwell (Oxford, 1966), p. 382. In a footnote Greg attributes the phrase 'the tyranny of the copy-text' to Paul Maas.

the aim of a critical edition should be to present the text, so far as available evidence permits, in a form in which we may suppose that it would have stood in a fair copy, made by the author himself, of the work as he finally intended it.   (p.x)

But if such a fair copy from the hand of Shakespeare himself had survived, it seems more likely that we should be dismayed by the innumerable variations in spelling, the incompleteness and inconsistency of the arrangement of acts and scenes, and the chaos of lineation in the verse. A holograph of a Shakespeare play would possess enormous interest as evidence of his manner of work. But it is not at all clear that it would be acceptable as it stood, and least of all in its accidentals, in a modern edition.

More than that, Greg's distinction between accidentals and substantive readings is incoherent if it is pressed in every instance. It is certainly possible to point to indubitable instances of one and the other. But punctuation, where it affects meaning between two possible readings, may cease to be an accidental feature and qualify as a substantive one, and much the same may be said of spelling. And when a case is found to stand astride this difficult borderline, Greg's distinction does not help the editor to take his decision. In Helen Darbishire's edition of *Paradise Lost* (1952), for instance, it is suggested that Milton regarded 'mee' as an emphatic spelling of 'me', and that, blind though he already was, he attempted to impose this distinction in the first edition of 1667. If this view is accepted, then the difference between 'mee' and 'me' in 1667 is substantive; if not, it is an accidental. But no individual instance of either usage can establish whether it is one or the other.

And finally, and more radically, the assumption that the last recorded intention of the author is in some sense sacred, that it takes primacy over all previous intentions, is the merest assumption. Nobody has ever shown that it is so, and it seems unlikely that anybody ever will. There is no absolute reason why it should be thought that last thoughts are always best; and if it is objected that 'best' is a matter of literary opinion, it may be answered that literary opinions may after all be considered and informed, and that they can be shown to be such. Anybody who supposes that Wordsworth's revision of his *Prelude* (1850) is better than the manuscript version of 1805 needs to be shown what Wordsworth's art at its most intense and vigorous is like, and how some of the cuts and reticent revisions of 1850 have weakened the authenticity of a great poem. Some of Keats's manuscripts provide a more complex example of the same truth: certainly an editor who began his task with the assumption that Keats's final intention was always to be adopted would be tying one hand behind his back. Henry James's elderly revision, or rewriting, of most of his novels for the New York edition of 1907–9 is a more controversial example. The New York edition is something like a total work of art in its own right, and it is admirable that it should be reprinted as a totality. But equally, many early novels such as *Roderick Hudson* (1876) possess a freshness of narrative pace and line which is obscured by later revision. The poems of W. H. Auden, which have suffered successive revisions at the poet's hands, may some day need to be restored by an editor to part at least of their original condition. In cases such as these, it is surely open to the editor to demonstrate on evidence that the early version is better than the last, and to reject the last intentions of the author as mutilations. An author cannot be said to own his own poem, unless in some strictly legal sense, and it is open to an editor in principle to reject even the corruptions of poets themselves. The single proviso is that he should convincingly explain what he is doing, and why.

The orthodox doctrine of following a copy-text (usually the first printed edition) and of inserting into it the author's last known revisions, is evidently in a state of some disrepair; and eclecticism and, still more surprisingly, modernization have now returned as scholarly possibilities. Progress has been extraordinarily rapid. In 1949 Greg spoke of the case for old-spelling editions as 'the view now prevalent among English scholars'. In the mid-1950s, as if imitating the process of de-Stalinization then afoot in eastern Europe, the rigour of the orthodox position suddenly dissolved. 'Compositors' preferences,' wrote one Shakespearean bibliographer, 'tell us nothing about the writer's. ... All that seems clear is that, in the metamorphosis of manuscript into print, compositors largely followed their own orthographical bent and that the trade showed no inclination to make spelling more phonetic. ... In accidentals, as in substantive readings, we need to be chary of supposing that compositors reproduced copy with the conservatism that has sometimes been assumed.'* And in 1958 Fredson Bowers declared himself in sympathy with the new school that was demanding the consistency of 'complete and absolute modernisation', though with a later access of caution he proceeded to advocate a text of Shake-

* Alice Walker, *Studies in Bibliography* (Virginia), viii (1956), pp. 110–11.

speare 'aimed at an audience somewhere between the bibliographical or textual specialist and the school-child', namely
'properly constructed critical old-spelling editions' formed by a
process of normalized spelling, so that 'in its texture of accidentals, as well as in its words, it conforms to the closest approxima-
tion to the author's own linguistic and orthographic characteristics that can be recovered'.* Evidently scholarship is not yet
utterly free of its Edwardian illusions that a *literatim* version of
Renaissance and later texts is recoverable, and worth recovering.
But it is now very near this point of admission – appalling as it
must seem to confess, after half a century of learned endeavour,
that the simple nineteenth-century preference for modernized
texts was after all justified. Recent researches in compositor-
determination in the Shakespearean First Folio of 1623 have
suggested that it is possible, by collating copies, to establish with
fair probability the work of five compositors, each of whom had
his own individual practices. An old-spelling edition would not
clearly or necessarily bring us nearer to Shakespeare, in fact: it
might merely bring us nearer to his printers. But by this stage in
the long controversy the last ditch of the orthodox school has
already been reached and abandoned. That stage consists of
admitting the force of all such arguments, while still insisting on
no certain evidence that some authorial features may have survived
among the accidentals of a Renaissance text:

We know that the compositor interfered; but we need to know a good
deal more about compositors and their habits before we can assume . . .
that they interfered to such an extent as to put the author out of the
picture altogether. . . . Of course we shall have the chaff along with the
wheat.†

It is tempting to suggest that when arguments for preservation are
reduced to this level of desperation, the subject is evidently poised
on the brink of revolution.

It may now be claimed that to edit modernized texts of most
English authors since Spenser is not merely more convenient
and, to the ordinary eye, more agreeable, but in a precise sense of
the word more scholarly too. Modernization forces the editor to
interpret: an old-spelling text, by contrast, offers him continual
excuses for not making up his mind. It is odd to reflect that until
recently it has been widely assumed that modernization is a task
for hacks and old-spelling editing one for scholars. But anyone

---

* Bowers, *Textual and Literary Criticism* (Cambridge, 1959), pp. 132, 140–41.
† Arthur Brown, *Studies in Bibliography* (Virginia), xiii (1960), p. 74.

who has ever attempted both will know that it is the old-spelling edition that is relatively mechanical and easy, especially if it is subjected to a rigorous version of the doctrine of copy-text. To modernize a text, by contrast, is often a high and exacting discipline. It demands that the editor should know his author and interpret the work to the depths of its detail. Unlike the old-spelling editor, the modernizer is not allowed to print nonsense. This truth is now partly recognized even by some sticklers for the older view:

Inherent in fully modernized text is the disadvantage that the transcriber must also constantly be an editor; he must interpret, and in so doing he may often alter the writer's meaning.*

The remark is revealing not only in its failure to see that the writer's meaning may already have been inadvertently altered by compositors or even by the author himself, but in the clear recognition it involves that the modernizer must 'constantly be an editor'. Old-spelling editors are traditionally allowed intervals in which they may be permitted to be mere copyists of the unintelligible.

Many mixed cases remain, and it may always be unclear how the editor should proceed where the author can be shown to have taken a partial interest in the accidentals of his text. Spenser's deliberate archaisms in the *Faerie Queene*, Milton's alleged interest in emphatic spellings, Pope's interest in certain aspects of printing practice, Swift's childish spellings in his *Journal to Stella* – all these present dilemmas for the most enlightened of modernizers. If authorial interest can be shown to exist, then such features become an aspect of the meaning of the work, and the modernizer will often wish to retain them. But if he does so, it will be objected, while modernizing other features which are without significance, he will produce a piebald text. It is altogether natural to revolt in the first instance from such a conclusion. But in revolting, it is worth noticing what is commonly overlooked: that all problematical texts tend to be edited in such a way as to produce a mixed result. The nature of the mixture may differ widely: but purity is not obtainable in the more difficult cases by any means whatever. When the old-spelling editor edits a Renaissance text by basing himself upon a copy-text such as the first printed edition, while correcting misprints and clearing up the outmoded confusion between i:j and u:v, he may offer his edition to

* Giles E. Dawson and Laetitia Kennedy-Skipton, *Elizabethan Handwriting 1500–1650* (New York, 1966), p. 22.

the world in good conscience as the nearest approach to editorial purity that the example allows. But his text is likely to be a mixture of several elements: the accidentals of the author himself, those of one or more compositors (in so far as these differ from the author's, and from one another's), the editor's emendations (which may conform to modern practice, or to a normalized view of Renaissance practice, or to the author's, or to one or another of his compositors); together with certain features of modern printing practice such as using 'j' for a consonantal 'i'. Such an editor may have produced this result honestly and in good faith, but he is not in a strong position in accusing others of eclecticism.

The plain fact is that mixture is usually inevitable and a degree of eclecticism an unavoidable duty. Once this is seen to be so, a still more radical prospect is opened to the editor: not only the prospect of scholarly modernized texts, but one of texts which are partly or largely modernized while yet retaining such features characteristic of their period or author as can be shown to be significant. The abolition of superseded forms such as 'yog' and 'thorn' in English fourteenth-century texts in favour of a familiar modern spelling such as 'gh' and 'th' is a mild and sensible example of what an informed eclecticism could offer. A largely modernized text of Spenser which none the less took note of deliberate archaisms and evidences of rime is another. The chaff does not always need to be kept along with the wheat. When the editor has identified an element to be without significance in the work, he is surely within his rights to reject it, regardless of whether it is authorial or not. If accused of improving, he may proudly agree that he is doing just that. A modern edition does not annul the evidences upon which it is based, after all, and the puzzling accidentals which the editor expunges remain in the original editions, and often in facsimiles, for anyone to consult. But until the modernizing editor gains the confidence to use such arguments boldly, the superior principles of the modernized text may continue in practice to attract only the inferior scholar.

THE COMMENTARY

It is remarkable how little formal attention has been paid in any language to the writing of a commentary. There is no philosophy of the footnote, though any editor with experience in establishing

a text and writing a commentary upon it will know that the
second function is usually more demanding than the first. And
the reader's experience will support this view. The vast majority
of readers take a text for granted: they assume, that is, whether
justifiably or not, that the text they are presented with is a
reasonable transcription of the author's so far as surviving
evidence may permit, and they usually show an understandable
reluctance to study whatever evidence of textual variation the
editor may have provided. But a good commentary is not
dispensable in the same way, and it is not a matter of general
indifference. Most literary texts are not self-explanatory, and they
often present readers with the alternatives of seeking help or
failing to understand. It seems inexplicable that a function as
indispensable as this should be so rarely considered. And yet
apart from four paragraphs near the end of Dr Johnson's Preface
to Shakespeare (1765), it would be difficult to point to a single
passage in which the problem has been attentively discussed; and
Johnson's hardly amounts to an example of an extended discussion. An editor is obliged in such circumstances to establish
his own policy in writing a commentary by sheer trial and error –
basing his practice, if he is well advised, upon examples which
he has learned to admire.

Johnson's account is both acute and contentious, and it contains
more than enough that is true to convince the hasty reader in its
entirety. Johnson could see that editing is not only a twofold
process, but that each part of the process, whether textual or
explanatory, depends upon the other: 'Not a single passage in the
whole work has appeared to me corrupt, which I have not
attempted to restore; or obscure, which I have not endeavoured
to illustrate.' The object of his commentary was to illustrate
obscurity: Johnson's own commentary to Shakespeare would
have been strictly better, one is inclined to add, though far less
revelatory of his personality, if he had confined its function in
this way. Where there is no obscurity – no difficult allusion to
explain, no textual or critical problem which gives rise to an
uncertainty of sense, no problem of language, whether verbal or
syntactical, which calls for elucidation – the editor certainly has
no duty, and arguably no right, to add a note at all. Johnson
does not altogether observe this rule, and perhaps would not
have agreed that it could properly be regarded as a rule at all.
When Malvolio in *Twelfth Night*, imagining himself in his vanity
married to Olivia, is overheard to say:

> *I frown the while; and perchance wind up my watch, or play*
> *with some rich jewel*   (II.v)

Johnson adds a note:

In our author's time watches were very uncommon. When Guy Faux
was taken, it was urged as a circumstance of suspicion that a watch was
found upon him,

which makes the point, helpfully enough, that a watch as well as
a jewel might be regarded as a symbol of wealth in Shakespeare's
time. But when in *2 Henry IV* John of Lancaster at Gaultree
Forest tricks the nobles who are rebelling against his royal father
into disbanding their army and then arrests them as traitors,
Johnson glosses the line

> *Some guard these traitors to the block of death*   (IV.ii)

with the reflection:

It cannot but raise some indignation to find this horrible violation of
faith passed over thus slightly by the poet, without any note of censure or
detestation.

But no obscurity in Shakespeare's text is 'illustrated' here: the
note is a pointless intrusion which solves no difficulty. Indeed,
since Lancaster's curtness of speech is in keeping with his frigidity
of character, there is no real difficulty to be solved at all.

Johnson might have remembered here, as he puts it memorably
in his preface, that an editor may always properly claim that
'where nothing was necessary, nothing has been done'. His
advice, however, remains excellent. Johnson is anxious as a
matter of principle that his reader should neglect his notes at the
first reading: 'when the pleasures of novelty have ceased, let him
attempt exactness, and read the commentators'. This is because a
great work is more than the sum of its parts, and needs to be seen
as a whole before examined in detail:

Parts are not to be examined till the whole has been surveyed; there is a
kind of intellectual remoteness necessary for the comprehension of any
great work in its full design and its true proportions; a close approach
shews the smaller niceties, but the beauty of the whole is discerned no
longer.

Johnson's anxiety is that a commentary may destroy by interposing itself between the reader and the work: 'Particular passages are cleared by notes, but the general effect of the work is weakened. The mind is refrigerated by interruption. . . .' But it is useful to recall here that commentary is not, and can never be, an aid to rapid reading. If the object of the reader is the perfectly proper object of 'surveying the whole', he is ill-advised to turn to a commentary at all. Some of the embarrassment of editors about the utility of what they are doing, unlike Johnson's here, is based upon their neglect of the fact that no single edition could ever ideally satisfy the demands that a whole variety of readers might make upon it. This is why it is natural that with a major author like Shakespeare there should exist many species of editions: facsimiles both of quartos and of the First Folio, *literatim* reprints, and attempts at old-spelling texts and at modernized texts, some with commentaries and some without. The mind that fears to be refrigerated by interruption, after all, has no need to use a text equipped with a commentary at all; and if he does, he is under no obligation to read it. But the fact remains that much literature needs to be explained, and that a commentary is among the most efficient ways of explaining in detail.

What does explanation involve? It surely involves the passage of information in a situation which is precisely known and formulated. It makes little sense, certainly, for an editor to determine in advance that he will explain everything that is difficult, or 'illustrate obscurity', as Johnson might have put it, unless he can also answer the question: 'Obscure to whom?' Johnson can afford to be noncommittal on such an issue, since the answer to such a question would have been obvious both to him and to his contemporaries. Obscure to the polite reader, he would no doubt have replied, meaning the reader of middling education, and preferably one with a copy of Johnson's Dictionary (1755) to hand and at least a vague recollection of the better known classical texts. Johnson is not editing for schoolchildren or for ignoramuses, on the one hand, nor yet for Shakespearean scholars on the other. This leaves him, in practice, as it leaves the modern editor whose object is the common reader, with three principal activities. First, he must explain linguistic difficulties, whether verbal or syntactical; and here, as if exhausted by his greater task as a lexicographer, Johnson is inclined at times to be ironically dismissive rather than unassumingly helpful. On *Henry VIII* V.iii. 10–12,

> *We are all men*
> *In our natures frail, and capable*
> *Of frailty . . .*

he writes playfully: 'This sentence I think needed no commentary. The meaning, and the plain meaning, is: *we are men frail by nature, and therefore liable to acts of frailty*, to deviations from the right. I wish every commentator, before he suffers his confidence to kindle, would repeat

> *We are all men*
> *In our own natures frail . . .'*

Second, there are social, historical and especially classical allusions to be explained, like Malvolio's watch, or a buried reference to Ovid, or a passing event of Shakespeare's day. On this last point, like later editors, Johnson is inclined to pride himself upon discoveries of his own: 'I am always inclined to believe,' he writes of *The Merchant of Venice* I.ii.48 and its reference to the Count Palatine, 'that Shakespeare has more allusions to particular facts and persons than his readers commonly suppose. The Count here mentioned was, perhaps, Albertus a Lasco, a Polish Palatine, who visited England in our author's time, was eagerly caressed, and splendidly entertained. . . .' And third, there are complexities and errors in the text itself to be unravelled and exposed, instances in which Shakespeare himself, and not merely his printers and editors, was probably confused or in the wrong. 'Shakespeare is here mistaken in his mythology,' Johnson writes magisterially of a line in 2 *Henry IV*,

> *Althea dreamed she was delivered of a firebrand* (II.ii.98)

'and has confounded Althea's firebrand with Hecuba's. The firebrand of Althea was real; but Hecuba, when she was big with Paris, dreamed that she was delivered of a firebrand that consumed the kingdom.' An inconsistency in Shakespeare's plotting draws a similar correction. Johnson's ironic disrespect for previous editors in the field is not counterbalanced, fortunately enough, by any idolatry for the bard himself.

These three species of explanation – language, allusion and authorial confusion – are likely to comprehend the major cases which the modern commentator may reasonably wish to gloss. But he still needs to be certain whom he is glossing for. One of the commoner defects of modern editing is to fail to understand that this question must be posed at an early stage and answered with some precision. It is hardly a matter to be decided in the course of writing a commentary. If it is not decided at an early stage, the editor runs the risk of two extremes of error which may easily damage the value of what he does: that of supposing his readers more ignorant, or more learned, than in fact they are. If the edition is designed for readers who are neither children nor specialists, for instance, then it is pointless to gloss words which appear in ordinary dictionaries; and equally pointless to forget that the reader, literate and intelligent as he may be, may yet be reading the work and even the author for the first time. It is easy for an editor to live so long with his text as to suppose that what is obvious to him is obvious altogether. The text of Donne's *Songs and Sonnets* is a case in point: allusions and confusions apart, the sheer complexity of Donne's language may often demand of the editor that he should do little less than paraphrase large portions of the more exacting poems. Explanation is a social activity: it demands a clear-eyed awareness of the state of mind of another. It is for such reasons, if for no other, that commentaries naturally tend to go out of date and to call for revision in the light of new circumstances. A situation like the late twentieth century, for example, in which knowledge of classical texts is probably lower than a century or two centuries ago, demands a higher level of explanation of classical allusion than some previous periods. Few readers today, probably, recognize an allusion which Byron expected his more educated readers to observe without effort in the opening lines of his first satire, *English Bards and Scotch Reviewers* (1809):

> Still must I hear? – shall hoarse Fitzgerald bawl
> His creaking couplets in a tavern hall
> And I not sing . . . ?

To reinforce the point the poet later added a footnote to his own poem confirming that the opening echoes the first lines of Juvenal's first satire:

> Semper ego auditor tantum? . . .

Byron intended the echo to establish the poem at the outset as a Juvenalic satire which justifies its abuse of contemporary poets and reviewers by classical precedent; but it is doubtful if more than a few readers in this century have taken the point at all.

Examples such as this confirm the significance of editorship in the critical task. No view of Byron's satire which failed to notice his open invitation to challenge comparison with Juvenal could be considered an informed view of Byron as a satirist. Equally, no one who was content with the easy and mistaken conclusion that Byron is merely writing Juvenalic imitations for Regency England could be said to have put such knowledge to its proper use. The moment at which the knowledge of a source widens into a question of the total status of the work itself is the moment at which the editorial activity widens into something else. An editor would ideally need all of Johnson's perception, and something even finer than Johnson's tact, to understand what are the moments when he should speak and what the moments when he should remain silent. But this delicate distinction, restrictive as it rightly is, is not the same as the mythical distinction between the work of a scholar and the work of a critic. The editor will need a fine critical sense to be an editor at all. The delicacy of the distinction reflects not so much a difference of attitude as a readiness to accept that any literary task has its proper confines, and that the proper confines of the editor are to expound rather than to dilate. The editorial art is the microscope of literary study. It differs from other aspects of literary knowledge not in the nature of the talent that it demands, and still less in any special view of what the study of literature is for, but simply in the supreme degree of detail which as an art it requires.

Part II

OTHER
DISCIPLINES

8

LINGUISTICS

The disciplines which compose the remaining part of this study – linguistics, psycho-analysis, sociology, the history of ideas and cultural history – share two properties which bring them within the scope of this book. First, they are studies which, though not altogether unknown in previous ages, are highly characteristic of the preoccupations of the intellectual West in the past hundred years in the form in which they are considered here; and second, they seem at face value to bear a direct relation to the study of literature. This face value is in every case the point of departure and no more than that. It is obvious, for instance, that linguistics ought to bear a direct relation to the study of literature, independently of whether in any given state of the subject, such as that which prevails in the twentieth century, it bears such a relation in fact or not. And to put the case as coolly as this is to suggest how far the endeavour is removed from either optimism or pessimism. It is easy to suppose in advance, as an optimist might, that literary studies are painfully isolated and await only the touch of modern linguistics or some other kindred discipline in order to make them fruitful. Or alternatively, the pessimist might insist upon claiming in advance of the evidence that literary studies are unique and properly so, and that it is for other disciplines to learn from them or to stay away. It is evidently important to avoid either view as a presupposition of argument. In these chapters I shall consider the relations, whether actual or potential, between literary studies on the one hand and five other humane disciplines on the other. The conclusions are unlikely to run parallel or even to prove harmonious. There is no reason to assume, that is to say, that an argument for coopera-tion in one field works similarly in any other.

Structural linguistics are essentially an invention of the

twentieth century, since they owe their existence to the lectures of the Swiss philologist Ferdinand de Saussure delivered at the University of Geneva between 1906 and 1911 and published posthumously in 1916 from notes taken down by his students. *The Course in General Linguistics*, if the text that survives represents Saussure's views fairly, is a radical and extreme attack upon what Saussure took to be a misguided obsession with chronology among students of language before his day. In any given language, at any given moment, in his view, 'succession in time is non-existent: it has become a state. The linguist who wants to understand that state must make a clean sweep of everything that has produced it and disregard the diachronic background.' 'Diachrony', or the study of language through history, is Saussure's chief target; the 'synchronic', or the study of a given state of a language, his most characteristic demand. Language, as was once claimed in a famous structuralist analogy, is like a game of chess. It does not matter where the pieces come from: all that matters is their present relation one with another. Hence the case for 'suppressing the past', as Saussure boldly put it: 'the interventions of history can only falsify the judgement'. Representing the study of language as a cross, with the 'axis of succession' intersecting the 'axis of simultaneity', Saussure held that it was simultaneity that must henceforth count for the modern student of language. More than that, the two lines cross at a point without magnitude, and it would be 'chimerical' to suppose that the one could be combined one with the other.

Saussure's synchronic view, extreme as it was, has become widely accepted in professional circles in the half century since it was published. Even compromise has hardly been fashionable. 'Panchronic' analysis, or the combination of the historical and structural, was something which Saussure had condemned as a chimerical enterprise, and is still rarely more than a prospect in the writings of most structural linguists, if indeed it is that. 'Language works synchronically and constitutes itself diachronically', as one structural linguist has put it, implying that this is about as far as he could compromise with the study of history. Nobody, it is true, doubts that the making of a language is an historical process; but it is still possible to deny that, in studying a language in any given place and time, it is useful to employ historical evidences. Whether the purity of structural theory is matched by its practice is another matter; but certainly the claims made against historical studies in principle have tended to be extreme and absolute.

But then it is clear that the extreme anti-historical bias of structural linguistics runs parallel to the mood called the New Criticism in English studies in the early twentieth century, and may help to explain why the linguist and the literary scholar have had surprisingly little to say to each other in the present age. An outsider might be inclined, none the less, to feel that the situation was ultimately nonsensical, and he would surely be right. Literature is written in language and in nothing else, and it is unlikely that any comprehensive study of literature that denied or disregarded the facts of language would be worth having. On the other hand, it is clear that linguists since Saussure have chosen the surest way of keeping clear of literature and of keeping literary scholars clear of them. This is because the case for reading literature synchronically, or without the use of historical evidences, is much less plausible than the case for studying ordinary language in this way. 'Language,' as Saussure asserted in his third chapter, 'is a system of pure values which are determined by nothing except the momentary arrangement of its terms.' But it is hard to see how a literary historian could tolerate such a view for an instant. In fact it is so implausible a view that it would have to be abandoned at the earliest stage of any considered study of literature. Literary style, as Valéry once said, is a deviation from a norm. A work of art is exceptional or it is nothing. It exists in a field of relationships outside as well as within itself, and it demands that these relations should be felt. One may fully sympathize with the linguist who wants to steer clear of literature in the early stages of his enquiry; but whether this entitles him to make claims concerning language in general which great literature falsifies is another question. More than that, literature survives to a unique degree, and in a way that spoken language does not, so that it is always likely after a lapse of time to call for the kind of historical explanation that critics and editors commonly supply.

These are already damaging arguments against any easy prospect of reconciling structural and literary disciplines. But the truth is still more general than this, and still more damaging to the synchronic case. For literature, more often than other uses of language, is notoriously prone to raid other language-systems at will, carrying off what it chooses and building alien materials into itself, while still insisting that the materials remain

recognizably alien. Eliot's *Waste Land* is a celebrated example of
the practice in this century; but the practice itself, which some
linguists call that of the 'partial' or 'incomplete' system, must
be as old as the tradition of poetry itself. It is by no means confined to simple examples like the quotations and allusions built
into *The Waste Land* or into Joyce's *Ulysses*, or to the deliberate
archaisms of *The Faerie Queene* or *The Ancient Mariner*. It applies
to cases as diverse as parody, where the language-system is
evidently partial or incomplete, and where completeness would
be self-defeating – parody cannot afford to be taken for the real
thing; or irony, where the same principle applies in a different
way, since irony cannot afford to be taken literally. But already
the argument has entered a region into which the structural
linguist will rarely wish to penetrate. If structuralists are to admit
the study of partial systems into their subject, indeed, then they
had better be on their guard. For such studies are historical or
diachronic in their very essence. They necessarily and inevitably
presuppose a memory of a pre-existing system.

What Saussure himself would have said about cases of this
kind remains unclear: he would probably have retreated behind
a reminder that his theory of language, after all, was designed
for the study of common rather than literary language. But
however far one might wish to push the anti-historical case,
one would be bound to admit that in reading *The Waste Land* it
is useful to know which words are Eliot's and which are not,
much as one could be bound to agree that in reading Spenser
or Coleridge it is helpful to be able to recognize the medieval-
isms; or that in reading a parody, it is useful to know what it is
a parody of; or that, in interpreting a masterpiece of irony like
the fourth book of *Gulliver's Travels*, it is useful to know where
Swift himself stood. None of these cases is in the least like a game
of chess, where only the existing relationships on the board
matter. Anyone who denied this would surely be mistaken in a
very obvious way, rather in the manner of the schoolboy who
complained that the play *Hamlet* was full of quotations. And yet
it is just because so much literature is involved in this apparently
minor category of the partial system that the literary student is
forced into the historical or diachronic study of language again
and again.

Perhaps it is becoming clear, then, why the synchronic study
of language has never been of much interest to those engaged in
studying literature, just as the structural linguists over the past

half century have often felt entitled to disregard the findings of those literary critics who are proceeding in their old-fashioned and diachronic way. But to talk like this invites a fallacy of an easy kind. It would be easy to suggest that really everything is as it should be, that after all the professionals are only doing what they do best – the linguists studying the language people speak, the literary scholars those extraordinary cases like Shakespeare and Milton. This would be a comfortable conclusion, but unfortunately it will not work. And this, in the end, is simply because common and literary language are hardly divisible: there are too many mixed or intermediate cases, that is, to allow the linguists and the literary scholars to go their separate ways. It is true that in spite of all this the distinction between 'common' and 'literary' is by no means worthless. On the contrary, it is often a useful distinction, and not only when it is plain which side of the fence we are on. *Hamlet* is literature: but it might be natural to describe many passages in it as 'common' or 'colloquial', and Donne's mastery of the cadence of common speech in his poems is a familiar critical point. The conversation one may have with one's dentist, by contrast, seems irreversibly an example of the 'common'; but it might, on a good morning, contain elements that would be well in place in a poem or novel, and partial systems like parody or irony might not be out of place in it. Neither profession, evidently, can in the end afford to declare its total independence of the other. Linguists and literary historians are in the end inevitably collaborators. If any comprehensive linguistic argument, including the argument for the purely synchronic study of language, is forced into denying that the common and the literary are intimately conjoined, or that a linguistic theory does not work for literature, then it has weakened itself beyond recall.

There are already some signs, however, that a more collaborative view is becoming possible. Literary scholars do not now seem as certain as once they claimed to be that what goes on in the language laboratories is none of their business: and some linguists have long shown a reciprocal tolerance. It is even possible that the long night of anti-historical linguistics is coming to an end. Two examples may prove illuminating. A few years ago an American linguist summarized a new movement of semantic theory by which meaning might be described as 'partial predictability'. 'Anything is totally predictable if its conditions of occurrence are so rigidly describable that its presence or absence can be known before the event,' in which case it is 'redundant or meaningless'.* At the other extreme of the scale, the totally unpredictable word or sound, being outside the given language altogether, or else inconceivable in the given context, would be equally meaningless. Meaning lies between these extremes of the utterly predictable and the utterly unpredictable. The process, which applies equally to listening to a conversation or reading a poem, has been further analysed in these terms:

When a hearer perceives the start of an utterance, he begins to form a silent sentence as nearly as possible like the one that he is hearing. He matches the two, step by step, keeping within the limits of the greatest probability, differentially affected by each item that he hears. When a match between internal sentence and heard sentence is reached, then understanding has taken place.†

This account seems to validate the procedures of literary study to a remarkable degree. 'Keeping within the limits of the greatest probability', if applied to the situation of an informed reader confronted with a printed poem, would mean interpreting the successive words on the page according to a system of probable significances which a poet of a given age and writing in a given set of conventions might have proposed. The account, too, seems to describe the essential dynamism of a literary experience in a revealing way. The apprehension of the poem by the reader as conceived in these terms is a process, not a single event: it begins and continues as an act of something approaching joint creation in which the reader, knowing whatever he may know of the given language-system, attempts to anticipate a poem which he does not yet fully know. And the action ends, in so far as it ever ends, with an awareness that, among the range of choices open to him, the poet has chosen these words and only these; and that these words in this unique combination, by the hindsight of one who for the first time apprehends the whole, have altered and enlarged what is known of linguistic probability itself. This last result may be presumed largely a characteristic of the literary experience as against an experience in the ordinary commerce of language; though a remarkable conversationalist might at times induce it as well as a poet. In ordinary conversa-

* Archibald A. Hill, *Introduction to Linguistic Structures* (New York, 1958), pp. 413 f.
† Hill, 'The Windhover Revisited', in his *Essays in Literary Analysis* (Austin, Texas, 1965), p. 111, quoting a remark by Martin Joos.

tion, that is, the probabilities usually diminish with every word that is uttered in any given phrase or sentence, and it is often this sense of diminution that gives shape and sense to the syntactical pattern. If this is so in literature, it may be less certainly and less characteristically so. The element of surprise is surely more natural to literature than to conversation. It would be unusual to tolerate in a speaker, or to tolerate for long, the precarious syntax and deliberate illusionism of logical pattern that Milton exploits again and again in *Paradise Lost*, where an expected conclusion – expected both by reason and by linguistic usage – is cunningly defeated at the last moment:

> *His spear, to equal which the tallest pine*
> *Hewn on Norwegian hills to be the mast*
> *Of some great ammiral, were but a wand*   (1.292-4)

No reader could be expected to predict the last four words, and Milton did not expect that any reader should: their predictability is almost as low as sensible meaning will allow. Milton's ingenuity here at least keeps the reader on his toes: the very notion of what constitutes probability in English is deliberately disturbed when a poet plays games like these. Not that the element of surprise, or of minimal predictability, need operate in merely detailed or trivial ways; but a detail such as this represents it more conveniently than a larger and more contentious example might do.

It is unfortunately true that examples of the principle of predictability employed by structural linguists themselves tend to be scarcely literary at all, being largely confined to minor phonetic cases. But it needs no extraordinary foresight to see that this doctrine, if accepted in its wider implications, means the end of the synchronic doctrine in its older and cruder form. If the meaning of an utterance, common or literary, depends upon our ability to predict it, or just to fail to predict it, then the conditions in which these partial predictions occur are aspects of meaning itself. And it is difficult to see how these conditions can be studied except in an historical or diachronic way. After all, the issue of the priority of events, the order in which the facts are known, expected or predicted, is crucial here. If it were not so, the schoolboy would have been quite right to complain that *Hamlet* is full of quotations. In a real sense, after all, it is. In correcting him, one would explain the priority in which the linguistic events occurred: how Shakespeare first wrote the play, and how years later people quoted from it phrases like 'To be or not to be' or 'Frailty, thy name is woman'. If the case demanded it, one might go on to ask him to use his historical imagination, to conceive of a situation in which such phrases were heard in the language for the first time in a London theatre around 1600. This, after all, is among the most familiar strategies of the literary historian. He enables the reader to see what the poem may have been like at the time, and re-creates the conditions in which certain utterances such as Hamlet's were (to put the matter in more technical terms) only partially to be predicted.

A second example of a hopeful movement in modern linguistics may be seen in the recent retreat from established certainties concerning the purely descriptive role of linguistics. On this matter the structuralist view in the twentieth century has until recently tended to be clear, dogmatic, and extreme. It was held to be one of the grand errors of pre-structural linguistics – an error shared by grammarians, lexicographers, schoolteachers and many others before the present century – to suppose that it was a function of linguistic study to behave 'prescriptively' or to try to impose correct usage; and a special degree of contempt was reserved for grammarians and others who tried to impose the rigour of Latin grammar upon a loosely evolving modern vernacular such as English. Linguistics, once a prescriptive discipline, was to be turned into a descriptive science in order to match the achievements of the natural sciences; and the misleading analogy of the natural sciences as they were imagined to be was allowed full play and won wide acceptance. 'The largely historical linguistic discipline evolved in the course of the 19th century,' so one highly characteristic summary runs, 'led to the creation of a considerable body of terms used to describe changes of a diachronic nature. It remained for the 20th century, with its emphasis upon synchronic, descriptive and structural linguistics, to evolve another, abundant terminology.'* But this hope of scientific certainty is already proving to have been ill-based. Its weakness can most rapidly be demonstrated, perhaps, by observing how little the behaviour of the structuralists conformed with their precepts. If modern linguists were to eschew prescriptive statements such as 'does' and 'don'ts', they would in all consistency be required to refuse in any circumstances to correct any

* Mario Pei and Frank Gaynor, *A Dictionary of Linguistics* (New York, 1954), preface.

usage committed by a native speaker. But no structural linguist, it seems likely, has ever practised what he preached in such matters. He is as aware as anybody that there are linguistic forms that are impossible, and others that are less than ideal and subject to improvement. If he hesitates to use such schoolmasterly terms as 'correct usage', it is none the less true that a standard of correctness is as fundamental to his own convictions about language as it was to older, diachronic forms of analysis. Indeed, by a supreme paradox, it now looks as if the ideal of the correct is more natural to structural linguistics than to the historical traditions of the nineteenth century. The structuralist, after all, is confined by his own choice to studying a language in its internal properties at a given state of time, so that it would be natural to his function to pronounce with some certainty that X was compatible with that state and Y not; whereas the historical linguist characteristically saw language in terms of flux, and ought, in all consistency, to have seen standards of correctness as being themselves subject to inconstancy and change.

Furthermore, it is beginning to appear as if pure structuralism is necessarily superficial. Its conviction that what applies to Latin does not necessarily apply to English may have been a sound and useful intuition, and in protesting against grammarians' rules, such as the discredited rule forbidding the split infinitive, it may indeed have been protesting against certain pointless excesses of rigour. But to limit oneself to a detailed and technical examination of the evidence of one's eyes and ears, salutary as such an experience may prove as an antidote to a period of exaggerated dogmatism, runs the risk of depressing the subject to the level of amateur botany. The collection and classification of specimens might provide a useful groundwork to an advanced enquiry into language, but it could not in itself attain the status of such an enquiry. Reflections such as these seem likely to reintroduce the modern linguist, by a long and circuitous route, back into his grandfather's study. Even the seventeenth-century quest by Descartes, John Wilkins of the Royal Society and others for a universal grammar – that most prescriptive of all linguistic enquiries, since it amounts to a search not just for the laws and rules of a single language but for those fundamental principles which govern human language altogether – now seems fated to experience an astonishing revival of interest. Half a century ago the Renaissance scheme of a universal grammar would have seemed to most linguists hardly more respectable than the search for the philosopher's stone or the elixir of life: now, by a sudden contrast, it is becoming clear that such an enquiry, wildly ambitious as it still is, represents a genuine attempt to examine the depth-structure of language; whereas most structuralism of the early twentieth century may have to be dismissed as pettily obsessed with the mere surface of linguistic phenomena. 'No descriptivist theory,' it has recently been suggested, 'can be reconciled with the known facts about the nature and use of language.' Language is genuinely governed by laws, rules or principles, after all – though all such terms are open to misconstruction in this context. When the organization of grammar is studied to its depth, it is likely to reveal patterns and principles not utterly unlike the rules of the older grammarians, however much the particular instances of such rules may be open to question; and in the end, even as linguists, 'we are led to a conception of language not unlike that suggested in universal grammar'.* Indeed such a conclusion seems inevitable when one reflects how much the ordinary commerce of language is itself concerned with prescriptive acts. When we correct a child or a foreigner, or note with admiration an unusually trenchant or felicitous usage in the remarks of a friend, or observe in a poem a conformity to ordinary usage that suffers through banality or triumphs by some subtle device of context, or note an oddity which works or fails to work, we are taking part in events perfectly normal to the use of language. Even the most severely descriptive view of linguistics would be bound, in the end, to take account of prescriptive acts such as these. They are facts to be observed in the experience of language itself.

The new literary turn of semantics, then, and the still more recent scepticism among linguists themselves concerning the purely descriptive preoccupations of traditional structuralism, are both events that seem to promise a possibility of future collaboration between linguistics and literary history. But such mutual aid remains essentially a fact of the future. To review past attempts at collaboration is only to realize how little there is to review. And one powerful reason for this paucity of achievement lies in the excessive modesty of literary studies themselves. It is very natural for the literary historian to assume that the linguist knows more about language than himself, and most attempts at collaboration begin from such an assumption. But

* Noam Chomsky, 'The Current Scene in Linguistics', *College English* (May 1966), pp. 590, 595.

as an assumption it is highly unsafe. For one, linguistics in this century have tended strenuously to neglect those aspects of language which can be dubbed prescriptive or normative, under the powerful impulse to confer upon the study of language as much as possible of the aura of objectivity that is commonly held to distinguish the natural sciences. In the act of doing so, linguistics has not only neglected what is, after all, a large fact about language itself: it has also tended to leave the student of literature with an undeserved monopoly of interest in matters of judgement. To analyse the manifest superiority of Dickens's dialogue over that of most contemporary novelists, for instance, is not the kind of subject which has in practice attracted the attention of a twentieth-century linguist. He is inclined to avoid literary examples in any case; and what is more, he is inclined to be superstitiously hostile to anything that smacks of a value-judgement. The effects of this superstition can be remarkably anti-educative. Most students of literature would probably be amazed at how little linguists know or care about the literary uses of words.

For another, structural linguistics has tended, almost of necessity, to concentrate upon detail. Indeed a large part of its charge against the grammarians of previous ages lay just here. It was tempting and even plausible to object against the older grammarians that they were both excessively dogmatic and at the same time almost wilfully ignorant of the minutiae of their subject. Saussure noted this: while remarking on the paradox that the grammarians had at least the merit of being strictly synchronic – 'they tried to describe language-states. . .; their method was therefore correct' – he was emphatic that they 'neglected whole parts of language, such as word-formation', as well as being 'normative, assuming the role of prescribing rules, not of recording facts . . .; often unable even to separate the written from the spoken word' (III.2). But the effects of this quest for greater and greater detail based upon increasingly technical procedures has led to an interest in language on the part of the professional linguist which often tends to be exclusively microscopic. He cannot see the wood for the trees, and often enough he does not want to see it. His interests may be phonetic, for instance – in which case they are necessarily minute; or they may be concerned with confined instances in the study of vocabulary by the use of such techniques as frequency-tests; or (more hopefully, from the literary point of view) he may be concerned with somewhat larger issues such as syntax or semantics. But in all these cases he is likely to confine himself to instances far smaller than an entire work of literature, and often smaller than an entire sentence. The literary student is inclined to suffer from claustrophobia in such a world. He may feel that such enquiries are being properly conducted, and yet reasonably despair that they could ever have much to do with him. And indeed if the cardinal question is posed: what literary work do we understand the better by reason of any discovery in the field of structural linguistics in the past half century? it is painfully clear that no highly convincing example can be presented. The revolution which has convulsed the study of language in the twentieth century has left the study of literary language almost untouched.

It follows that an attempt to convert the terminology of one discipline into that of the other is not likely to be the best mode of approach. When the literary historian learns the terminology of structural linguistics, for instance, he is not likely to be learning anything that explains anything he needs to know. One may apprehend the nature of Saussure's distinction between *langue* and *parole*, for instance, where *langue* (or a language-system used in its totality by a community) is contrasted to *parole* (or a single use of language by an individual in a given case). But this is not in itself to understand anything that the literary historian does not already know. Victorian English is *langue*, Hopkins' 'Windhover' is *parole* – what does the literary historian know now that he did not understand already? He is in a better position to read the works of the structural linguists, indeed: but it is yet to be shown that he is in a better position to read and expound the poem. When we call the style of an author his ideolect, we indulge ourselves in a similar fantasy. It may be added that there is nothing new in this situation: the terminology of Renaissance rhetoricians was often pseudo-knowledge of a like sort. To know such things may be a proper enquiry of intellectual history, and to know the jargon of a modern discipline may be a matter both of convenience and of courtesy. But it ought not to be confused with understanding the subject itself.

And yet this, though admittedly a sceptical view, is not offered as a counsel of despair. The converging lines now represented by linguistics and literary history, on an optimistic view, seem likely to converge on a point at which the anti-historical dogmatisms both of Saussure and of I. A. Richards have been abandoned in favour of a renewed respect for what the historian calls history and what the linguist calls diachronic analysis. It is in a sense of the pastness of the past, and only there, that an alliance can hopefully be attempted. The reasons for this are broadly similar for literature as for linguists. The literary scholar can now see with increasing clarity that his concern for the meaning of a work cannot be divorced from issues of source, provenance, historical context and authorial intention. Such evidences may in particular instances prove irrelevant or even misleading: but this no longer looks like convincing reason for abandoning them utterly. The linguist may follow a similar pattern of argument, compelled by remarkably similar reflections. He may now feel dissatisfied with Saussure's blank assertion that 'succession in time does not exist in so far as the speaker is concerned; he is confronted with a state', or that it is the duty of the linguist to enter the mind of the speaker by 'suppressing the past'. To demand that is like asking someone in a conversation to neglect all considerations of context – what he knows of the speaker's character, of the social conventions governing the meeting, and the past quality of his relationship with the speaker – and simply to regard every sentence that he hears on its face value. Such a demand would be not only plainly unnatural but very near to an impossibility. If language is to be held significant at all, then it needs to be regarded in its specific human context. And to know the context is to know the past.

More than that, language needs to be regarded from more angles than one. The status of a *parole*, whether a remark or a poem, can hardly be considered as a single and unvarying substance. It depends, as people say, on how you look at it. One considers and re-considers it in the light of information which it does not itself contain. The difficulty of collaboration here lies in the fact that structural linguistics obstinately began by denying just this:

> It would be absurd to attempt to sketch a panorama of the Alps by viewing them simultaneously from several peaks of the Jura; a panorama must be made from a single vantage-point. The same applies to language: the linguist cannot describe it, or draw up standards of usage, except by concentrating on one state. When he follows the evolution of language, he resembles the moving observer who goes from one peak of the Jura to another in order to record the shifts in perspective.
>
> (Saussure III.2)

But neither linguist nor critic should be content to hear himself compared with a sketcher of mountain views. On the contrary, he is decidedly what Saussure called a 'moving observer'; and if the Alpine analogy is to be retained, then he is less like a sketcher than a geographer. Where the object is to learn to know the Alps as a geographer might need to know them, there can be no reason to remain on a single peak. And the critic too wishes to know what is behind the view. Such enquiries, it is important to notice, are in no way pedantic or peculiar to the function of the literary history: they occur in ordinary conversation too, as when one asks oneself 'What is behind that remark?'; and, as in the act of reading, one may supply a provisional answer which modifies itself as the speaker proceeds and as one recalls more and more about his social rank, his setting and his history. It is too easily forgotten that the scholarly techniques of the literary historian are versions of techniques of interpretation which even an illiterate uses every day of his life.

The collaboration of linguist and critic, then, would surely be a collaboration in modes of interpreting complex and shifting patterns of language where the object of finality can hardly apply. This is not to deny that literary interpretations, like other kinds, may be decisive. But if it is a question of assisting in the day-to-day labours of the literary historian who is engaged upon some problematical aspect of the past, it would be important that the linguist should not attempt to import into the situation any of the false analogies of laboratory certainty. Such analogies induce both unrealistic hope and unrealistic despair, and the literary historian stands in no need of measuring himself against such objectives. If his conclusions appear to the outsider to be indecisive, it does not follow that he is failing in his task. The great and familiar problems of literary history, such as 'What did Swift mean by the fourth book of *Gulliver's Travels?*', do not lend themselves to a single and a simple answer. But to despair at this discovery is to abandon oneself to the naïve view that the complex realities of literature are there to be interpreted and solved as a man might solve a crossword puzzle.

In any case, the function of knowledge in the interpretation of language is very different from interpreting the 'system of pure values' of which Saussure spoke. Linguistic values are not pure: they take colour and significance not only from the context in which they are used but also from one another. And in this case the analogy of the chessboard may prove less misleading than it usually does. That analogy is usually held to show that the provenance of a linguistic element is not an aspect of its meaning at any given time: much as the significance of the position of a chess-piece in no way depends upon where it came from. This analogy is false; but it may help to explain how it is that, in literature especially, the replacement of a word in a new position sets up new fields of force and alters the significance of the whole. In a largely uninflected language such as English, the phenomenon is peculiarly striking, but it is no doubt observable in other languages as well; and if the linguist could help to clarify some of the complexities of syntax and word-order, he would be working in a field which the literary historian too might in part regard as his own.

But the prime difficulty in all hopes of collaboration remains in the blunt fact that literature is extraordinary. And the fact seems to be universal. If a work were not in some way linguistic-ally exceptional, then it could hardly qualify as literature at all. It is entirely natural for the linguist to object that this is not the end to start at. A reply which is now becoming possible, and even appropriate, on the part of the literary historian is that structural linguistics are now half a century old and something well past the beginning of their labours. If the time has not yet come in which the exceptional language of literature is to be considered, then it surely cannot be delayed indefinitely. If the linguist is still concerned with the norms and variants of vulgar speech, he need not forever confine himself to that point. It is precisely one who is trained in the normal, after all, who is best equipped to see the exceptional for what it is. And the problems of literary interpretation will challenge him by posing the prob-lem of what it is to work in larger units and in wider forms. In the end, after all, and even for the linguist, nothing less than the whole work will do.

9

PSYCHO-ANALYSIS

The literary prehistory of psycho-analysis before 1900 is abundant, just as the doctrine of the subconscious is itself older than the present century. But it will always be clear to intellectual historians that the revelations of Freud and his early successors in the first years of the century were new, and in two ways: in their attempt to rationalize the irrational in a convincingly scientific way; and in the hope they offered not only of analysis but of cure. Freud dated his decision to analyse his own dreams to a day in July 1895; *The Interpretation of Dreams* was largely written in the years 1897-9, to appear in the last months of the nineteenth century, late in 1899, and it was this work which included his controversial account of infantile sexuality and of the Oedipus complex. The achievement is aptly hinged on the turn of the centuries, and in fact psycho-analysis is among the most significant links in intellectual history between the two ages. As a formal doctrine it is known only to the twentieth; but viewed in historical perspective, it looks more like the ultimate phase of the 'romantic agony' – of that late romantic obsession, at least as old as the poems of Baudelaire, with the intimate relations held to exist between neurosis and creativity. Thomas Mann's *Buddenbrooks*, a novel also composed in the late 1890s and published in 1900, helps one to measure the degree of Freud's intellectual dependence upon his time and place. In the supreme value it places upon self-knowledge and analytical egoism, Freudianism stands as the final and most intense expression of literary romanticism and the long tradition of Rousseau.

And probably the literary approach, in the end, is here the best. There is surely no discipline external to literary studies so intimately involved with the response to literature in this century as this. Freud made the link explicit in one of his most

quoted remarks: 'Not I, but the poets, discovered the unconscious.' In any case, he was in himself a highly characteristic
product of a mid-continental culture of the nineteenth century
which looked to Goethe and to Shakespeare for its models and
which saw in literature the supreme example of the conscious
organization of mysterious and unconscious urges. Freud's
loose, almost novelistic account of Leonardo (1910) is hardly a
representative example of his artistic interests, which were more
traditional, literary (in a Victorian sense) and self-consistent than
this single and eccentric essay might suggest.* Since his death in
1939, the therapeutic claims of psycho-analysis have grown less
and less precise, even to the point where they are not always
insisted upon by practitioners themselves, and it may eventually
emerge that the literary effects of the movement have proved
more significant and more permanent than any other. As a
branch of medical science it may have failed; but it has undeniably
advanced the cause of human self-awareness to a point that
seems bound to leave a lasting mark upon the literary responses
of the Western world.

The 'Victorian' quality of Freud's thought touches upon
literary studies acutely at many points, but nowhere so paradoxically as in its intense consciousness of the past. Freudianism, with
its deep roots in nineteenth-century Germanic culture, is a
whole world away from the anti-historical reaction which is to
be observed in so many of the humane disciplines of the twentieth
century. The doctrine of the subconscious is itself, in its own
strange way, a doctrine of history. It holds that the significance
of human acts and desires is to be interpreted by seeking motives
and impulses anterior to those of which the patient is in the first
instance aware. In the late essay *Civilization and its Discontents*
(1930), Freud even compares the human mind, where 'it is the
rule rather than the exception for the past to be preserved', to
the city of Rome as it might appear if most of its ancient monu-
ments had not vanished, with pagan temples standing among
medieval and Renaissance buildings and modern thorough-
fares. In history itself, the past may die and leave no trace. But in
the individual mind, in the Freudian view, memories are stored
and stand ready for use. Looked at from the angle of the literary
historian, such a view seems like an ecstasy of Victorian historical
enthusiasm. The most biographical critic before Freud –
Sainte-Beuve, for instance – would not have ventured so far as

* Cf. E. H. Gombrich, 'Freud's Aesthetics', *Encounter* (January 1966).

to suppose that remote infantile experience, and even pre-natal experience, could be formative in what ultimately appears as a work of literature. He would have been content, more modestly, with the outward facts about the schooling, reading and acquaintanceship of the poet whose portrait he drew. The Freudian critic would intensify these biographical elements to the point of seeing the poem as minute evidence of the past of the poet; not of one past only, or the experience immediately preceding the act of creation, but of a whole succession of states of mind stretching back into childhood and causally interconnected.

Causation, indeed, even more characteristically than history, is the essence of the new doctrine as it impinges upon the study of literature. Most literary historians would probably be content with something like agnosticism on this subject. They might agree, under pressure, that human acts and desires are likely to be linked in causal chains that stretch back into infancy, but they would hardly think it any part of their professional duty to hold such a view, or for that matter any other view; and they would certainly not regard it as any necessary part of their duty to demonstrate what the psychological causes of a poem may have been. If such causes present themselves as a way of solving a problem of interpretation, well and good: but it would be something else to conceive of the continual duty of the literary historian in these terms. Even critics deeply influenced by Freudianism are inclined at times to be perturbed by the intensity of Freud's doctrine of mental causality. The debate in the 1940s and 1950s about the 'intentional fallacy' was in some of its aspects a debate about this. The critic under Freudian influences might concede the whole of the case for therapy, and yet feel that Freud and his British disciple Ernest Jones, when they venture into the realm of artistic interpretation, are exaggerating the biographical element to an absurdity; that they 'do not have an adequate conception of what an artistic meaning is. . . . The meaning of a work cannot lie in the author's intention alone. It must also lie in its effect'.★ Even I. A. Richards, in spite of a professional training in psychology, drew back at the last moment from the prospect of a psycho-analytical school of criticism: 'Whatever psycho-analysts may aver, the mental processes of the poet are not a very profitable field for investigation. They offer far too

★ Lionel Trilling, 'Freud and Literature' in his *Liberal Imagination* (New York, 1950), from an essay first published in an earlier form in 1940.

happy a hunting-ground for uncontrollable conjecture.'* It is an astonishing fact, in view of the enormous vogue of Freudianism on both sides of the Atlantic between the two World Wars, that psycho-analytical criticism somehow failed to emerge as a school. Even the most convinced Freudians have often refused in matters of literary judgement to follow where their master has beckoned.

It is equally clear that Freudianism has not been totally frustrated in its literary effects by its failure to achieve its predictable influence upon the study of literature. But the evidences for its success, though convincing enough in the short run, remain scattered and oddly formless. One might expect, for instance, that psycho-analysis and the stream-of-consciousness novel were causally connected: but Proust is not known to have read Freud, and Joyce not known to have read him early enough to influence the *Portrait of the Artist* (1916), though he mentions 'the new Viennese school' once in *Ulysses* (1922) and often speaks of Freud and Jung, not very respectfully, in *Finnegans Wake* (1939). It seems likely that the contemporaneous rise of the scientific interest and the fictional in western Europe in the first two decades of the twentieth century owes its coincident origin to some common source. Other kinds of novelist seem to have been only spasmodically affected: D. H. Lawrence, for instance, has been shown to have discovered Freud in 1912, when he first met his future wife Frieda, and when *Sons and Lovers* (1913) was already in first draft; so that the novel was first written in ignorance of the Oedipus complex of which it presents so faithful a picture, and perhaps revised in the knowledge of it. But Lawrence's fiction as a whole is hardly analytical in a Freudian sense; and Mann's early interest in neurosis makes it clear that much that could pass as Freudian in literature could as easily derive from remoter origins. Often, too, Freud provoked only resentment. Kafka, a novelist whom one might have expected to feel himself in profound harmony with the new doctrines, wrote in his diary in a hostile spirit that self-awareness can only be an evil – 'psychology is impatience; all human mistakes are impatience, a premature breaking-off from the methodical' (1917–19). The direct effects of Freudianism upon literature do not seem much more impressive than its effects upon literary criticism. Its most powerful influences, probably, have been in the realms of popular intellectualism: not among those who write literature,

* I. A. Richards, *Principles of Literary Criticism* (London, 1924), ch. 4.

in fact, or among those who write about it, but among the millions who simply read.

What have these effects upon literary response been like, and what do they hold in prospect? The first part of an answer has already been suggested: that being deeply convinced of mental causality, as psycho-analysis is, it offers the intriguing but still largely unexplored possibility of a more intensely historical form of criticism than any that has yet been attempted – one, perhaps, in which the 'uncontrollable conjecture' which Richards feared has been brought within reasonable control by means of sharper and more pertinent biographical analysis. The difficulty here is the one which Richards presumably had in mind: that poetic creation in Freudian terms, though decidedly purposive, lies in large part beneath the level of consciousness. It is true that Freud was not a modernist in aesthetic matters. He had little sympathy with merely self-expressive works of art, such as the products of Surrealism seemed to him to be, and was always emphatic about the importance of deliberate and conscious shaping in the work of art. But he also emphasized that what the artist was deliberately shaping was material of which he had repressed his awareness. The function of the psychological critic, then, would be to reveal significances of which the poet himself was unaware and which (at least in the first instance) he might even strenuously deny. Such a view might be said to enlarge the traditional notion of artistic intention rather than to breach it: one can accept, on reflection, that 'subconscious intention' is an intelligible concept, and that a poet might have willed into existence a work whose true significance, if explained to him by a perceptive reader, might surprise or distress him. And it has not yet been demonstrated that conjectures of this sort are necessarily and in their nature uncontrollable. The plausibility of psychological conjectures about literature surely rests on similar foundations to the plausibility of any other kind of historical conjecture. It is the business of the critic, that is to say, to validate his interpretation in the text and in what he knows about the text, to show that it works. When we see individual examples of psychological interpretation overturned by argument, as Freud's own view of Leonardo has been overturned by fresh evidence, we are observing examples of how such validations and invalidations may properly operate.

An absolute case against psycho-analysing the poets through their works, then, does not seem to have been clearly made.

Two of the commoner objections, certainly, will hardly bear investigation. The first is that we commonly do not know enough. But if in a specific instance not enough is known, this is only an objection to analysis in the specific instance: it leaves the general propriety of literary psycho-analysis exactly as it was. And this remains true even if the specific instances where we do not know enough are in a majority: they would not count, that is to say, against those cases where enough is known to advance a reasoned and informed conjecture. The question of Swift's sanity is perhaps such an example. It was an actively debated question in the eighteenth century itself, so that it cannot be charged against it that it is an example of mere modern inquisitiveness. It is at times an active question in the works themselves – so much so that it seems merely hypocritical to claim that, in reading Gulliver's account of the Yahoos, the question does not naturally cross the reader's mind. And this is where the second objection commonly arises. There are always those who will insist, at such moments as these, that questions concerning the mental health of an author are in their very nature improper. But to this one can only reply that no convincing reason has yet been offered why anyone should suppose anything of the kind. After viewing all the evidence, one might properly conclude in some given instance that that answer cannot certainly be known. But to review the evidence for the question is in itself to concede that the question is an admissible one. The notion that works of art are properly self-explanatory, that they bear (or ought to bear) all the necessary evidences for interpretation within themselves, seems to run counter to every ordinary experience of literature. Nothing in practice is commoner than to find that one cannot understand what one reads and that explanations fortunately exist. If an understanding of the role of the Yahoos depends upon knowing more about the quality of Swift's mind in general, it seems merely philistine to refuse to listen.

But then psycho-analytical criticism in these terms, such as the study of the mind of Swift in his life and writings, is merely an extended version of the most familiar forms of biographical criticism. The modern analyst would often demand more: in fact he might be inclined to speak in terms of something like an infinite regress in the patient's mind, of layers below layers extending downwards towards birth and even beyond. When Ernest Jones, in his study of *Hamlet*, speaks in characteristic terms of 'the deeper working of Shakespeare's mind', one is hardly in the ordinary world of biographical interpretation. Jungian doctrine is remoter still from familiar historical processes. When Jung writes of the unconscious as 'the totality of all archetypes' and of the 'things that from immemorial times have lain buried in the depths', of 'those far-away backgrounds, those most ancient forms of the human mind',★ one is in a world where the literary historian may suddenly feel himself in possession of a perilous and unaccustomed liberty. The ambitious doctrine of a collective unconscious which is common to the human race and which manifests itself, independently of influence, throughout the literatures of the world, is certainly seductive enough. But it re-opens the question of mental and emotional causality in an utterly dizzying and uncontrollable form. Even Freudianism, to the biographical critic, may seem something of an infinite regress – but at least it allows the analyst to limit himself to the lifespan of the patient. The Jungian system of archetypal patterns and primordial images seems to offer no handgrips where the climber may so much as pause. It is a free fall. This is not offered as a view in any way derogatory to its fascination: in fact it seems to be the very property on which its fascination is based. It commands a world where the literary historian might easily feel at home, a world of forms of a kind which he already knows: the secret garden, the hero-god, the eternal feminine, the chase or the quest. But its weakness, for the historian, lies in the simple fact that it offers not too little but too much. And when it offers as much as this, the normal processes of explanation tend to go into reverse: the explanation, that is to say, is likely to be more mysterious and more difficult than the work which it claims to explain. A Freudian explanation of a poem often makes the poem look simpler than it is: but then making poems look simpler than they are may be among the useful things a critic can do. To relate a poem to 'things that from immemorial times have lain buried in the depths' is to perform an opposite function. One might readily concede that it could be so, and yet honestly wonder why anyone should think that any literary discussion could be advanced by conceding or denying anything of the sort.

The effects of psycho-analysis upon literary response, then, are likely to be overwhelmingly Freudian; and the Jungian

★ C. G. Jung, 'Mind and the Earth', in his *Contributions to Analytical Psychology* (London, 1928), p. 108 f.

digression seems productive of literature which demands to be
seen in its own light as a contribution to the poetry of the
archetype rather than as a system of explanations calculated to
alter the view of literature itself. And certainly the Freudian
view has already altered, and perhaps permanently, the quality
of literary response in this century. But the nature of its influence
has been deeply paradoxical. One might have expected the
notion of causality in the emotional life of an individual to have
deepened and complicated a relatively simple response to
literature. But Freudian criticism is not in practice usually more
subtle or complex than other kinds: on the contrary, it is often
characterized by a rude simplicity all its own. When a Freudian
critic speaks of the 'insane or possessed people of Sophocles',
for instance, the virtues of such an interpretation are the virtues
of a simple, bold diagram imposed upon a drama of baffling
subtlety and complexity. Left to oneself, one might have hesitated
over taking a decided view about the mental health of Sophocles's
heroes and heroines; but if they are simply mad, then the whole
matter is really much easier:

Electra is what we should call nowadays schizophrenic: the woman who
weeps over the urn which is supposed to contain her brother's ashes is not
'integrated', as we say, with the fury who prepares her mother's murder.
And certainly the fanaticism of Antigone – 'fixated' like Electra, on her
brother – is intended to be abnormal, too.*

This certainly leaves Sophocles looking tidier than ever before,
though much less interesting. And it seems undeniable that an
eagerness to label the complex realities of literature in just such a
bold and schematic way is a characteristic aspect of literary
Freudianism. The new psychology is after all a system, and its
fascination lies precisely in being systematic. Realities in poetry
or in life which to the non-Freudian seem vague and debatable
tend, for the convinced Freudian, to look plain and simple: and
perhaps it is because he wants the world to look plainer and
simpler that the Freudian is what he is. It is also true that simplification is only a vice if it supposes itself to be something else. If
the Freudian critic is aware that he is simplifying, and if he signals
this awareness to the reader, no real harm may be done. But if he
does neither, then the process of explanation may be reductive in
a damaging sense. It would be one thing to emphasize the
terrible polarities of Electra's mind and the intensities of her loves

* Edmund Wilson, *The Wound and the Bow* (Boston, 1941), p. 261.

and her hatreds by the word 'schizophrenia'. But Electra, after all, is not mad; and if, along with Antigone, she is 'abnormal', it does not follow that she would be more admirable if she were otherwise. To be heroic is in itself to be unlike most men and most women. Audiences unversed in the doctrine of the common man must always have been utterly clear about that. It is one of the sadder characteristics of the Freudian mind to suppose that abnormality is a condition inviting only regret, rejection or – most condescending of all – cure.

And latter-day Freudianism, including some of Freud's own pronouncements, can in practice be senselessly reductive both of human emotion and of human rationality. To consider the emotion first: when the Electra of Sophocles is dubbed a schizophrenic, or Hamlet a victim of the Oedipal complex, it is rarely or never the case for such accusations to be, in effect, anything less than that. Such hypotheses are never demands for an enlargement either of our human sympathies or of our notions of what heroism can encompass. Nobody, in practice, ever thought Hamlet the more heroic for secretly nursing a repressed desire for his mother. And yet the reasons why anyone should think the less of Hamlet for such a reason, though they may indeed be good reasons, are seldom fully presented in any account either of the complex itself or of Hamlet as a character. It is probable that silence of this order of regularity has a significance of its own. Freudian critics are unlikely to be engaged in a conspiracy to keep from the world a secret known only to themselves which would, if debated, reveal why suppressed desires are in some sense unheroic or normal men and women better than abnormal ones. It is much more likely that there is at least the shadow of a rational explanation underlying the regularity of these assumptions. On the matter of repression, indeed, Freud is well-known to have shown his hand: the objection to repression is the claim for rationality itself as the proper basis of human behaviour; and the patient is invited to terminate repression, if necessary by means of analysis, in order to bring a wider and wider range of his motives into the light of reasonable interpretation. And this cannot in itself be called an argument reductive of humanity or of human dignity. Indeed it seems remarkably optimistic, and perhaps absurdly optimistic, concerning the prospect of rationality in human behaviour. The difficulty is that Freud's own notion of rationality tended in itself to be contemptuous. Arguments, he could at times claim, are merely an expression of repressions which, necessarily and always in any given individual, lie deeper than the repression that is in process of being exposed to the light. 'Man's judgements of value,' as he put it in *Civilization and its Discontents*, 'follow directly his wishes for happiness; . . . accordingly, they are an attempt to support his illusions with arguments' (ch.8). In this view the aim of analysis is hardly to expose an illusion to the light of reason: in the end, it is merely to subject the obscurity of one illusion to the greater and profounder obscurity of another.

It is at extremes of the Freudian argument such as this that psycho-analysis seems to operate as an agent hostile not only to any rational view of literature, but to any rational view of anything whatever. The breaking-point in the argument comes here, as it came for Jung (according to his own account in his autobiography), in the period of their disagreements soon after their first meeting in 1907. When Freud was challenged with the objection that his view of human civilization was 'an annihilating judgement' which reduced it to the level of 'a mere farce, the morbid consequence of repressed sexuality', Freud only replied: 'So it is, and that is just a curse of fate against which we are powerless to contend.'* But on this point there can hardly be a compromise: either man's judgements of value in literature and elsewhere are genuinely subject to argument or they are not. Freud's view was that they are not and cannot be so. To offer a reason for admiring what one admires, in his view, could only be to offer a pseudo-argument: and this view would presumably apply however cogent the argument in itself and however sincere the motive of the critic who employed it. 'Sincere', that is, in a conventional sense of the word; in an ultimate sense, for the Freudian, all judgements of value are insincere, since they are not the genuine reasons why the reader thinks what he does, though he may suppose that they are. The study of literature by the usual exchange of argument, on these principles, could only be considered as an exchange of pseudo-arguments. The arguments might be in some sense valuable in themselves: but they could not be the reasons why anybody thought as he did.

Nobody, in all probability, would be prepared to defend for long a study of literature conceived in these terms. It is true that the subjectivist case is often argued in terms remarkably similar to these: that literary preferences are merely matters of individual judgement, that arguments are merely diversionary,

* Jung, *Memories, Dreams, Reflections* (London, 1963), p. 147.

or ways of spending time in sociable terms, or mental gymnastics which are self-justifying by reason of being beautiful or intellectually muscle-building. But then the literary subjectivist, like Freud himself at this point of his argument, does not behave as if he believed any of this, and his scepticism is surely well justified. If Freud really believed that man's judgements of value are based not upon arguments but only upon pseudo-arguments, then he would also believe that his own judgement about man's judgements in this very instance was similarly based. But it seems very unlikely that he believed anything like this. He was a confident and insistent controversialist, and took proper care that his views should be disseminated and reiterated. Why should he have taken such care over arguments which he believed only to be spurious?

Freudianism, then, and especially in its literary manifestations, is plagued by certain internal contradictions of its own. On the one hand it is rationalistic in its ambition to investigate and reorganize the profoundly instinctual and pre-rational sources of human motive; on the other, it is profoundly sceptical of rationality itself. But this contradiction, if such it is, is visible only to the outsider. To the Freudian critic neither proposition is acceptable in quite these brutal terms. He is surprised, even incredulous, to be told that Freud was suspicious or hostile to matters concerning the human instinct. To many who have fallen under the spell of psycho-analysis, Freud has signified the great liberator of the instinctual element in man, of the 'drives' which compel a man to live as he does. 'One is always aware in reading Freud how little cynicism there is in his thought,' as one Freudian critic has written. 'His desire for man is only that he should be human, and to this end his science is devoted.'* But then the constraining prudery of Freudianism has always been an aspect of the system of which disciples themselves were unaware. It would not occur to a Freudian, in the vast majority of instances, to ask why it is better to be normal than otherwise. The enclosed world of the middle-class Vienna of the Habsburg Empire in which Freud lived and worked cannot have supposed this to be a real question, and modern Freudians have usually been content to accept the silent assumptions of a doctrine fitted for a closed and conformist community. This is not a system either for the hermit or the hero. It is a faith of those who have lost faith itself, the censor-system of those who deny the authority of official or parental

* Lionel Trilling, 'Freud and Literature', *op. cit.*

censorship. Orwell once called the Marxism of Western intellectuals in the 1930s 'the patriotism of the deracinated'; and Freudianism, in its literary effects, is often enough the morality of the deracinated. Those who adopt it in these terms rarely notice how absolute its demands upon their thoughts and actions are: they suppose that because they have freely chosen to believe in it, they must be in a state of freedom in accepting what it teaches.

And yet the potency of Freudianism in systematizing the awareness even of those who are not disciples cannot be in doubt. Its function is not to deepen or subtilize the complexities of life or literature, but rather to devise simplifying formulae that make all things clear. And so long as this function is understood for what it is, there seems no reason to object and every reason to accept. Perhaps a literary example may clarify how Freudian simplification works. In the course of *The Bride of Lammermoor* (1819), Scott tells how the Lord Keeper, Sir William Ashton, whose daughter Lucy was the 'constant playmate' of her father, greeted his visitor the Marquis of A—. The Marquis

answered with courtesy the courteous inquiries of the Lord Keeper, and was formally presented to Miss Ashton, in the course of which ceremony the Lord Keeper gave the first symptom of what was chiefly occupying his mind by introducing his daughter as 'his wife, Lady Ashton'.

Lucy blushed; the Marquis looked surprised at the extremely juvenile appearance of his hostess, and the Lord Keeper with difficulty rallied himself so far as to explain. 'I should have said my daughter, my lord; but the truth is that I saw Lady Ashton's carriage enter the avenue shortly after your lordship's.'   (ch. 22)

The story is a plain example of what Freud, in the fifth chapter of his *Psychopathology of Everyday Life* (1901) calls 'mistakes in speech' and what the world now calls 'the Freudian slip'. Freud cites case after case of 'self-betrayal' in actual conversation, adding examples from literature, including one from Schiller's *Piccolomini* (I.5), another from Shakespeare's *Merchant of Venice* (III.2), and a third and fourth from Meredith's *Egoist*. The phenomenon illustrates the most helpful of all possible relationships, probably, between Freudianism and literary response. It is an exact model of Freud's dictum that his doctrine is all in the poets. Shakespeare, Schiller, Scott and Meredith all know that what they are portraying are examples of slips of the tongue which reveal more of the truth than the speaker intended. Freud is not drawing attention to an unknown phenomenon, or claiming to do so. But his simplifying formula of the speech-blunder, by grouping cases together and noting what they have in common, still offers something more than the poets give – namely a comprehensive view of how such blunders work, and in what circumstances: 'People make no mistakes when *they are all there*, as the saying goes,' Freud concludes, after reviewing the evidence. Freudian slips are characteristic of moments of confusion and uncertainty, of 'the stifled voice of the author's self-criticism'.

But if Freudianism works well in a minor, finite example such as the significant speech-blunder, why does it help so little in respect of its larger and more crucial doctrines, such as the alleged origins of adult repressions in infantile sexual trauma? The answer probably lies in the fact that Freud's doctrine of infantile sexuality, unlike the Freudian slip and the Oedipus complex, is hardly to be found in the poets at all. On this point Freud surely underrated, and perhaps knowingly, the novelty and radicalism of what he was proposing. When Jung broke with him over his obsession with the sexual basis of repression – or so Jung's own account would have it – it was precisely because this obsession seemed to Jung extravagantly dogmatic and exclusive. It seemed to him to deny ordinary experience, to leave out far too many of the cases under review and to base itself on a mystical attraction for sexual experience rather than upon a cool assessment of evidence. If this is a fair account of Freud's character at the time of the breaking-point between the two men, then it is rather different from the character that Freud turned outwards upon the world. In public he was a scientist, eager to support his assertions with case-histories, emphatic that the doctrine of infantile sexuality was based upon ordinary observable fact and well known to every mother and every nursemaid. And yet, however that may be, it remains clear that it is not a fact of Western literature: Freud, not the poets, discovered infantile sexuality. If it were not so, the world could hardly have been as shocked and derisive as it was, in the first decade of this century, to hear the hypothesis suggested as a scientific truth. As for its actual status as a fact, that is irrelevant to the present argument. But it is surely clear that, whether the literary historian accepts the doctrine or not, he is in no position to employ it in his own investigations of literature without imposing upon the poets a knowledge which they did not possess.

It is the sheer originality of Freudianism, in fact, that limits its uses in the study of literature. Suppose the Freudian critic to have been given his head in an interpretation of the *Electra* of Sophocles. It is perilously easy to imagine an interpretation far less Sophoclean than that in *The Wound and the Bow*. Nothing could be so plausible, for a post-Freudian, than to suppose Electra, deprived in infancy of her father Agememnon and brought up in terror of her mother Clytemnestra and her mother's lover Aegisthus, to have been the victim of a sexual trauma in infancy. The three Greek tragedians who handled the theme, indeed, were none of them blind to the horror of her upbringing; and Euripides especially would not have doubted that her personality had been scarred by experience. But sexual trauma in infancy is in excess of anything that any of them can be shown to have recognized in Electra. If the Freudian critic is to offer such a suggestion at all, then he must offer it as an addition to the plays themselves. He is presenting a possibility in the story, or something more than that, which Aeschylus, Sophocles and Euripides all failed to observe.

It would be easy, in cases like these, to assume that Freudianism can deepen our awareness of works of literature at a profounder level than the poets themselves were capable of. But to suggest this is to misconceive both the function of the critic and the function of the psycho-analyst. For the analyst as such, literary examples cannot be said to possess any special virtue or interest. It is pleasant, even reassuring, to remark upon the ancestry of one's own observations, and when Freud quotes four literary examples of the significant speech-blunder he is decorating his argument in much this way. But his argument would be just as sound if it depended entirely upon cases observed from life itself. He does not need literature at all. As for the critic, it has still to be demonstrated why he should wish to deepen his awareness of a work *ad infinitum*, irrespective of the possible or probable awareness of the poet himself. It may be fully admitted here that awareness includes subconscious awareness; and if Freudianism has directed a more informed attention upon the paradox that a poet may both know and desire at a profounder level than conscious knowledge or conscious desire, then this paradox must be numbered among the most useful of Freud's attempts to formulate and to systematize. But the odd, indeed awkward fact remains that Freud adds or invents as much as he systematizes; that whatever mothers and nursemaids may know, poets before this century, with the rarest exceptions, cannot be demonstrated to have possessed an awareness of infantile sexuality at any level whatever.

This discussion has tried to show what aspects of the Freudian heritage may prove useful or useless to the literary historian: how it may help him to speak of what the poets knew, and how some formulations accurately describe what it was that they knew. But this is to neglect the influence which psycho-analysis may in the future exercise upon literature and upon the response to literature. If the situation could be frozen as it is, it would be possible to content oneself with the systematization of existing knowledge, some original additions to that knowledge, and the modest influence of the system upon literature in the earlier twentieth century. But Western literature today is proudly aware of existing in a situation of permanent revolution, and Freudianism and its successor-doctrines, so far as they continue to be noticed by poets and readers, are themselves among the active agents of that revolution. Psycho-analysis, indeed, is an unusually exact model of the principle of successive languages: as Freud analysed himself, and was later analysed by Jung and others, so the drives and motives of the successors are themselves analysed by those who follow later still. In the long course of such a process, those who unprofessionally pride themselves upon their psychic awareness, as many poets and novelists may wish to do, may develop a continuing hierarchy of poetic languages by which to describe their own condition and that of their fellows. The intense knowingness of much contemporary literature, its pride in its own self-awareness and its determination to question all motives and seek sources for them, has by now long since passed the point at which Rousseau or Byron would still recognize their influence as their own. It is also true, paradoxically, that beneath the 'clinical awareness' of the modern poet there often lies a deep reservoir of easy sentiment; and certainly the vogue of psycho-analysis can operate to support a condition of facile and self-regarding sentimentality. But the interaction of poetry and critical response now seems to have entered into a spiral of self-awareness to which there may be no end, unless the end should prove to be sudden reaction in favour of healthy ignorance. Thomas Mann, in his Vienna lecture of 1936, has spoken of the 'analytic revolution' of Freudianism which 'infiltrates life, undermines its raw naïveté, takes from it the strain of its own ignorance, de-emotionalizes it'; and a recent critic has written approvingly of the modern poet's 'cool, analytic attitude to his own distress' as something which he openly shares with his readers: 'the more ruthless he is with himself, the more un-shockable the audience becomes'.*

The prospect is admittedly uninviting, especially when one reflects that 'unshockable' in such contexts probably means 'ready to discuss' rather than 'ready to tolerate'. The sharp moralism of the post-Freudian shows little sign of diminishing: he does not characteristically take the view that to understand is to condone. A literature arrogantly aware of its own awareness and determined to exercise its claims to knowledge as a technique of moral instruction or intimidation is the gloomiest prospect of the influence of psycho-analysis upon literature. It promises nothing like the liberation of which the first analysts dreamed and which their first enemies, in the early years of this century, so openly feared. It would make its own prison of the mind, a closed system of perpetual self-censorship where an experience is no sooner to be felt than it is labelled and judged. From such a prison, in which many now choose to live, only a moral intuition as striking and as systematic as Freud's own could ever set them free.

* A. Alvarez, *The Times Literary Supplement* (23 March 1967).

10

SOCIOLOGY

A sociology of literature might mean any one of several things. If it means the study of social history and its application to literature, then it may safely be said that it already exists, and that the study of that most social of all literary forms, the novel, has long been inconceivable without it. *The Dickens World* (1941) by Humphry House would be a distinguished example. If it means that sociologists should themselves study literature – to take account, say, of the vast encyclopedia of knowledge about society embodied in the nineteenth-century novel – then the prospect can only be applauded; indeed the neglect of literary evidence by sociologists, sometimes approaching a kind of contempt, must be regarded as something of a scandal. If it means the application of 'laws' of social action, of what Mill long ago in his *System of Logic* (1843) called a 'general science of society', a science designed to reveal the 'uniformities of coexistence' and the laws of social progress (VI.x–xi), then the case still needs to be made. In this chapter I shall neglect the first possibility, rewarding as it is, since the uses of social history in the study of literature are probably too familiar to be worth describing; which is not to say that critics use social history enough, but rather that they are not inhibited from such use by doubts or confusions of principle. The employment of literary evidence by sociologists, by contrast, is a matter of some urgency; and its urgency is linked with my third possibility, which I propose here only in order to dismiss, since the expense of energy upon the search for a phantom concept of a 'general science of society' is precisely what, in all probability, has diverted sociologists from the subtler and unquantifiable truths that great literature has to offer.

Sociology is among the most Victorian of all humane studies, and its sudden vogue in the mid twentieth century must be regarded as a tribute to the continuing potency of Victorian values in the Western intelligentsia. There is a long prehistory stretching back at least a hundred years, to Montesquieu, but the rise of the subject can fairly be dated to the 1830s and 1840s: to Comte, who invented the word and apologized for his invention; to Mill, who tried to relate it to the achievements of the classical economists; and to Marx and the Marxists, who linked it with the political programmes of the class war. The ensuing half century and more, up to the First World War, saw a grand critique of Marxism from radicals like Bernstein, a German Social Democrat who by the 1890s had lost faith in Marx's historical prophecies; Emile Durkheim, a French democrat who in the same period saw through the scientific pretensions of Marxism; and Benedetto Croce, the Italian Liberal philosopher who began and ended the 'Marxist parenthesis' of his life in the same decade. In the early years of the new century the study took on a new and violent dictatorial colouring, as in the works of the Frenchman Georges Sorel, who died a Leninist in 1922 and demanded, in his disillusionment with parliamentary democracy, a return to heroic and even barbaric values; or Pareto, an Italian professor at Lausanne who saw political action as a struggle between *élites*, advocated a tough-minded conservatism and probably influenced the young socialist Mussolini. The imposing exception was the Prussian democrat Max Weber (1864–1920), who feared that the bureaucratization of Western society might naturally lead to Caesarist dictatorship and who fought for political democracy and social justice without the tyranny of Socialism. His study of the causal relations in human affairs in the early years of the century, following a breakdown in 1898, led him into conclusions already familiar in practice to students of literature: that in order to escape from the pseudo-scientism of Comte and Marx, the sociologist should construct or invent a purely hypothetical analysis based on a 'model' or ideal type; and that in such enquiries the point of departure is necessarily and rightly arbitrary. By the time of Weber's death sociology was already established as an academic discipline, at least upon the Continent of Europe, and its invasion of universities in the English-speaking world since the thirties has been one of the acknowledged triumphs of scholarly adventurism.

Two strands emerge even in this summary account: the historicist or predictive view of social studies which apes some of the more imposing achievements of the natural sciences, seeks even for the study of man in society a scientific framework of 'laws', and pursues the will-o'-the-wisp of a science of man; and the other, soberer study of living societies in all their complexity, as in Weber and his successors, by means of subtler, more tentative and less ambitious tools. Comte had held that 'social phenomena are subject to natural laws admitting of rational prevision'; and the tendency of his teaching, and of Marx's, was to erect a vast and systematic pattern which claimed to explain everything. Mill in the *System of Logic* puts a more cautious case when he distinguishes two kinds of sociological enquiry: 'the general science of society', on the one hand; and on the other, particular enquiries such as what would happen in a given society if one were to abolish, for example, the monarchy or the Corn Laws. Mill was prepared to believe that social laws might be formulated – laws both of 'coexistence' and of succession or progress – in the sense that causation itself was susceptible to study. But he cautiously denied that such study should allow itself to become necessitarian, and emphasized the vast and unpredictable significance of the individual. 'We cannot foresee the advent of a great man,' he insisted; and 'I believe that if Newton had not lived, the world must have waited for the Newtonian philosophy until there had been another Newton or his equivalent' (VI.xi). Mill's fascination with the principle of causation in human affairs, and his reluctance to submit to any crude version of determinism, can readily be paralleled in English fiction in the same age; such concerns mark one significant difference between the novels of George Eliot, for example, whose interest in human causation is avowed, and such immediate predecessors as Dickens and Thackeray.

Perhaps the area where sociology and literary fiction most naturally relate and overlap lies in the study of social inequality, that universal fact of human societies of whatever age or continent which, though constant as a fact, is always shifting in the forms that it assumes. In the following analysis I shall take the English novel as my principal example, since English, along with French, is perhaps the most social of all literatures, and the English novel especially insistent in its social preoccupations. No other literature, in all probability, has studied its own society for so long and with such delicate precision, so that in advancing the English novel as a prime example of social analysis in literature there seems no possibility of being unfair to the literary side of the case. Rather the contrary: it is more likely to be objected that this discussion amounts to rash advocacy of literature as a hopeful rival to sociology in its present form, and in the very field of social analysis itself. That would be a bold and, at first glance, an implausible claim, since it would amount to preferring the amateur to the professional, and it is not a claim to be made without a sufficiency of documentation. But then the sociologist, whose labours are today in no danger of being undervalued, will not reasonably expect the study of society to be considered an enclosed preserve. He knows better than most that it is a subject upon which everyone, even the illiterate, often holds views of a developed kind. Many of his own techniques, indeed, depend upon his recognizing just this, since enquiries about rank, class and status are commonly and justly based upon conversation and interviews as well as upon silent observation. Studies of social inequality do not limit themselves to quantifiable factors such as income but, where they make any claim to completeness, include reports on the attitudes of individuals within groups. Even snobbery, which is one of the many forms that an interest in social inequality can take, though it may be thought a petty and even a malignant state of mind, cannot be said to be in any ordinary sense crude or simple. The snob, as the term is commonly understood, is always an amateur; but many a professional student of society might do well to bow before the mass of social observation that underlies his convictions, mistaken as they may be, and the subtlety of argument by which social detail is related to category.

Two grand theories of social inequality perhaps underlie all others, and these I shall here call the doctrine of rank and the doctrine of class. The doctrine of rank, understood in its widest sense, is utterly familiar to Western man within literature and outside it, since it is the assumption of the great poets and novelists of the past and equally of any ordinary snob in contemporary experience. It conceives of social inequality as a stepped pyramid in which the upper ranks number few individuals and the lower many, so that social promotion commonly means an ascension into ever narrower limits.* (In modern industrial society, with its expanding middle class, the pyramid may come to look something more like a diamond.) As for the

* My concern here is with the doctrine of the social pyramid as such rather than with still more complex questions concerning whether, or rather how far, the doctrine conforms to the facts of society before the Industrial Revolution or since. For a critique of the pyramid model, cf. Lawrence Stone, 'Social Mobility in England 1500–1700', *Past and Present* (April 1966).

number of such ranks, it is certainly very great and perhaps infinitely great. Moreover, rank is established not by any single or simple factor such as wealth, but rather by a wide complexity of factors which even those who accept the theory are at difficulty to explain; perhaps 'status' is the simplest explanation to be offered, though it is an explanation which is largely question-begging. Literary examples of the doctrine of rank are beyond numbering, since the literature of the West before 1800 knows hardly any other doctrine than this. Chaucer, who calls rank 'degree', offers a succinct account of the social pyramid in his General Prologue to *The Canterbury Tales*, though it does not claim to be complete even in outline, rising no higher than a knight and descending no lower than a ploughman; and a complete account would no doubt include kings and beggars as well. Chaucer certainly means the reader to place individuals on the scale of social hierarchy, and offers sufficient detail to enable this to be done, apologizing with mock humility for having failed to do it himself:

> *Also I prey yow to foryeve it me,*
> *Al have I nat set folk in hir degree*
> *Heere in this tale, as that they sholde stonde.*
> *My wit is short, ye may wel understonde.*   (A.743–6)

Shakespeare often shows his English characters acting within a known social hierarchy and, at the same time, explaining and justifying themselves in so doing; as Henry V, on the eve of Agincourt, leaves his royal brothers, borrows a cloak from one of his knights, and sits unrecognized among his common soldiers, defending the theory of sovereignty until he loses his temper. And similar assumptions surely underlie the works of the earlier British classical economists. Adam Smith, it is true, saw 'three great, original and constituent orders of every civilised society' in his *Wealth of Nations* (1776), but he adds that the 'revenue of every other order is ultimately derived from these three', who live by rent, wages and profit, so that the list of orders is evidently much longer than a list of three. Cobbett in the 1820s speaks approvingly of the 'chain of connection' between rich and poor, and the chain evidently has many links. If the English novel before the 1840s is considered for its evidence of social inequality, it seems only to confirm the doctrine of rank. It is true that *Robinson Crusoe* (1719) has been ingeniously subjected to Marxist interpretation in terms of the single and essentially simple relationship of master and man that exists between Crusoe and Friday; but then the situation of a desert island is an extraordinary one. Novels which Defoe sets in England, such as *Moll Flanders* (1721), show figures moving up and down a tall and complex hierarchy; rather as in a game of snakes and ladders, it is always clear whether the movement is up or down; and clear, too, that while the economic motive is powerful it is much less than fully determinant. Moll as a thief is prosperous, after all, but even in her own eyes debased. *Tom Jones* (1749) may serve as an unusually lucid example of the function of rank in the classic English novel: Tom's upward movement from an indeterminate status in Squire Allworthy's house to his final recognition as the legitimate nephew and heir to the estate is traced by a variety of social indicators: most plainly of all, perhaps, by the three mistresses whom Tom enjoys before winning the hand of Sophia, since the first is a village trollop, the second a woman of middle rank, and the third a lady of high society. And once again the economic factor is less than fully determinant: the position that the hero wins by finding himself heir to an estate requires money to maintain it, indeed; but the rank is a fact in itself, and would not be rendered altogether void if money to sustain it were not there. The centre of interest lies not so much in the fact that Tom wins an estate as in the fact that he reveals himself by a multitude of acts as being already worthy to possess it.

If rank is described in terms as broad as these, as a complex hierarchy governed by status, then it seems an almost universal doctrine both of life and of fiction before the nineteenth century. But in the earlier decades of that century a rival doctrine of class was invented and propagated by certain European intellectuals of Left, Right and Centre. According to the new doctrine, which was precipitated by the Industrial Revolution, society was losing its hierarchical stability and transforming itself into something far less harmonious, a battleground (or at least a potential battleground) of two or at the most three vast classes: a decaying aristocracy, a rising industrialist class and a wage-earning or proletarian class. Saint-Simon, who pioneered the doctrine, interpreted French society after Waterloo as essentially tripartite, and declared his allegiance, though himself an aristocrat, to the new and dynamic industrialist order. Mill saw the doctrine of class as a new and productive tool of social analysis. Disraeli, as the sub-title to *Sybil* (1845) has it, saw England as 'Two Nations', and demanded political action to re-unite them

under a transformed Conservatism. Marx saw the same impend-
ing civil war as a blessing, and in any case an inevitability, and
rejoiced at what he took to be the imminent prospect of a
bloodbath between the classes to usher in a dictatorship of the
proletariat. For over a hundred years the language of class has
been the familiar currency of Western sociology and political
science.

Two aspects of the origins of the doctrine of class are worth
emphasizing here. First, it is not, in its origins, a literary doctrine,
and with occasional exceptions such as the novels of Disraeli it is
not sustained by literature. It is the invention of political and
social scientists. In this it differs sharply from the more ancient
doctrine of rank which, whatever its ultimate origins, is the
doctrine (or, more often, the unspoken assumption) of whole
societies and of the poets and novelists who have written for
those societies. Second, class is not in its origins a socialist doctrine:
its earliest advocates, such as Saint-Simon, Mill and Disraeli,
make the fact clear. Marx inherited the doctrine and gave it a
socialist stamp, and if that stamp now seems ineffaceable it is
because political movements other than socialist have in the past
century tended to abandon or under-emphasize it. In the Victorian
age, at all events, it is entirely possible for a Tory like Disraeli to
advocate the doctrine of class and for a Radical like Dickens to
oppose it. But if it is the English novel that is in question, then
terms like Tory and Radical are too blunt to be of much use.
What is remarkable is that the doctrine of class, fashionable as it
has been for more than a hundred years, has influenced fiction so
little. Disraeli has already been admitted as an exception; but
even in Disraeli's novels class is a special phenomenon to be
visited, tourist-like, in certain cities of the north of England; it
lies outside the normal range of the novelist's experience and of
his reader's. In *Mary Barton* (1848), again, Mrs Gaskell clearly
regards the social apartness of rich and poor in Manchester as a
sudden and unprecedented threat to the traditional unity of the
English people; a threat apparently confined to certain industrial
areas – uncharacteristic of the more traditional South, in fact –
and still in her view susceptible to cure by Christian charity. This
is all very unlike the socialist belief in the class-war as both
inevitable and beneficent: in fact Mrs Gaskell is explicit that only
a fool would be a Socialist or 'Owenite' (ch. 37). These views
seem to match neatly with those of Charlotte Brontë, whose
biography she wrote, and of Dickens, who became her editor;

and if these resemblances are purely accidental, in the sense that social inequality was a question which remained undiscussed in the acquaintanceship of these three novelists, the coincidence of view may be considered all the more significant for that reason. Charlotte Brontë, in a novel of the following year, makes her heroine Shirley speak of any talk of class as 'dangerous nonsense':

'All ridiculous, irrational crying up of one class, whether the same be aristocrat or democrat – all howling down of another class, whether clerical or military – all exacting injustice to individuals, whether monarch or mendicant – is really sickening to me: all arraying of ranks against ranks, all party hatreds, all tyrannies disguised as liberties, I reject and wash my hands of.'   *Shirley* (1849), ch. 21

Shortly after, Dickens embodied in *Bleak House* (1853), the most impressive of his social novels, a vision of an England which was indeed one, though its inhabitants may invite catastrophe by refusing to acknowledge the state of unity in which they inescapably live. The total logic of the book, which reveals the links that bind the individual plaintiff to law and a cumbrous administration, the squire to the slum-dweller and city to country, monumentally exemplifies much of the argument of this discussion. Perhaps the greatest novel of society that the language can show, *Bleak House* solves with daring ingenuity the almost insuperable problems of representing a whole society within the limits of a narrative of individuals. And certainly the doctrine of social unity is passionately explicit here as well as a fact to be demonstrated in human action. The subtle infection of disease, which unites high and low in suffering and death, establishes the fact of unity as no mere aspiration, and offers in the death of the crossing-sweeper an occasion for an assertion by Dickens of his own radical faith:

There is not an atom of Tom's slime, not a cubic inch of any pestilential gas in which he lives, not one obscenity or degradation about him, not an ignorance, not a wickedness, not a brutality of his committing, but shall work its retribution, through every order of society, up to the proudest of the proud, and to the highest of the high.   (ch. 46)

'Even the winds are his messengers', a reminder of the force of disease, is a remark that leaves no room for sentimentality. In the following and inferior novel, *Hard Times* (1854), Dickens represents an honest labourer ground to dust between the mills of organized capital and organized labour, and vilifies those who, like the odious Mrs Sparsit, regret the rise of trade unions while provoking their rise by condoning unions of employers:

> 'It is much to be regretted ... that the united masters allow of any such class combinations. ... Being united themselves, they ought one and all to set their faces against employing any man who is united with any other man.'   (II.i)

George Eliot puts a similar view in a less passionate and more reflective way in a review published two years later, where she characteristically accuses the theorists – sociologists, politicians and the rest – of an ignorance of particular cases, of a weakness at the very point where literature is at its strongest:

> Probably, if we could ascertain the images called up by the terms 'the people', 'the masses', 'the proletariat', 'the peasantry', by many who theorise on those bodies with eloquence and who legislate for them without eloquence, we should find that they indicate almost as small an amount of concrete knowledge. ... When Scott takes us into Luckie Mucklebackit's cottage [in *The Antiquary*], or tells the story of 'The Two Drovers' – when Wordsworth sings to us the reverie of 'Poor Susan' – when Kingsley shows us Alton Locke gazing yearningly over the gate which leads from the highway into the first wood he ever saw, ... more is done towards linking the higher classes with the lower, towards obliterating the vulgarity of exclusiveness, than by hundreds of sermons and philosophical dissertations. Art is the nearest thing to life ...
>
> *Westminster Review* (July 1856)

It would be interesting to consider who wrote those 'philosophical dissertations' and was guilty, in George Eliot's view, of the 'vulgarity of exclusiveness': the answer, whatever it may be, seems unlikely to be a political party, since the doctrine of class was common in that age to intellectuals of various political allegiance. The passage is evidently a protest by a future novelist against certain emerging aspects of the social sciences. Its protest against class and in favour of social unity, of 'linking the higher classes with the lower', is in direct lineage from Mrs Gaskell, Charlotte Brontë and Dickens; its claim that 'art is the nearest thing to life', superior not just to bad social science but to social science absolutely, is an aspect of the growing confidence of the novelist in the nineteenth century, and not only in England, as one charged with a mission of truth which is in its nature unique. 'The historian of manners', as Balzac had put it in his preface to *Les Paysans* (1844), obeys harsher laws than those that bind the historian of facts. He must make everything seem plausible, even the truth; whereas, in the domain of history properly so called, the impossible is justified by the fact that it occurred.

It is sometimes suggested that the intellectual hatred of class characteristic of certain Victorians, such as Dickens's dislike and distrust of trade unions, is an oddity of the age and absurdly out of keeping with the radicalism which such novelists protested. If this is widely felt, it is perhaps because the currency of a diluted Marxism in the twentieth century has left many with a sense that class-protest is the inevitable lever of social reform: 'without conflict', as Marx himself put it, 'no progress'. But it is worth noticing that intellectual objections to class in that age were remarkably successful in practical terms: or at least, since it is perilous to estimate the influence of literature upon political action, that the Victorians by and large fail to exemplify the conflict predicted or demanded by Disraeli and Marx, and that they successfully illustrate in large measure Dickens's vision of a united society. United is not the same as equal: a society might be widely diverse in terms of ownership and income, for instance, and yet remain united in the sense that it avoided civil war, escaped organized class conflict of a kind that characterized many Western countries in the 1930s, and met the challenge of great national emergencies such as foreign wars. Considering that England had already suffered the first industrial revolution in human history, a revolution incapable of learning from the mistakes of any predecessor, the Victorian avoidance of social revolution was an impressive feat of political skill. The murmur of English self-congratulation that followed the continental convulsions of 1848 is certainly open to the charge of complacency; but those who make this charge often omit to notice how much of that complacency was justified on the facts. No doubt it would be beyond the evidence to suggest that the Victorian novelists prevented class-war in their generation; but it may still be plausible to suggest that they helped to create a climate of opinion which successfully prevented it. When Gladstone declared in 1886 that 'all the world over, I will back the masses against the classes', he was restating in bold oratorical form a view more fully and subtly expounded by novelists and others who, in the 1840s and after, had set their faces against a sundering doctrine. And the literary effort towards social reconciliation has continued in twentieth-century novels like

E. M. Forster's *Howards End* (1910) with its motto 'Only connect'.

Almost as striking as the open rejection of class by English novelists of classic status has been the nearly total neglect of the doctrine of class by English novelists in general, even in the twentieth century. The Marxist novel, for example, is surprisingly hard to find: the more surprising when one reflects how many English novelists between the World Wars believed themselves to be Marxists. Christopher Isherwood's *Mr Norris Changes Trains* (1935) and *Goodbye to Berlin* (1939) are studies of English life in the 1930s transposed into the world of pre-Hitler Berlin – comedies of manners written by a novelist who, at the time of writing, was avowedly a member of the Communist Party. But no reader of these novels, it seems likely, has ever expected to see any of his characters categorized by their creator in Marxist terms; and though Mr Norris is ultimately shown to be a member of the Party, this is evidently the least interesting thing about him. Another novelist of the same school, Isherwood's undergraduate friend Edward Upward, has belatedly emerged with a novel *In the Thirties* (1962); but the book denies what may be supposed its initial impetus by narrating the disillusionment of a poet with his party membership. Lionel Trilling's *The Middle of the Journey* (1947) is an earlier and more distinguished example of the same phenomenon, and Arthur Koestler's *Darkness at Noon* (1940) another. Certainly English can boast an ex-Marxist novel: but it seems incapable of producing a major novel that enacts the Marxist analysis of society and the reality of class-conflict. French has done a little better, with André Malraux's *La condition humaine* (1933); but the novel is set outside Europe, in the China of the 1920s, so that the exacting demands which a French reader might have made of a Marxist novel on French society are easily evaded.

But then the avoidance by English novelists of Marxist 'realities' in their fiction, even by those novelists who happen themselves to be Marxists, is a fact of significance far beyond the familiar dilemmas of the Marxist intellectual and his nagging inability to relate principle to practice. Suppose instead the question to be widened to enquire whether any system of social analysis imported from outside the novelist's art can be shown to have influenced any English novelist of distinction. One large positive answer has already been allowed: the doctrine of rank or degree, based upon a complex system of status. Even this answer, safe as it looks, may be open to question, in the sense that it may seem an odd use of language to speak of Fielding as 'importing into' *Tom Jones* a system of rank learned outside it. And certainly there is no need to think of Fielding as learning the system of rank from the works of any social or political scientist: that doctrine was common knowledge in the English society of his day, and what Fielding knows is, in outline at least, what every Englishman knows or takes for granted about the processes of social promotion in the mid eighteenth century. And terms like 'doctrine' or 'system', in such a context as this, may seem odd as well. To say that Fielding has a doctrine of society is surely to suggest that his social intelligence was more conceptual than the evidence allows. Certainly he knew what he thought about certain social issues, both as a magistrate and as a novelist; and if we impute a doctrine to him, as is common enough, it is for the purposes of summary explanation and clarification. He may be thought to believe, for example, that the status of a country gentleman is the highest that existence has to offer to any commoner, and that the traditional virtues of the country gentleman, if properly understood, are the noblest of all virtues in any real contemporary situation. To say even that is to say a great deal in the way of distinguishing him from other novelists: these are not, for instance, views one would impute to Defoe or Richardson. But Fielding does not make any assertions as broad as these; and if he did, we might not naturally allow to his assertions about society the same weight that we allow to the novels themselves. 'Fielding's social doctrine' is a summary and a clarification not so much of what Fielding says about society as of what he shows us about it. If there were any question of conflict between the showing and the telling, it would be natural to neglect or dismiss what the novelist explicitly has to say.

And here, in all probability, an utterly characteristic contrast between fiction and sociology emerges at last. It is conceivable that one might wish to neglect or dismiss as incomplete, inaccurate or even mendacious a view offered by a novelist about society as being genuinely his own. This is hardly a conceivable procedure in interpreting sociology. If Weber tells us that, beyond and above an economically determined class-situation, there is a situation governed by status and expressed by a style of life, then this remains indisputably Weber's view. There may be reason to dispute the view, but none to dispute that it is Weber's. But if Jane Austen announces, as she does at the beginning of

Pride and Prejudice, that 'it is a truth universally acknowledged that a single man in possession of a good fortune must be in want of a wife', the reader accords to the observation an altogether more provisional significance. Irony apart, its function is unlikely to be purely informative. If the ensuing novel were to demonstrate a somewhat different truth about social reality, as in the event it does, the reader feels himself neither cheated nor amazed.

It is tempting to conclude, then, that novels do not provide social knowledge. But this sceptical view, which may be held with many degrees of scepticism, seems to run counter to two considerations which few, in the last resort, would wish to contest. The first is that it seems obvious on reflection that society and fiction are causally related. When it is noticed, for example, that Dickens's novels often represent a pattern of social promotion through the acquisition of wealth, that the hero rises in fortune and accordingly in status in *Oliver Twist*, *David Copperfield* and *Great Expectations*, it would seem an impossibly sceptical view to suggest that the social promotion of the heroes of these novels bore a purely accidental relationship to Victorian society. The liberal ideals of kindliness to the oppressed and unprotected like the infant Oliver, of self-reliance, manly endeavour and hard work, like Copperfield's, and of hatred of snobbery, like Pip's, are hardly intelligible out of their social context; and a richer historical awareness of context, such as appropriate information about Poor Law and prison reform, is likely to deepen any understanding of what is there to be seen. Probably no one wishes to deny this if it is soberly stated; and when sociologists and historians deny that novels are social evidence they exaggerate a natural scepticism about the uncertainties of literature to a point at which it ceases to be plausible. The other consideration is the other side of the question: if society influences fiction, so does fiction influence society. Dickens's social campaigns in his novels often failed to have the effects he most ardently hoped of them; but it seems impossibly over-sceptical, again, to suggest that they had no effect at all. In fact an historian of Victorian prison-reform who omitted the contribution of Dickens would evidently be failing in his ordinary duty as an historian.

And yet when the case for scepticism is exaggerated, as it often is in the present instance, to the point of utter implausibility, there are probably nagging dissatisfactions and fears which are worth considering. The neglect of fiction by sociologists is broadly a fact, and it is perhaps an increasing fact: as the study of society grows more technical, sociologists may come to think even less than they now do of the prospect of fruitful relations between their own studies and literature. The implausibly sceptical view might easily in such circumstances become an established view, and both studies might suffer from a divorce entered into upon insufficient grounds. The objections to literary evidence, then, may be worth reviewing. One objection applies broadly to documentary evidence from the past of any kind: that it is in its nature usually incomplete and not in itself subject to completion. The social historian might concede, for instance, that Mrs Gaskell in *Mary Barton* was an honest and informed observer of the life of the Manchester poor in the Hungry Forties, and yet reasonably complain that neither the novel itself, nor even the totality of literary documents surviving from that age, offer any certain guide in ascertaining how far the life of the Barton family was representative of its place and time. The preference of the sociologist for enquiries in the present tense is intelligible enough in these terms. So far as the present age is concerned, evidence may be extended by increasingly sophisticated techniques of mass-observation. For the past, by contrast, one depends upon what happens to have survived in records. And to this objection against literary evidence as a prime source of social knowledge there can be no reply. It is natural to concede that the sociologist should seek his evidence where it survives most abundantly.

But where the study is itself a study of the past, a different situation applies. I assume here, for convenience, what is in practice nearly always the case: that in historical enquiries about the structure of societies the raw materials of surviving records, such as census-returns and parish records, are less complete and less informative than the historian would wish. It is precisely this incompleteness, indeed, that has been known to turn historians into sociologists. If we consider questions of common interest to historians of society and historians of literature – questions such as the structure of the family in fifth-century Athens, the average marriage-age in Renaissance England, or the quality of capital–labour relations in the Manchester of the 1840s – then the first objection to literary evidence that I have considered does not apply. The historian may want more precise and reliable information about society than the plays of Euripides and Shakespeare or the novels of Dickens and Mrs Gaskell appear to supply. But he is in no position to manufacture his evidence. He has the painful choice of using the literary evidence with professional reluctance, or of neglecting it on a matter of principle.

It is the matter of refusal of literary evidence on principle that poses the problem of the future relations between literary and social studies in their most acute form. The sociologist – a term which includes, in this context, the historian of society who is employing in some measure the tools of modern sociological analysis – has in such cases two recognized sources of doubt. One is that a work of literature is indeed all too 'literary': that it offers not a plain view of social reality as if seen through plate-glass, but rather one refracted and coloured by literary convention and individual personality. If Shakespeare marries his Juliet to Romeo before she is fourteen, or if Mrs Gaskell causes John Barton to commit a murder out of class-hatred, how can the historian be certain that either event reflects any observable reality of the 1590s or of the 1840s? And the other objection is a more demanding version of the first, and concerns the stubborn indeterminacy of literary evidence. Even if such events as these occurred in life, it may be argued, how can the sociologist judge the degree to which they were representative acts? How can the social evidences of literature ever be quantified?

It is highly characteristic of arguments of this kind to assume that vagueness and indeterminacy are necessarily forms of in-accuracy. Sociology does not easily blend with the popular view that statistics are lies, or even 'damned lies', even though much of the progress of the subject since the 1890s has been based upon a readiness to retreat sceptically before some of the more extrava-gant expectations of precision held out by Comte and Marx. The subject is two-faced. At one moment it speaks hopefully of the prospect of creating what Mill called 'a general science of society', with laws and variables that might one day explain all the facts. At another it speaks more cautiously, like Weber, of 'hypothetical analysis' as an escape from the dilemma of pseudo-scientism, of arbitrarily identifying the decisive factor in a social evolution, of employing hypothetical creations such as 'models' or ideal types. It is with the second species of sociology that the literary student can come to terms. About the first he is almost professionally required to feel something like the scepticism of George Eliot concerning the 'small amount of concrete know-ledge' that characterizes those who eloquently theorize. The future of collaboration does not lie with these. But to the scientist of society who can see that the facts of social relations inevitably include much that is fleeting and still more that is unquantifiable, the resistance of literary evidence to statistical summary will not seem a disadvantage. On the contrary, the careful scientist might reasonably conclude that it is the novelist's refusal to quantify his data, and his insistence, at the best, upon telling only what he knows for certain while leaving its significance in the total scheme of society in the vague, that offers some reason for taking his evidence seriously at all. It is the observer who claims to know how to quantify the unquantifiable or to square the circle, he may properly feel, whose credentials need most urgently to be scanned.

The juxtaposition of three passages, two from English novels and a third from a sociological essay, may help to clarify the nature of collaboration between the two disciplines:

Another moment, and Fanny was in the narrow entrance-passage of the house, and in her mother's arms, who met her there with looks of true kindness, and with features which Fanny loved the more, because they brought her aunt Bertram's before her; and there were her two sisters, Susan, a well-grown fine girl of fourteen, and Betsey, the youngest of the family, about five – both glad to see her in their way, though with no advantage of manner in receiving her. But manner Fanny did not want. Would they but love her, she should be satisfied.

She was then taken into a parlour, so small that her first conviction was of its being only a passage-room to something better, and she stood for a moment expecting to be invited on; but when she saw there was no other door, and that there were signs of habitation before her, she called back her thoughts, reproved herself, and grieved lest they should have been suspected . . .

Fanny was almost stunned. The smallness of the house, and thinness of the walls, brought every thing so close to her that, added to the fatigue of her journey, and all her recent agitation, she hardly knew how to bear it. . . . There were soon only her father and herself remaining; and he taking out a newspaper – the accustomary loan of a neighbour – applied himself to studying it, without seeming to recollect her existence. The solitary candle was held between himself and the paper, without any reference to her possible convenience; but she had nothing to do, and was glad to have the light screened from her aching head, as she sat in bewildered, broken, sorrowful contemplation.

Jane Austen, Mansfield Park (1814), ch. 38

Mr and Mrs Veneering were bran-new people in a bran-new house in a bran-new quarter of London. Everything about the Veneerings was spick and span new. All their furniture was new, all their friends were new, all their servants were new, their plate was new, their carriage was new, their harness was new, their horses were new, their pictures were new, they themselves were new, they were as newly married as was lawfully compatible with their having a bran-new baby, and if they had set up a great-grandfather, he would have come home in matting from the pantechnicon, without a scratch upon him, French-polished to the crown of his head.

For, in the Veneering establishment, from the hall-chairs with the new coat-of-arms, to the grand pianoforte with the new action, and upstairs again to the new fire-escape, all things were in a state of high varnish and polish. And what was observable in the furniture was observable in the Veneerings – the surface smelt a little too much of the workshop and was a trifle sticky.   Dickens, *Our Mutual Friend* (1865), I.2

The decisive role of a 'style of life' in status honour means that status groups are the specific bearers of all conventions. In whatever way it may be manifest, all stylization of life either originates in status groups or is at least conserved by them. Even if the principles of status conventions differ greatly, they reveal certain typical traits, especially among those which are most privileged. Quite generally, among privileged status groups there is a status disqualification that operates against the performance of common physical labour. This disqualification is now setting in in America against the old tradition of esteem for labour. Very frequently every rational economic pursuit, and especially *entrepreneurial* activity, is looked upon as a disqualification of status.

Max Weber, *Essays in Sociology* (1948), p. 191

All three passages are directly concerned with styles of life, and more particularly with the ways in which evidences of status are seen to surpass in significance the purely economic issues of wealth and poverty. In the first Jane Austen describes the return of her heroine Fanny Price to the reduced circumstances of her family home in Portsmouth after years of upbringing in a large country house; and here the purely physical facts of relative poverty – 'the smallness of the house, the thinness of the walls' – are represented as more significant than a virtuous and affectionate girl had at first innocently thought likely: 'Would they but love her, she should be satisfied.' In the second, Dickens acidly itemizes the life-style of a parvenu London family which seeks by money alone to establish itself in society – a family that buys everything, even guests for its dinner-table, while remaining too ignorant of the true style of aristocratic existence to achieve its essential nonchalance. In the third Weber summarizes and regulates much of the social information of which passages such as these by Jane Austen and Dickens are examples.

The three passages are hopefully offered as representing a relationship. The paragraphs drawn from *Mansfield Park* are Jane Austen at her finest, the detail placed with an accuracy that never leads to overloading, the intelligent reader being allowed and encouraged to recognize the social significance of detail just a step ahead of Fanny herself in the course of a growing disillusionment. The reader is enabled to stand between Jane Austen and her heroine: if Fanny is bewildered, we are not. The Dickens passage is admittedly less than Dickens at his finest, and the surplus of detail, suggestive as it is of his hand, does not altogether encourage the reader to suppose that he knows much more about the real quality of aristocratic life than the Veneerings do. Will the furniture pass when it is a little older? one is inclined to ask; and the answer ought ideally to be No, since the Veneering taste needs to be shown as decisively bad and not merely expensive. As for the passage from Weber, it is in essence as stylistically graceless in translation as its German original. But this objection, being merely accidental, is in all generosity well worth neglecting. It is an over-notorious fact that sociology is in practice ill-written, perhaps because socio-logical works which are not ill-written are commonly thought of as something else. The point does not need to be laboured: there seems to be no reason in principle why sociology should not be expounded with lucidity and grace.

What is the logical relationship between the Weber on the one hand and the two passages of fiction? Certain preconceptions may be quickly laid to rest. The difference is not that which obtains between narrative and discursive prose, since the Dickens is scarcely more narrative than the Weber. Nor is the difference that which obtains between invention and observed truth, since the Jane Austen and the Dickens are clearly based upon observation, and upon observation of a closer sort than any which, on the evidence of these passages alone, need underlie the account of status offered by Weber. The notion that sociologists behave like scientists in the popular imagination, proceeding from observed facts to hypothesis to tested hypothesis to laws, whereas the novelists make it up as they go along – such a notion of contrast between the two disciplines will not bear examination for a moment. A novel may be much more than a narrative, and much other; and even when it is narrative, as in Jane Austen, it may employ narrative for an expository purpose. What Fanny Price observes is what is there to be observed, and it is narrative in the sense that it is told in the order in which she observed it; with the single, untidy exception of the detail of the borrowed newspaper, which represents a piece of information she is un-likely to have acquired at just that moment. For the rest, the technique might be described as a narrative exposition. If one were to pose the question 'What is it like for such a girl with such an upbringing to return to such a home?', this passage is evidently an answer to that question, and a very sufficient answer.

But does the sociologist most characteristically pose questions of this sort? Probably not; and the fact that he does not is likely to be the significant fact of difference. It is certainly easy to imagine a sociologist dealing with an observed situation such as Fanny's return home. The case might figure as a case-history in a study of cross-cultural situations. But its function would then be that of an example serving among others as evidence towards a general conclusion. It is true that Jane Austen too has her general conclusions. She believes, with Sir Thomas Bertram in the last pages of the novel, in 'prizing more and more the sterling good of principle and temper' rather than 'ambitious and mercenary connections'. Probably most sociologists would agree with this conclusion: certainly the difference between Jane Austen and themselves is not usually of this nature. But if they were offered the novel as a contribution to their subject, they might offer certain puzzled objections. However close and acute they might concede the social observation to be, the total fictional form presents difficulties in distinguishing the observation from the fiction. *Mansfield Park*, regarded as a whole, is after all Cinderella as well as social observation. The mixture does not puzzle in the act of reading: but it puzzles as a work of science. Is Jane Austen suggesting that such girls in such situations commonly marry as well as Fanny does? and if so, is this view itself based upon social observation, or is it the mere wish-fulfilment of a Hampshire spinster? Or is it something more than either, the conclusion of a moral design?

The last answer is evidently right – the only answer, indeed, consistent with the revealed intelligence of the great novelists themselves. Neither they nor their readers seriously suppose that novels simply tell of the world as it is. Even George Eliot, with her celebrated concern with accuracy of detail, revealed in her notebook that art is not only 'the nearest thing to life' but equally a form of moral exhortation: 'It is for art to present images of a lovelier order than the actual, gently winning the affections, and so determining the taste'. The degree to which this ambition of her art conflicts with the equally serious ambition of accuracy of detail is among the most delicate problems of reading many works of fiction of the last two centuries. They inform and they exhort: and here they differ from the works of the sociologists, which inform merely. But to the extent that sociology does inform, the knowledge it provides cannot in the end fail to change the world that the novelist sees. As for the novel, and the knowledge that it has to give, it is clear that the scientific dignity of such knowledge has been diminished by the informality with which it is presented and by the superior single-mindedness of the social sciences. But the dangers of using what it has to give have none the less been exaggerated. In the very act of exaggerating such dangers, indeed, the clues for interpreting such knowledge are often unwittingly provided. When we protest of a novelist that he is an unreliable social reporter for reason of this prejudice or that ignorance, we provide the best reasons for thinking that prejudices and ignorance can be identified and allowed for. And to argue like this is to re-assert, often unknowingly, the sense in which the social evidences of fiction are like other kinds of documentary evidence of the past. To make allowances of this sort, after all, is a familiar and essential feature of historical studies of every kind.

11

THE HISTORY OF IDEAS

The history of ideas is a new and flourishing aspect of the study of literature. It is true that the tradition of intellectual history in the nineteenth century is recognizably an ancestor. But Arthur Lovejoy, writing in 1938, could reasonably speak of the discipline to which he devoted his life as 'barely in its adolescence',* proposing at the same time a collaborative enterprise of scholarship in which at least twelve existing subjects might all play their part: the histories of philosophy, science, language, religion, literature and comparative literature, and of other arts, economics, education and politics, as well as parts of folklore and sociology. The most characteristic and controversial aspect of his programme, perhaps, was a demand he had already made in the first of his lectures of 1933, *The Great Chain of Being* – the demand that the historian of ideas should penetrate the what he called 'familiar names ending in *-ism* or *-ity*' which are 'trouble-breeding and usually thought-obscuring', being complexes of many doctrines, and that he should proceed to isolate and study the 'unit-ideas' which allegedly compose them. Such unit-ideas, in his view, might prove to be a variety of historical phenomena: assumptions common to an age, tricks of reasoning, appeals to emotional responses, or the 'sacred words and phrases' of periods or movements. This ambitious programme is what the history of ideas has since come to signify; and it remains clear that, regarded as a whole, it is an original one, and certain that it has influenced literary studies since the thirties in a momentous way. English literary studies, at least, though familiar with intellectual history in a general sense, did not previously regard ideas as possessing histories of their own which could usefully be narrated. Apart from J. B. Bury's *Idea of Progress* (1920), it would

* Arthur O. Lovejoy, *Essays in the History of Ideas* (Baltimore, 1948), p.10.

be difficult to name an English book devoted to such a subject before the Second World War, though Leslie Stephen's *History of English Thought in the Eighteenth Century* (1876) and its sequel *The English Utilitarians* (1900) represent with distinction a passion for intellectual history of an expansive kind that was highly characteristic of the mid and later Victorian age.

And yet the scepticism which the history of ideas provokes remains powerful, however much it may prove to be based on misunderstandings. The most radical misunderstanding of all is also the most ancient, being Platonic: that ideas-as-truth, such as a philosopher might deal in, are necessarily and always a different matter from the poet's concern with ideas-as-beauty. The artist, as Plato put it in the *Republic*,

knows nothing of the reality, but only the appearance. . . . Does he ever have either knowledge, or correct belief? . . . And so what can be said of the poet's wisdom concerning what he writes about? . . . He can only reproduce what pleases the taste or wins the approval of the ignorant multitude. . . . Art is merely a form of play, not to be taken seriously.

(x.600–1)

If ideas in literature are merely a form of play, this would constitute not only a massive reason for refusing to take them seriously, but also a potent objection against confusing the study of literature with the study of the history of ideas. It has often been noticed, and even over-emphasized, that poetry does not demand credence in any ordinary sense: that nobody needs to be an Epicurean to admire Lucretius or a Christian to admire Milton. But then it is not always noticed in such arguments that studies of the history of philosophy, science, religion and the rest do not demand credence either; so that a property which, at first glance, seems to distinguish literary history from other historical studies turns out, on examination, to be merely another point of similarity. Only a very inexperienced student of philosophy would suppose that the great philosophical texts from Plato to the present day are to be studied with an attention proportionate to the truths they can be demonstrated to embody. It is true that it sometimes astonishes the youthful student of philosophy to discover that his teachers believe the great philosophers of the past to have been wrong in thinking what they thought. But those who retain this sense of astonishment for long are not likely to excel in the study of philosophy. Stephen Spender has wonderingly described what he calls the 'Obstacle Race way of teaching philosophy' at Oxford between the wars, but his account is only an exaggerated version of what schools of philosophy commonly practise:

> The next philosopher is Locke. We were told what he thought and then why he was wrong. Next please. Hume. Hume was wrong also. Then Kant. Kant was wrong, but he was also so difficult to understand that one could not be so sure of catching him out.*

No doubt the youthful assumption that a philosopher is someone who tells you without prevarication what the whole truth is like might be too rudely shocked by procedures like these. But a shock of some kind seems called for, however delicately administered. And equally, the student of literature who is astonished to discover with Plato that poetry may be excellent without being true needs to be shown without delay that this is a property which poetry shares with many other intellectual endeavours of mankind.

Another objection to the historiography of ideas is a refinement of the first. Plato held that poetry was untruthful, and that if it told the truth it did so only by accident. The modern exponent of this view is inclined to adopt what he takes to be a less vulnerable position. He is more inclined to say, quoting Sir Philip Sidney out of context, that 'the poet nothing affirmeth, and therefore never lies' – that the question of the truth or falsehood of literature hardly arises, since poetry is in its nature noncommittal. This certainly misrepresents Sidney, who held that the poet works through fictions to teach true doctrine. The characters and events in his fictions are not true in the sense that historical events are true: but they 'show the way' to true virtue. 'Who readeth Aeneas carrying old Anchises on his back that wisheth not it were his fortune to perform so excellent an act?' The *Aeneid*, rightly considered, does not affirm that events occurred in history, but rather that certain models of action are better than others. This is certainly to affirm – and Sidney is not one of those who supposed that moral judgements were merely matters of personal opinion. Virtue, in his view, was a truth which God has forever shown to man; and if a poet fails to recommend it, or recommends something else, then he is failing in a poetic duty as much as in a moral one.

The noncommittal view of poetry is certainly more modern than this. It more usually takes refuge in facile confusions

---

* Stephen Spender, *World within World* (London, 1951), p. 40.

between 'idea' and something like 'total philosophical system' or 'ideology'. When T. S. Eliot said of Henry James that he 'had a mind so fine that no idea could violate it', he was drawing memorable attention to the delicate agnosticism of much of James's moral world. But to emphasize the perilous difficulty of taking moral decisions in a complex situation, and to expound the very complexity which any actual situation reveals, is certainly to advance an idea about human morality – an idea, moreover, which possesses its own traceable ancestry in Protestant and agnostic ethics. It may be supposed that Eliot would not have wished to deny any of this, and that he was merely drawing attention to a difference between the delicate and the dogmatic moral intelligence. But it ought not to be supposed that these considerations remove James, or any other unviolated mind, from the sphere of intellectual history.

More than that, the fashion in the present century for discovering paradox and 'tension' in literature has sometimes misled critics into supposing that great poetry is often noncommittal in the special sense of revealing both sides of an argument and leaving the matter unresolved. Again, it is not usually noticed in such arguments that great philosophers as well as great poets may do precisely that. An 'irritable reaching after fact and certainty' is a fault commonly ascribed by the literary mind to the philosophical, though it is not so often ascribed by philosophers to themselves. But in practice philosophical language can be as tentative and as inconclusive as any other kind. When the critic emphasizes that the greatest authors 'seem not so much to reflect the intellectual system of their age as to express . . . its inherent contradictions',* he may find himself passing a judgement which, on examination, proves to be true of Bacon, Hume and Sartre as well as of Shakespeare and Wordsworth.

A further and more ingenious refinement of the Platonic argument may be observed in the view that the poet does not speak in his own person. This notion, considered as a total dogma of literature, is hardly known before the twentieth century, and was probably conceived in reaction to what in the 1930s and 1940s was regarded as the excesses of biographical interpretation. The biographical critic had supposed that to discover the poet was to enrich one's view of the poem: Sainte-Beuve even speaks at times as if the discovery of the poet in the totality of his

---

* Ian Watt, 'Joseph Conrad', in *The English Mind*, edited by H. S. Davies and George Watson (Cambridge, 1964), p. 257.

personality were the end of criticism which a study of the poems merely serves. In the 1930s and after, the New Criticism challenged this view in a variety of ways; and one of these ways was to deny that poets speak for themselves. The poet was replaced, for the purposes of exposition, by a series of intermediaries between himself and the work: a dramatic speaker, a pose, a role, a mask. 'We ought to impute the thoughts and attitudes of the poem immediately to the dramatic speaker; and if to the author at all, only by an act of biographical inference.' Even the reader, in more sophisticated versions of the theory, was not what he seemed:

The actual reader of a poem is something like a reader over another reader's shoulder; he reads through the dramatic reader, the person to whom the full tone of the poem is addressed in the fictional situation.*

And the theory flourished on a wealth of undeniable examples of poets speaking in the voices of others: dramatists of necessity, novelists in their dialogue, Victorian poets in their dramatic monologues, Yeats in his self-avowed doctrine of masks, and poems like Eliot's *Waste Land* that owe much of their technique to the monologues of Tennyson and Browning.

The doctrine of the dramatic speaker, though open to many difficulties in itself, may not seem of special concern to the cause of intellectual history. An idea, it might be argued, is none the less there whether the poet commits himself to believing in it or not. The doctrine of 'degree' as a principle underlying not only human society but the entire created universe is one which Shakespeare in a famous speech in *Troilus and Cressida* attributes to the character of Ulysses, and it might be suggested that it hardly matters for the intellectual historian whether Shakespeare himself believed in it. This is a mistake; but it is of some importance to recognize the point at which such an argument crosses the border-region that divides plausibility from error. It is undeniable that poets have often written in voices other than their own. It is also true that literary historians have at times culpably failed to notice that this is so – that they have credulously attributed the views of the poet-lover in the sonnets of Shakespeare to Shakespeare himself, for example, or Gulliver's views to Swift. It does not follow that all or most literature is like this. As for the view that the poet's presence in his poem is always and

---

* W. K. Wimsatt Jr and Monroe C. Beardsley, *The Verbal Icon* (Lexington, Kentucky, 1954), pp. 5, xv.

necessarily that of a dramatic speaker, such a view seems acceptable only in a truistic sense. When Dante writes that 'in His will
is our peace', or when Wordsworth concludes his *Prelude*:

> *what we have loved*
> *Others will love; and we may teach them how;*
> *Instruct them how the mind of man becomes*
> *A thousand times more beautiful than the earth*
> *On which he dwells* . . .

nobody will seriously wish to doubt that these views represent
the most passionate convictions of Dante and Wordsworth
themselves. The sense in which one might allow oneself to doubt,
that is to say, could only be in the form of a scepticism of a
peculiarly total kind, like the Freudian scepticism which doubts
whether arguments can ever represent more than attempts on the
part of the speaker to rationalize some ever deeper and more
obscure desire or urge. But radical scepticism about human discourse as such, whether such scepticism is Freudian or other, is
open to two large objections. First, it is not justified on the facts:
human beings do sometimes manage to say what they believe,
and Dante can be demonstrated on abundant historical evidence
to have believed the theology of the *Divine Comedy*. And
secondly, such radical scepticism has nothing much to do with
literature. It is a suspicion alleged against human discourse as
such. One might indeed choose to 'impute the thoughts and
attitudes of the poem to the dramatic speaker' much as one
might claim to interpret what a friend may say in conversation
as not representing his real self. But this seems a hopelessly over-
subtle view in much of art as in much of life. The notion of a
reality underlying everything to be seen and heard has an
enticing air of profundity about it; but those who pretend to be
in favour of applying it to the whole universe of literature never
seem to practise what they preach. In practice they are as ready
as the next man to attribute ideas to poets.

And it is evidently important that they should. No doubt it is
barely possible to conceive of an historian of ideas who accepted
the whole doctrine of the dramatic speaker in literature while
remaining genuinely indifferent to the question whether the
poets themselves believed what they wrote or not. The remoteness of this possibility points to the dangers as well as to the
absurdities of the doctrine itself. Of course there is no such historian, and in all probability there never will be. If ideas in poetry

are merely entertained by poets rather than held, then the dignity and interest of such ideas can only be enormously trivialized by that very fact. This is often denied: not because it is often doubted, on the whole, but rather because it is often felt to be difficult to explain. Why should we care whether poets believed in what they wrote or not? It is often tempting to argue as if what one cannot readily explain is simply untrue. But it is still a common experience, in art as in life, that ideas offered with a sense of conviction impress as no others can do. An obvious explanation is that an idea entertained as an hypothesis rather than held as a conviction has presumably failed to pass the first test. It has not even convinced its spokesman: why should it convince anyone else? If the Great Chain of Being were a doctrine from which Plato, Abelard, Milton, Pope and the rest had ultimately withheld their consent, it would hardly have attracted the enduring interest of any historian.

This discussion must draw to an end the review of objections to the history of ideas which might, in a general sense, be called Platonic – though they are Platonic not in the sense that Plato proposed them, still less in the sense that those who now propose them are Platonists, but merely in that they seem to be logically connected with the attack upon poetry in the *Republic*. The last of such objections concerns the cogency of argument in great poems. It is often suggested that poems do not need to be convincing as arguments; and, as before, it is a usual assumption of those who put this view that philosophy and history need to be convincing in a sense that poetry does not. It is surprising that those who argue like this have never observed how little our acceptance of Plato, Hobbes or Hegel as great philosophers depends upon our accepting the cogency of their arguments or of any part of their arguments. It is entirely conceivable, for instance, and even rather common, for students of philosophy who disagree with every proposition characteristic of Hobbes to insist, with no sense of contradiction, that he was indeed a great philosopher. Students of literature do not usually find this spectacle very puzzling; but they are oddly inclined to suppose that the same phenomenon, when transferred to literature, is significant in some special sense:

It is not a weakness in 'Lycidas' . . . that the final stage of the meditation is connected with the beginning by no intrinsic dialectical necessity, but only by the poetic inevitability of such an outcome.*

* Ronald S. Crane, *The Idea of the Humanities* (Chicago, 1967), vol. i, p. 187.

What is meant here, in all probability, is that the weakness of 'Lycidas' as a total argument is not a weakness utterly fatal to the poem: that the poem survives as a masterpiece, much as Hobbes's *Leviathan* does, even though on reflection it may fail in all its aspects to convince. But to claim that the weakness of its argument is not a weakness at all is something well in excess of this. It is to suggest that the poem would not be better if the argumentative connection between the beginning and the end were strengthened. That would be an extraordinarily rash hypothesis. It seems more plausible to say that 'Lycidas' is a poem that readily survives its weaknesses; but that its weaknesses are none the less perfectly real. It is easy to be misled by a masterpiece into supposing that there is some special law like 'poetic inevitability' that turns its defects into something else. But to observe Milton rendering the manifest defects of 'Lycidas' into matters of minor significance is not a lesson in the special logic that is sometimes supposed to govern poetry. It is rather an example of how poetry, like philosophy itself, can survive by virtue of ideas which are formidable enough to demand an answer, whether they are right or wrong: an example of how poetry can survive failures in organization which are incidental rather than radical to the merits of the work.

It seems clear, then, that the historians of ideas in literature are not chasing phantoms: that the ideas are there, that they are significantly there in the sense that they often and properly occupy a major share of interest, and that it matters, much as it matters in non-literary discourse, whether they are right or wrong. It does not follow that literature is excellent to the extent that the ideas it embodies are so – still less that to invalidate the idea is to invalidate the poem itself. An historian working in this field will surely have passed the point of sophistication at which he needs to be told that ideas do not come in two sorts, the true and the false; just as advanced students of literature rarely need to be disabused of the notion that there are only two kinds of poems, the good ones and the bad ones. There are ideas which can be shown to be false which are none the less intensely worthy of respect, and not only because many men have believed in them. Much of the suspicion that the historiography of ideas still invites is based upon careless notions of the relation between literature and other forms of intelligent discourse and upon a mistaken assumption that intellectual history demands credence on the part of those who practise it in a way in which the historiographies of philosophy, science or religion do not.

But a larger and subtler difficulty, and one more characteristic of the twentieth century than of Plato, still overhangs the status of ideas in literature, and is often believed even by intellectual historians themselves. This is the doctrine or assumption that an idea in literature is likely to be nothing more than a second-hand version of something which exists outside the world of the poem: something that the poet has borrowed and exploited to a literary end. Oddly enough, those who reduce the intellectual role of the poet to that of a mere purveyor of what philosophers and others have achieved do not usually offer this highly reductive view of poetry with the sense of desperation that one might expect. Sidney in the *Apologie*, for instance, offers it proudly as a first line of defence against those who rate poetry too low:

> The philosopher teacheth, but he teacheth obscurely, so as the learned only can understand him; that is to say, he teacheth them that are already taught. But the poet is the food for the tenderest stomachs, the poet is indeed the right popular philosopher ...

Leslie Stephen, in his essay on 'Wordsworth's Ethics' (1876), speaks warmly of a poem that 'holds a number of intellectual dogmas in solution'; and Lovejoy, in a more famous and telling phrase, has spoken of ideas in literature as 'philosophical ideas in dilution'. And it is true that the practice of decorating or diluting philosophical ideas in poetry is a perfectly familiar one: Pope's *Essay on Man* would be a clear example, and Dr Johnson's comment on that poem in his Life of Pope was a succinct and cutting recognition that it was so: 'Never were penury of knowledge and vulgarity of sentiment so happily disguised.' Unfortunately, however, it has often been assumed that the functions of Bolingbroke's ideas in Pope's poem are a model of what the relation between ideas and literature is normally like. Sidney's notion of the poet as a 'right popular philosopher' has tended to become the assumption by which twentieth-century historians of ideas have been content to work.

But two further possibilities need to be considered as well. The first, and less significant of the two, is that poetry might be philosophy in epitome rather than in dilution: more concise, and not always less obscure, than the philosophical prose which it interprets. Lovejoy might have noticed, in the course of his *Great Chain of Being*, that his poetic examples were not always more diffuse than his philosophical examples. If Lucretius's sources in *De rerum natura* were altogether like the surviving prose of Epicurus, then the difference between them could not be described by suggesting that Lucretius was diluting anything. Shelley's Platonism is a similar case; it is not always noticed that the famous passage in 'Adonais',

> *Life, like a dome of many-coloured glass,*
> *Stains the white radiance of Eternity,*
> *Until Death tramples it to fragments . . .*

is not only a striking summary of Plato's doctrine of forms, but also a highly accurate one. It would be an absurd condescension to suggest that it dilutes. Where, in the dialogues, does Plato offer so much of his doctrine in such a nutshell?

The other and much more significant possibility is that the ideas of poets might be simply original. It is surprising that historians of ideas take so little account of this possibility. One might concede that it was a natural part of their duty to exhaust the search for intellectual sources: but having taken these natural precautions, they ought to be ready to admit, and even to proclaim, that what they see is new. An obsession with intellectual daisy-chains, with the ways in which 'unit-ideas' have been handed down from age to age or subjected to individual variations within a single age, has often tended to exclude the still more inviting prospect of studying the mind of a great poet in its original vigour. Lovejoy seems to have been surprisingly content to exclude the possibility of an original mind. The history of ideas, in his view, was 'a history of trial-and-error', as if nobody has ever been known to get anything right; and his main concern was not with what individuals have discovered for themselves but rather with what he called 'literary and philosophical public opinion' in a given age or succession of ages. And in this elaborate search for a consensus, a masterpiece may be merely a nuisance:

Your minor writer may be as important as – he may often, from this point of view, be more important than – the authors of what are now regarded as the masterpieces.*

But this, if it is to be regarded as the essential business of the historian, is surely to trivialize intellectual history. If the object of the historian's enquiry is accepted as the more ambitious one

* Lovejoy, *The Great Chain of Being* (Cambridge, Mass., 1936), pp. 19–20, 23.

of discovering and interpreting individual achievement, he will be justified in insisting that mere intellectual background, though useful enough, is best kept in its natural place. It is after all the foreground that more naturally commands his attention.

But the principal resistance to admitting the sheer originality of literature more probably lies in a widespread misunderstanding concerning what an original idea in literature is like. The literary partnership of Wordsworth and Coleridge is a notable model of such a misunderstanding. Coleridge's idea of a great philosophical poem, which he urged again and again upon Wordsworth in the years around 1800, was one which he described years later in his *Table Talk:* a kind of versified successor to Locke's essay on the human understanding. Wordsworth was to draw up a scheme of human perception under a system of categories and then to expound it in blank verse; he was invited by Coleridge to

assume the station of a man in mental repose, one whose principles were made up, and so prepared to deliver upon authority a system of philosophy. He was to treat man as man – a subject of eye, ear, touch and taste, in contact with external nature, and informing the senses from the mind, and not compounding a mind out of the senses.   (21 July 1832)

And Coleridge added engagingly: 'It is, in substance, what I have been all my life doing in my system of philosophy.' But Wordsworth was understandably nervous at the prospect of writing such a poem, and wrote the autobiographical *Prelude* of 1805 instead; a poem not about mind in general, a theme which to the end defeated him, but about his own experience: 'the growth of a poet's mind'.

It is highly characteristic of the *Prelude* that general ideas are only intermittently proposed in it; and even more characteristic that, when they are proposed, they often represent cautious and tentative explanations of particular events rather than the convictions of one whose 'principles were made up'. Wordsworth does not usually understand the full significance of the climactic events of his life which form the subject of his poem, and he is reassuringly eager to confide his uncertainty to the reader:

> *My brain*
> *Work'd with a dim and undetermin'd sense*
> *Of unknown modes of being . . .*   (I.418–20)

> *I should need*
> *Colours and words that are unknown to man*
> *To paint the visionary dreariness*
> *Which, while I look'd all round for my lost guide*
> *Did at that time invest the naked pool . . .*
>
> (XI.309–13)

The events are certainly significant: but significant of what? It would hardly be true to say that Wordsworth is at a loss for an answer. He is abundant with answers. But the answers certainly do not form what Coleridge asked for: a system of philosophy delivered upon authority. The authority of the *Prelude* may be thought all the greater for this reason: it is the authority that belongs to one who knows what he is talking about and who is not prepared to assert more than he knows. Its doctrine of the 'vivifying influence' to be won from the climactic events of past experience and enriched by a process of recollection is not proposed as a nostrum but gently proffered as an experienced fact. It is ironic to reflect that Coleridge, even after listening to the *Prelude* in 1807 from Wordsworth's own lips, still hoped that his friend would some day write his philosophical poem, and that Wordsworth to the end seems to have believed that the 'Prelude', as his widow called it, was no more than that. Neither poet realized that it was the thing itself, or that the truths about experience which it offers are all the more authoritative because they have not been compelled into a systematic form or dogmatically reinterpreted. It is a fact familiar in law-courts that a witness who does not claim to understand what he has seen is usually more reliable than one who believes that he does. Wordsworth is the first kind of witness. He tells what he knows.

Intellectual history, in the last analysis, can hardly afford to shirk examples of this order of originality. If in the end it is concerned with thought itself, it cannot content itself with minor problems concerning the ways in which thought has been transmitted from mind to mind. If it is objected that ideas are not what make poems excellent, and this for no better reason than that the ideas of some great poems have been demonstrated to have been wrong, then the wide similarities between literary history and other kinds of history will need to be re-asserted. If it is objected that ideas can be extracted from poems only by violence, and that those who practise this kind of analysis upon literature are indulging themselves in a brutal species of surgery, it may be replied that the survival-power of literature is greater than such objections seem to comprehend: that literature can certainly survive analysis as violent as this, and worse. There is no cogent reason for refusing to extract ideas from poems. The summary is not the poem, but it may none the less do the work for which summaries are meant. 'No figure in the carpet is the carpet';* and yet the pattern is none the less there, and worth recording.

But there is still a vestige of sense in the view that poetry, though it may prove itself to be of formidably philosophic interest, is not itself philosophy; much as Coleridge may have had some good reason after all to feel that the *Prelude*, however good, was not the poem he had hoped for. The broad similarities which connect the study of literature with the histories of philosophy, religion and the rest are similarities and not identities. The differences between them are usually exaggerated; but it is still true that we do not read poetry just as we read Kant or Mill. If Wordsworth's *Prelude* is of philosophical interest, then it would seem absurd to say the same of Kant's *Critique of Pure Reason*. Much of the argument of this chapter has been concerned with reducing the gap between what is commonly held to be of philosophical interest and what is held to be philosophical. But even when the gap has been reduced, it may still be found to exist. Leslie Stephen, at the beginning of his essay on 'Wordsworth's Ethics' (1876), has spoken soberly of the difference as consisting in the fact that 'the poet has intuitions, while the philosopher gives demonstrations'; and this would be an acceptable summary, provided it is understood that the difference between the intuitions of the poet and the demonstrations of the philosopher is not the difference between the inconclusive and the conclusive. A philosopher might conclude from his argument only that he could not draw a conclusion; he might even conclude that it was of the nature of the question not to be conclusively answered. This procedure might disappoint, but it would not be necessarily true that the philosopher was failing in his duty by behaving in such a way – still less that he had ceased to practise philosophy and had become a poet. An intuition may convince, after all, and a demonstration fail to convince. Most readers of the *Prelude* would agree that Wordsworth has revealed his intuitions about human perception and memory in such a way as to impose conviction. To be shown 'why Locke was wrong',

* C. L. Barber, *Shakespeare's Festive Comedy* (Princeton, 1959), p. 4.

if he was, is not to be shown that he was not a philosopher. It is the formality of his procedures rather than the truth of what he tells that makes him what he is.

Can an idea be said to have a history – a history that can be narrated? This question is not posed as possessing life-and-death importance to the study of the history of ideas. History, it may be suggested again, does not need to be narrative. It may be a proper function on the part of any sort of historian to describe a single state of a given phenomenon as it has existed in the past, and the horizontal study of intellectual history is already a familiar function. To study the European Enlightenment, or Romanticism, might well fall more readily into an analytical than into a narrative form. But the prospect of the vertical design for a history of ideas is naturally tempting. And if the preceding argument concerning ideas in poetry is broadly right, then the answer can only be a favourable one. Since poets are fully engaged in ideas, and not merely in diluting or popularizing them, the sequence in which ideas have been discovered, modified and propagated is a genuine sequence, and the 'collaborative enterprise' between literary historians and others which Lovejoy demanded can be shown to match a collaborative enterprise in the past between the minds of poets and the minds of philosophers or religious sages. This is a collaboration between equals, to put it conservatively. 'It must puzzle us to know what thinking is if Shakespeare and Dante did not do it.'* Ideas emphatically have a history, independently of whether they are inside literature or outside it. Anybody who attempted a history of Christianity would necessarily and inevitably find himself using literary sources in the most confined sense of the term 'literary'. But the historians of ideas in this century have not always been content with this easy position. Lovejoy has spoken of familiar abstractions such as Romanticism and Christianity as 'unstable compounds', and accused them of breeding trouble and obscuring thought. He does not mention what trouble they have bred or whose thought they have obscured; but to judge from his attack upon the term Romanticism, it seems likely that one of his objections is based upon the view that the historian of ideas should confine himself to terms which are susceptible to verbal definition. But even this objection, mistaken as it is on general grounds, would hardly cover the case of Christianity, which is surely susceptible to verbal definition; and if one were

* Lionel Trilling, *The Liberal Imagination* (New York, 1950), p. 287.

to call such a term an unstable compound, it would presumably be in order to point to the highly significant fact that, while there may be an irreducible minimum common to the belief of all Christians in all periods, there is also a large variety of beliefs in addition to this minimum upon which certain sects and individuals have at times insisted. It does not seem to follow from this, however, that a history of Christianity cannot be written: in fact this variety would be the very stuff of such a history. It is strange, too, that Lovejoy could not see that the 'unit-ideas' which he preferred to such unstable compounds as Christianity were themselves unstable in much the same sense. His valuable article on '*Nature* as Aesthetic Norm', for instance, attempts to analyse the various uses to which the term 'nature' has been put in aesthetic debate, mainly in the seventeenth and eighteenth centuries. This analysis demonstrates the 'instability' of the compound 'nature', which Lovejoy calls 'a verbal jack-of-all-trades'; and the object of his analysis is to 'make clear the logical relations and . . . the common confusions' between the many senses in which the word in these centuries was used. Lovejoy's tone in the course of distinguishing a wide variety of senses of 'nature' is characteristically severe, and his air is that of a man firmly setting out to tidy a room which he feels ought never to have been allowed to get into such a mess: 'the multiplicity of its meanings has made it easy, and common, to slip more or less insensibly from one connotation to another, and thus in the end to pass from one ethical or aesthetic standard to its very antithesis, while nominally professing the same principles'.

It would be a pity if historians of ideas were commonly to behave as if the use of the same word in different senses were either an exceptional or a regrettable occurrence. It is certainly not exceptional. To say 'now' may mean, according to context, 'this minute', or 'today', or 'this week' or 'this month', or 'this year', or 'in this age or century'; but nobody thinks 'now' an unstable compound or even an ambiguous term, though there may be contexts in which it is ambiguous or worse. It may be objected that the complexity to be observed over the centuries in the uses of 'nature' is a higher order of complexity than this, and so in a sense it is: not, in all probability, because 'nature' has a greater number of senses than 'now', but because the senses of 'nature' are what Lovejoy calls 'pregnant . . . in the terminology of all the normative provinces of thought in the West'. 'Nature' is not odd, in fact, in the variety of the senses it has been allowed to bear, but merely significant to an extraordinary degree for the purposes of the literary historian.

But the suspicion survives that those who believe in unit-ideas rather than in ideas as such feel there is something unsatisfactory in such variety. Lovejoy speaks of seventeenth- and eighteenth-century Englishmen and others who have employed the word 'nature' as 'slipping more or less insensibly from one connotation to another', and the impression remains that they would have been better advised not to do so. But this is not as obvious as he may have supposed. It may be assumed that no historian of ideas believes that people ought to have thought the same thing in all ages, whether about aesthetic norms or anything else, so that the changes in aesthetic doctrine that Lovejoy records is not in itself a matter for regret. Equally, it cannot be said that Dryden, Addison, Pope, Reynolds and the rest were misusing language, since it is not in itself a misuse of language to use a word in more senses than one, or in a sense different from that of a predecessor. And they were certainly not using the word obscurely; if they had been doing so, Lovejoy would have been unable to classify the instances they provide him with. The gentle accusation contained in the phrase about having 'slipped more or less insensibly from one connotation to another' does not appear to have much force; there does not seem any good reason to doubt that the writers concerned understood 'nature' in the senses that are being ascribed to them, and that they could have said of other senses, if challenged: 'That is not what I meant.' To behave like this is not to behave insensibly to language. It is simply to use language as language is used.

It is altogether likely that the search for 'units' has proved something of a time-wasting digression in the study of intellectual history. If it is allowed to suggest, as it often is, that the great doctrines of the Western mind are merely compounds built out of certain ultimate and indivisible ideas, rather as matter is composed of atoms, and that the task of the historian is to isolate, define and illustrate these atoms of meaning, then it would be right to protest that this misdescribes both the Western mind itself and the function of the historian in relation to it. A doctrine is not a material object like a body, and anatomy is not usually the best way to analyse it. But the historiography of ideas since Leslie Stephen already offers better models than these prescriptions would suggest for the exercise of a great historical art. That art presents features reassuringly familiar to those who already know what history is like and how it can best perform its functions. It possesses an abundance of knowledge awaiting interpretation; the possibility of tracing the evolution of phenomena as a narrative or of analysing them in single states; and the excitements of shifting perspectives in which discovery may reveal not only a new fact in intellectual history, but a relationship which may radically shift the significance of what is already known.

12

THE IDEA OF
CULTURAL HISTORY

The relation between literature and the other arts poses special problems for an inhabitant of the French- or English-speaking worlds. In these countries, as seldom elsewhere, civilization is overwhelmingly a matter of literature, so that alliances among the arts cannot be expected to flourish as partnerships between equals. And it seems altogether likely that his situation of inequality will continue. Nobody, certainly, should be confused by claims that the mass media represent a fatal threat to literature. Such claims are usually based upon a simple error of fact and upon a confusion of terms. The error of fact is to suppose that radio and television diminish the habit of reading, and there is already clear evidence that this is wrong. (They were once thought likely to kill conversation, and that does not seem to have happened either.) The confusion concerns what literature is. It is certainly not the same as a printed book or even a manuscript. It is surely plain that an ancient Greek tragedy was a work of literature even if nobody but the dramatist and the actors had ever seen a written copy of it. It did not become a work of literature only when copies were made and disseminated, otherwise the copyists could qualify to be regarded as the creators of literary works. In the same way a broadcast play which is never printed is already a work of literature. It is subject, both in principle and as a matter of fact, to the existing procedures of dramatic criticism. In so far as it provokes such criticism in print, as it often does, it is itself among the causes of the increasing writing and reading of printed texts. If it is itself printed, as it sometimes is, or if it is based upon some existing play or novel and stimulates interest in an existing printed text, then a further stimulus to the printed work is provided. The vast and rising scale of printing in the Western world makes exaggerated claims for the effects of the newer mass media something of a joke. The probability is that there never was an age as subject and as vulnerable to literature as this. Some of that literature, it is true, is purveyed by means other than the written or printed page. But the continuing rise of literacy does not suggest that this proportion is an increasing one, difficult of calculation as such matters must be. What is known about medieval and Renaissance drama, or the nineteenth-century habit of reading books aloud in a family circle, does not encourage the view that there is in itself anything new in a situation in which millions are content to receive literature in ways other than by reading it from the printed page. This is not to suggest that the mass media make no difference to the study of literature, but rather that those differences are readily and often misdescribed.

Literature in the existing situation is not threatened. On the contrary, it is the master-art that threatens all the rest. This makes the claims of cultural history the more plausible and the more inviting to a literary historian, at least in French and English, since it allows him to feel with some confidence that his own qualifications for describing a whole civilization, perilous as such a task must always appear, may be better than anyone else's. What is at issue here is a practical fact which happens to concern two great civilizations: it is in no sense a necessary or even natural condition of civilization in general. But for as long as it is a fact of French and English, the fact is bound to loom large. One can readily imagine an historian of literature writing a cultural history of France in the age of Louis XIV or of England in the age of Victoria; but if a musicologist or an art-historian were to attempt tasks like these, one would be inclined to fear for the consequences. The degree to which the language of criticism in music, painting, architecture and sculpture in France and England is parasitic upon literary criticism has often been noticed. A high degree of dependence by music and the visual arts upon literature is also observable. The vast influence of psycho-analysis upon abstract painting in the last half century is none the less real for the fact that Freud himself disliked such works and preferred representational art, and anyone attempting a history of abstract art would wish to take account of the twentieth-century passion for self-analysis which Freud helped to provoke. It seems much less plausible, by contrast, to say that anyone who takes an intelligent interest in the modern psychological novel is bound to take an interest in the visual arts contemporaneous with it. A reader of novels might visit art galleries to some advantage to himself, but he would not feel his literary understanding doomed if he did not. The sculpture of Henry Moore is said in some degree to have its literary sources:[*] but how many poems are known to have a Moore sculpture as their source?

There are convincing reasons, then, for supposing that the literary historian is in a uniquely favourable position as an historian of civilization. His claim is only rivalled by that of the historian in the wider sense; and certainly the stage is always set for a Jakob Burckhardt with the range and skill to work the civilization of one age and country into an historical pattern. But whether the task more properly belongs to the historian or to the literary historian, a question fundamental to the prospect of composing cultural history always remains. Is there any intimate or necessary relation between the arts in any one place and at any one time? It has often and plausibly been doubted that any such intelligible relation exists. 'How can one make of phenomena having no common character but that of not being contemporary with us the matter of rational knowledge? . . . Can one imagine a complete science of the universe in its present state?'[†] This is an intelligently sceptical view, and the question might be restated in a still more sceptical form. When one considers the inconsistencies of form and substance that may co-exist in the work of a single artist, how can it be supposed that a whole civilization could be demonstrated to possess a coherence of its own?

A review of the existing condition of cultural history, and principally of the relations to be drawn between literature and the visual arts, may bring scepticism of this sort into clearer perspective. The ancient doctrine of poetry and painting as sister arts – Horace's '*ut pictura poesis*' – failed to lead to an active tradition of cultural history either in classical or in neo-classical criticism, perhaps because the argument was conducted on a level of generality which did not encourage the analysis of particular similarities or differences of style between the arts. Dryden, for instance, in the first treatise on the visual arts ever written by an English poet, the 'Parallel of Poetry and Painting'

[*] e.g. D'Arcy W. Thompson, *On Growth and Form* (Cambridge, 1917).
[†] Marc Bloch, *Apologie pour l'histoire* (Paris, 1949), ch. 1.

(1695), makes a number of familiar points about the portrayal of heroic virtue in the epic and its equivalents in seventeenth-century court painting. But the parallel is remotely Platonic rather than detailed or analytical: both the arts of poetry and painting are 'not only imitations of nature, but of the best nature, of that which is wrought up to a nobler pitch; . . . images more perfect than the life in any individual'. Dryden was acutely aware of the differences between the arts and of the difficulties of relating them to one another; though he is not bold enough to conclude, as Lessing was to do three quarters of a century later, that the Horatian parallel between poetry and painting is simply a matter of 'false transference':

I must say this to the advantage of painting, even above tragedy, that what this last represents in the space of many hours, the former shows us in one moment. The action, the passion, and the manners of so many persons as are contained in a picture are to be discerned at once, in the twinkling of an eye; at least they would be so if the sight could travel over so many different objects all at once, or the mind could digest them all at the same instant or point of time.

This is a highly concessive argument at every point, and makes the parallel look more like a contrast. It suggests an intelligent awareness of the difficulties of cultural history rather than any real eagerness to solve them.

The first serious attempt to create such a tradition is likely to have been Winckelmann's in the *History of Ancient Art* (1768), a work which is among the earliest experiments by a European in writing art history in continuous relation to the history of a civilization in general. But Winckelmann left one profound intuition to his nineteenth-century successors: he failed to see that methods of representation characteristic of artists or even of whole ages – the great matter of 'style' itself – was the way to relate cultural movement to intellectual progress in general. With his remote and reverent view of the heroic properties of ancient art, he saw the surviving masterpieces of ancient sculpture as ideal forms to excite modern admiration rather than as an expression of an individual artist working in a single and impermanent historical situation. 'Great art must have no flavour, like perfectly pure water,' he once wrote. This engaging view worked in the direction of taking art out of time and leaving it isolated, often magnificently enough, as pure form in a series of pure forms. It was left to the nineteenth century to seize the chance of perceiving art in its full historical relations, and both professional historians and dedicated connoisseurs worked in that age to create the familiar tradition of the histories of great styles. It is to Winckelmann's successors, and not to him, that the present century owes its understanding of terms such as 'High Renaissance', 'mannerist' and 'baroque'.

Jakob Burckhardt of Basle, before any literary historian, may be shown to have laid the foundations of modern cultural history. Burckhardt never wrote the history of Italian art to which the whole effort of his life seemed to be directed. But it is appropriate that a civilization as little dominated by literature as the Italian should find an art historian to recount the history of its great age. Burckhardt's guidebook *Cicerone* (1855) and his *Civilization of the Renaissance in Italy* (1860) are imposing introductions to a history he never lived to write. His doctrine of 'art history as the history of mind' developed through the conscientious sifting of evidence into a cool historical enquiry – a procedure strikingly different from the practice of his English contemporary Ruskin, who was notably less interested in the past for its own sake, and who used its works as instruments in a passionately conducted campaign against what he supposed the evils of his own industrial age.

No English historian, at least, can call himself the worthy successor of Burckhardt, and the grand design that he tried to raise is still largely unfulfilled. Cultural history in the twentieth century does not begin to rival social and political history either in the scale of its achievement or even as a task to generate enthusiasm. 'Cultural background' is merely matter for an end-chapter in many established historical handbooks; and literary historians among the rest are unable to point to any convincing model of how the work should be done. Even the proposals made by Burckhardt for history have rarely been thought practical. Wölfflin, who was his pupil at Basle and who succeeded to his chair in 1893, interpreted his master's achievement as sceptical on this very issue. In his lectures, according to Wölfflin, Burckhardt had denied that connections between art and civilization were generally demonstrable, unless 'loosely and lightly'; 'art', he is reported to have said, 'has its own life and history'.* This view would make cultural history difficult to sustain even in principle, and Wölfflin fully adhered to it, whether it properly belonged to his master or not. Art, in his view, developed accord-

* Heinrich Wölfflin, *Gedanken zur Kunstgeschichte* (Basle, 1941), p. 24.

ing to laws internal to itself, and not under the pressure of historical events in general. 'What has the Gothic style to do with feudalism and scholasticism?' as he put it in his first book, *Renaissance and Baroque* (1888). Wölfflin's notion of the dynamic urges within a civilization was one of forces common to the visual arts but confined within them, and he is rarely concerned even with the loosest parallels between such sister arts as painting and literature. The aim of art history, as he explained it in his preface, is to discover the ultimate laws underlying an artistic style, to 'provide an insight into the intimate working of art'; and style, which is the hero of his writings as no individual artist such as Leonardo or Michelangelo ever is, is conceived as a power which pre-exists those works of art which are its examples, and one which wills them into being and life.

The notion seems at first glance too mystical to be Anglo-Saxon, but surprisingly it is not. More than one Victorian was stirred by the idea of a moving principle behind cultural history, and perhaps behind history in general – a demon in the machine which worked as a creative force behind a whole society. Ruskin in later life believed that the history of a people's art was more revealing and more trustworthy than the history of its politics or of its literature. 'Great nations,' as he put it in the introduction to *St Mark's Rest* (1884), 'write their autobiographies in three manuscripts: the book of their deeds, the book of their words and the book of their art,' and he went on to argue that the 'book of art' was in some ways the most truthful of the three. Leslie Stephen looked for the demon elsewhere, in social history, and thought that intellectual and literary history might some day be shown to be mere by-products of social evolution, 'the noise that the wheels make as they go round'.* But the search for a principle within human history, characteristic as it is of much nineteenth-century utopian thought at its most ambitious, was more productive of casual effects than of a conclusive and revolutionary discovery of the kind that it earnestly sought. The new science of iconology, for instance, arose out of detailed and technical studies in the early twentieth century by Aby Warburg of Hamburg and, after his collection had been brought to London by Fritz Saxl in 1934, by a number of disciples concerned in England, France and the United States with the study of pagan survivals in Renaissance art; and in the 1930s it began to develop some of the features of general cultural history in its

* F. W. Maitland, *The Life and Letters of Leslie Stephen* (London, 1906), p. 283.

search for the symbolic values of works of art and the relations
of these values with intellectual history in general. The purely
descriptive function of 'iconography' soon gave way to something more ambitious. It was one thing to see Leonardo's fresco
of the Last Supper as thirteen men grouped in a certain spatial
relationship around a table; another to see it as a document of an
age and as a climactic point in the supersession of many ages:

When we try to understand it as a document of Leonardo's personality,
or of the civilization of the Italian High Renaissance, or of a peculiar
religious attitude, we deal with the work of art as a symptom of something else which expresses itself in a countless variety of other symptoms,
and we interpret its compositional and iconographical features as more
particularized evidence of this 'something else'.*

And the same historian goes on to distinguish the interpretation
of such significances in a work of art – values symbolic of the
personality of the creator and of the civilization he worked in –
as the prime feature of iconology as opposed to the severer and
simpler discipline of some older traditions in the history of art.

Some of the accidental aspects of the new discipline of iconology impress the historian of literature as of instant significance.
One is the fact of mid-continental origin, which is a matter not
merely of the ultimate sources of iconology but of its continuing
impulse as well. In many ways the most active tradition in
cultural history which the Western world has to show in the
present century, iconology still remains linked, in some of its
emotional preoccupations, with a nineteenth-century will to
nationhood in central Europe, where national characteristics
were felt to be the more deeply engrossing because of an historic
lack of what France and England have for centuries possessed:
the visible symbols in state and church of a realized community.
Nietzsche, at the conclusion of his *Birth of Tragedy* (1872), had
spoken in prophetic tones of the union of music and tragic
myth as 'an expression of the Dionysiac talent of a nation', and
the operas of Wagner seemed for a time to offer a hope of
reviving the cultural unity of ancient Athens in modern Germany.
The fascination of the great scholar-exiles of the 1930s and after
with the elusive qualities of a national art continued the tradition
of a search for a visible unity and order that may be seen to

---

* Erwin Panofsky, from his introduction to *Studies in Iconology* (New York,
1939); reprinted as 'Iconology and Iconography' in his *Meaning in the Visual Arts*
(New York, 1955).

unite a whole people and a whole civilization. Iconology is
international in its range and scope, and readily pursues its
symbolic values across frontiers, periods and forms of art. But
its rootlessness is matched by a longing for roots. To compare
Ruskin's writings on Venetian Gothic with a work like Nikolaus
Pevsner's *The Englishness of English Art* (1955) is to sense the
quality of this difference at once. Ruskin writes as an Englishman
who believes that he has found in a remote and alien culture,
the Venice of the later Middle Ages, something that Victorian
England needs: a masterly blending of the commercial and artistic
life of a maritime nation. Pevsner, by contrast, sees in the evolving tradition of the visual arts in England over many centuries an
emotionally engaging unity, a common stylistic property or set
of properties which asserts its attachment to one people and one
place. It is hardly conceivable that an Englishman should write
such a book. To compose cultural history as rich in confident
generalizations as this requires a sense of distance from the object
under review: the distance of an anthropologist, one is tempted to
add, on a visit to a savage tribe.

Another aspect of the new study of iconology is the plain fact
that it is practised by historians of art. There is nothing natural,
still less necessary, about such a circumstance. If iconology stands
on the borderland where literary, artistic and intellectual history
meet, then there is no clear reason, in the abstract, why the
literary historian should not take part on equal terms. But in
practice he has rarely done so, and literary histories that employ
the evidence of the visual arts are still surprisingly rare. This lack
of symmetry in the relationship between the two subjects remains a striking fact even in the present age. Probably no
historian of art would now presume to approach his subject
without a familiarity with the surviving literary evidence, and a
work like Edgar Wind's *Pagan Mysteries of the Renaissance*
(1958) shows how natural and fruitful such a relation can be.
But to ask why it was written by a student of Botticelli rather
than by a student of Spenser is to realize again how confidently
exclusive the tradition of literary studies in some Western
countries remains to this day. The sense of assured nationhood
relieves the English literary historian, for the most part, of any
compulsion to see his civilization as a whole or to distinguish
its characteristic features; and one of these features, its intensely
literary quality, may easily distract him from any sense of concern for evidences presented by the other arts.

What remains, then, of the argument for seeing an entire civilization, such as the Italian High Renaissance or Elizabethan England, as a single and coherent whole? It is sometimes argued that those who are most intent on seeing coherences of this sort are also suspiciously given to stretching the evidence, and that the stretching usually consists of seeing phenomena of the most diverse kind as belonging, regardless of diversity, to a single pattern. An art-historian like Wölfflin is as open as anyone to charges of this kind, since the end of his enquiry is always the discovery of a common or uniting factor in the diverse master-pieces of a single epoch:

> Grünewald is a different imaginative type from Dürer, although they are contemporaries. But we cannot say that this destroys the significance of the development: seen from a larger range, these two types reunite in a common style, and we instantly recognize the elements which unite them as representatives of their generation.*

The procedure is certainly open to the accusation of indifference to the sanctity of the individual instance; though Wölfflin's own analysis of the difference between artistic forms in Europe in the sixteenth and seventeenth centuries forms an argument too detailed and too ingenious to be open to any ordinary charge of ignorance. The analogy he draws between progress in the arts, such as the rise of the baroque style in the seventeenth century, and the loosening of grammatical forms in languages is especially suggestive and ambitious. But the complaint against forced coherence needs a more powerful answer than the single example of Wölfflin's *Principles* can offer; and the *Principles* themselves, rewarding as they are, expose themselves at times to traditional doubts. 'Seen from a larger range, [Dürer and Grünewald] reunite in a common style': it remains tempting to object that any range of vision as large as that could make any diversity whatever merge into a similarity. When the historian draws parallels between the language of *Paradise Lost* and the ingenuities of *trompe-l'œil* effects in late seventeenth-century architecture, or between architectural functionalism, abstract painting and the language of Eliot's *Waste Land* in the earlier twentieth century, the difficulties of demonstrating such parallels may be thought insuperable.

But this scepticism may in the end prove to be exaggerated, and may perhaps best be shown to be so by comparing the

* From the *Principles of Art History*, preface to sixth edition (1922).

personality of a whole civilization with that of an individual. Wölfflin's intricate parallel between the loosening of grammatical forms and the relaxation of High Renaissance into baroque, daring as it is, is hardly more daring than the explanations one readily accepts about the workings of a single mind. The coherence of an individual personality is not obviously a more difficult concept than this. If one accepts as evidence for a wider coherence, in a friend or acquaintance, the wildest divergences of word and conduct, it is because an individual is known, in advance of any information, to be just that, and no evidence concerning what he may say or do could be strong enough to destroy conviction concerning his essential individuality. When he behaves inconsistently or unpredictably, new evidences of his personality are simply accommodated, with whatever difficulty they may occasion, into a larger knowledge of the man. The cultural historian may be said to behave in a similar way; and if he appears to force the evidence that he sees, it is because of a prior conviction that some pattern or other is there to be found. A civilization is after all some kind of an entity, however diverse. When Wölfflin argues with all the force of paradox to demonstrate a common style that unites the works of Grünewald and Dürer, it is because he knows that they are contemporaries and the products of a single culture. The ingenious solution will seem over-ingenious only if the premise of cultural unity is denied. But anyone who persists with denials of this sort may be challenged with the answer that his sense of what constitutes coherence in the behaviour of a whole people is more demanding than in the case of a single individual.

If this perilous licence is granted, then, to the cultural historian, and the difficulties and dangers of his task frankly admitted from the start, the possibilities of a form of history wider than the history of a single art such as literature seem more than ever open and inviting. History in these terms might represent an attempt to achieve for modern and advanced civilizations what anthropologists in the past century have attempted for the primitive. And certainly the achievements of anthropology in the past century, from J. G. Frazer's articles on taboo and totemism in the 1880s to Claude Lévi-Strauss's accounts of the primitive mind in the years since the Second World War, may be suggested as indirect examples of a slowly increasing optimism towards the possibility of cultural history. That anthropologists should choose to limit their enquiries, to an overwhelming degree, to the habits of pre-industrial man is an oddity which the subject seems bound to outlive. But it has the strange effect of leaving the science of man, so far as an industrial and literate world understands it, to the more informal investigations of the historian of modern culture who is usually, in the first instance, a literary scholar. And certainly, in the existing situation, the literary historian who widens his horizon, and seeks to interpret the total function of a creative civilization such as Elizabethan England, cannot be justly complained against that he is invading the sphere of another. Nobody in the present state of academic enquiry is readier or better equipped for such tasks than he.

The anthropological obsession with primitive culture has so far tended to exclude cultural history from its range of interest. But the assumption of coherence unites the two disciplines too powerfully to allow them to be considered apart, slight as may be the debts that the one in the present situation owes to the other. It seems likely, moreover, that recent movements in anthropology have intensified this connection, in that it was once easier to attribute habits of mind to primitive man so alien to the modern spirit as to render him intelligible only as a spectacle for wonder. Frazer, with the confidence of a Victorian rationalist, saw human history as a progress in awareness analogous to the evolutionary progress of the species before it attained to human dignity – a 'long evolution by which the thoughts and efforts of man have passed through the successive stages of Magic, Religion and Science', as he put it in *The Golden Bough* (1890). Lévi-Strauss, in *The Savage Mind* (1962), has rendered the progressive view of human knowledge less secure by producing evidence to suggest that the mind of primitive man was already proficient in the arts of classification. The second view, if it is correct, certainly offers some hopes of rendering the enquiries of the anthropologist more like those of the cultural historian in more and more respects. The earliest man may be shown to possess something like a civilization, and the study of one civilization may increasingly benefit from the study of another. For the moment, such connections are only tenuous. But limiting as must be an enquiry into the remotely primitive, it might instruct the modern world about itself if it were conducted in terms that allowed for the existence in all ages of an exercise of rational principles and of the search for evidence.

And certainly a renewed confidence in rationality is among the first and most urgent causes to be contested for in the study of literature. It would be easy to abandon the literary discipline, with an easy sense of liberation, to those who are victims of an autistic fallacy and who hold that the literature of the past exists in our minds alone, that it is and can only be what we choose to make it, or that what it ought to say is more significant than what in fact it says. The present century is tragically familiar with systems of tyranny that offer themselves as liberation, and the doctrine of an eternal present in literature is a freedom little better than theirs. But the danger remains real enough in a situation in which literary studies are in universal demand. The literary scholar is subject to easy temptations; and to abandon the study of literary texts in favour of a science of communications or a study of contemporary culture is often to ensure oneself an easy hearing. And yet to liberate oneself from history, to view the past only out of respect for what it may have to say about present concerns, is to consent to remain a victim of the instant in time in which we are forced to live. And to exchange an abundant past for a single present is to advantage nothing but the cause of simplicity. In the same way, to demand a single key that might explain the past altogether is to ask for the abolition of diversity and the reduction of intelligence into mere self-importance. The bitter truth is that the past has not survived in order to enlighten the present. It has survived, often accidentally enough, for no single reason that the present can truthfully name, and it speaks as often of what we are not as of what we are.

SELECT BIBLIOGRAPHY

The place of publication is noted,
unless it is London, following the short title.

I. THE LIBERTY OF JUDGEMENT

Since the Second World War the most controversial restatement of the
problems of commitment in literature has been Jean-Paul Sartre,
Qu'est-ce que la littérature (Paris, 1948). On the conquest of the past
by literary historians since the eighteenth century, the pioneer phase in
England has been recounted by René Wellek in *The Rise of English
Literary History* (Chapel Hill, 1941). John Churton Collins, *The Study
of English Literature* (1891) is a plea for its recognition by British universities, and includes a proposed curriculum and quotations from Gladstone,
Pater, Matthew Arnold and others drawn from the *Pall Mall Gazette*
questionnaire of the 1880s; and D. J. Palmer, *The Rise of English Studies*
(Hull, 1965), traces the story of the academic study of English up to the
foundation of the Oxford English School in 1894, while E. M. W.
Tillyard, *The Muse Unchained* (1958), describes the creation of the
Cambridge English School from the early twentieth century till about
1930. There is an account of the German achievement, Friedrich Stroh,
Handbuch der germanischen Philologie (Berlin, 1952).

2. REASON AND VALUE

Among many recent accounts of the status of historical study, two may
be especially noted: Marc Bloch, *Apologie pour l'histoire* (Paris, 1949),
translated as *The Historian's Craft* (Manchester, 1954); and E. H. Carr,
What is History? (1961). For Plato's view of poetry, E. A. Havelock,
Preface to Plato (Oxford, 1963) is a useful clarification.

On the alleged contrast between literary and scientific processes,
Karl Popper, *The Logic of Scientific Discovery* (1959) has been highly
influential. A view characteristic of the New Criticism is fully expounded

in René Wellek and Austin Warren, *Theory of Literature* (New York, 1949, revised 1956); while Laurence Lerner, *The Truest Poetry* (1960) argues persuasively for a cognitive view of poetry. For the post-war French debate, Raymond Picard, *Nouvelle critique ou nouvelle imposture* (Paris, 1965) is a brief and devastating attack on the critical subjectivism of Roland Barthes and others, and has provoked a reply by Barthes, *Critique et vérité* (Paris, 1966). William Righter, *Logic and Criticism* (1963) puts a sceptical view of the relationship; and John Casey in *The Language of Criticism* (1966) a Wittgensteinian one.

3. THE LANGUAGE OF VERSE AND PROSE

Studies of metre since George Saintsbury, *A History of English Prosody*, 3 vols (1906–10) have been numerous; many are listed by Karl Shapiro, *A Bibliography of Modern Prosody* (Baltimore, 1948), with a glossary of terms. Two notable articles are A. Hensler, Roman Jakobsen and others, 'Metrica', in *Enciclopedia Italiana* (Rome, 1934); and C. T. Onions, 'Prosody' in *Cassell's Encyclopaedia of Literature*, ed. S. H. Steinberg, vol. I (1953), both with bibliographies. There is a reasoned defence of traditional against 'free' verse by Yvor Winters, 'The Influence of Meter on Poetic Convention', in his *Primitivism and Decadence* (New York, 1937), reprinted in his *In Defense of Reason* (Denver, 1947). W. K. Wimsatt, 'One Relation of Rhyme to Reason', in his *Verbal Icon* (Lexington, Kentucky, 1954), is an original contribution largely based on the example of Pope's couplets, supported by 'The Concept of Meter' in his *Hateful Contraries* (Lexington, 1965); while John Thompson, *The Founding of English Metre* (1961), is concerned with the fifteenth and sixteenth centuries. As a manual of English metre, there is Karl Shapiro and Robert Beum, *A Prosody Handbook* (New York, 1965), with a glossary of terms. Paul Fussell, *Poetic Meter and Poetic Form* (New York, 1965) is a critical study of English metre through examples.

There is a sensitive account of examples of English poetic language in Winifred Nowottny, *The Language Poets Use* (1962). Studies of prose are less common and less confident: for Latin theory and practice in prose, A. D. Leeman, *Orationis ratio*, 2 vols (Amsterdam, 1963). Earlier articles by Morris W. Croll mainly on English Renaissance prose have been collected as *Style, Rhetoric and Rhythm* (Princeton, 1966), to which Brian Vickers, *Francis Bacon and Renaissance Prose* (Cambridge, 1968) is in part a reply; and there are two studies of the language of French fiction by Stephen Ullmann, *Style in the French Novel* (Cambridge, 1957) and *The Image in the Modern French Novel* (Cambridge, 1960). Christine Brooke-Rose, *A Grammar of Metaphor* (1958) is a study of the structure of metaphor; and there is a collection of studies on the subject, *Metaphor and Symbol* (1960), edited by L. C. Knights and B. Cottle.

4. THE LITERARY PAST

André Morize, *Problems and Methods of Literary History, with Special Reference to Modern French Literature: a Guide for Graduate Students* (Boston, 1922), is a rare example of a methodical account of the procedures of the literary historian, unfortunately outdated in its references. A briefer but more modern version is James Thorpe, *Literary Scholarship: a Handbook for Advanced Students of English and American Literature* (Boston, 1964). For the rise of literary history, see under Chapter 1, above. An article by W. K. Wimsatt and Monroe C. Beardsley, 'The Intentional Fallacy', which first appeared in a periodical in 1946, was revised and collected in Wimsatt, *The Verbal Icon* (Lexington, Kentucky, 1954), and acknowledges a debt to an earlier exchange on a similar theme between C. S. Lewis and E. M. W. Tillyard, *The Personal Heresy* (Oxford, 1939). There could hardly be a single record of the vast expansion of literary history since 1800; but René Wellek, *A History of Modern Criticism 1750–1950* (New Haven, 1955–), is largely concerned with its progress in Europe and North America. On biographical elements, Leon Edel, *Literary Biography* (Toronto, 1957, revised New York, 1959); and for an anthology of the views on biographies themselves, *Biography as an Art*, edited by James L. Clifford (Oxford, 1962).

5. THE THEORY OF KINDS

The debate, which has been conducted in the present century mainly by classical scholars, has tended to concentrate on the *Poetics* of Aristotle; G. M. A. Grube, *The Greek and Roman Critics* (Toronto, 1965), demonstrates the extent and variety of ancient views of this subject among others. In recent times the most ambitious attempt to renew an interest in the literary kinds has been Northrop Frye, *Anatomy of Criticism* (Princeton, 1957). Modern critical texts rarely pay much attention to the matter: exceptions are Graham Hough, *An Essay on Criticism* (1966), sections 87f.; and E. D. Hirsch, *Validity of Interpretation* (New Haven, 1967), ch. 3, 'The Concept of Genre'.

6. COMPARATIVE LITERATURE

F. Baldensperger and W. P. Friederich, *Bibliography of Comparative Literature* (Chapel Hill, 1950) is a guide that may be supplemented by the sections on 'Literary Relations with the Continent' in all three volumes of the *Cambridge Bibliography of English Literature* (Cambridge, 1940 etc). For examples of modern comparatism, Renato Poggioli, *The Spirit of the Letter* (Cambridge, Mass., 1965), which posthumously collects his essays on European literature; and René Wellek, *Confronta-*

tions (Princeton, 1965), on Anglo-German relations in the nineteenth century.

Modern interpretations of the art of literary translation are abundant. T. F. Higham, in his preface to the *Oxford Book of Greek Verse in Translation* (Oxford, 1938), offers a discussion of interest beyond the confines of classical studies; and T. H. Savory, *The Art of Translation* (1957), is perhaps the best modern study in English. *On Translation* (Cambridge, Mass., 1959), a symposium edited by Reuben A. Brower, collects essays by Richmond Lattimore, Edwin Muir, Vladimir Nabokov, Roman Jakobsen and others, and a critical bibliography by B. Q. Morgan of works on literary translation since Cicero, with quotations and summaries. *The Craft and Context of Translation*, edited by William Arrowsmith and Roger Shattuck (New York, 1964), includes an appendix of texts from Cicero to Samuel Johnson.

7. THE EDITORIAL ART

Samuel Johnson's preface to his edition of Shakespeare (1765), together with a selection of his notes, has been edited by Walter Raleigh as *Johnson on Shakespeare* (Oxford, 1908, corrected 1925). On the transmission of classical texts in manuscript, the standard work is Paul Maas, *Textual Criticism* (translated Oxford, 1958), first published in German (Leipzig, 1927, revised 1957). On the tradition of Lachmann and his concept of the archetypal text, cf. Giorgio Pasquali, *Storia della tradizione e critica del testo* (Florence, 1934, enlarged 1952). A. E. Housman, *Selected Prose*, edited by John Carter (Cambridge, 1961), includes extracts from Housman's introductions to Manilius (1903, 1930) and Juvenal (1905), as well as reviews of classical editions and the 1921 lecture 'The Application of Thought to Textual Criticism'.

The principal periodicals in English are *Library* (1889–) and *Studies in Bibliography* (Charlottesville, Virginia, 1949–), the latter including valuable restatements of the old-spelling view by W. W. Greg and R. C. Bald (1950), and the new case of modernization by Alice Walker (1956). The foundation-work on English bibliography is R. B. McKerrow, *An Introduction to Bibliography for Literary Students* (Oxford, 1927, corrected 1928), with an English Renaissance emphasis; its successor-works are notably Percy Simpson, *Proof-Reading in the Sixteenth, Seventeenth and Eighteenth Centuries* (Oxford, 1935) and Greg, *The Editorial Problem in Shakespeare* (Oxford, 1942, revised 1954), *The Shakespeare First Folio* (Oxford, 1955), and *Collected Papers*, edited by J. C. Maxwell (Oxford, 1966), including his 1949 paper 'The Rationale of Copy-Text'. Fredson Bowers, *Principles of Bibliographical Description* (Princeton, 1949), formalizes bibliographical description and extends its application into the nineteenth and twentieth centuries; the task is continued in his two lecture-series, *Textual and Literary Criticism* (Cambridge, 1959) and *Bibliography and Textual Criticism* (Oxford, 1964). On compositor-determination in Shakespeare and the probable five compositors of the First Folio, Charlton Hinman, *The Printing and Proof-Reading of the First Folio of Shakespeare*, 2 vols (Oxford, 1963); and on the special problems of editing texts after 1800, *Editing Nineteenth-Century Texts*, edited by J. M. Robson (Toronto, 1967). Vinton A. Dearing, *A Manual of Textual Criticism* (Berkeley, 1959) offers a more technical approach.

S. H. Steinberg, *Five Hundred Years of Printing* (1955, revised 1961), is a good introductory history of printing in the West; and John Carter, *ABC for Book-Collectors* (1952, revised 1966), a masterly handbook in alphabetical form. For printed directions to editorial and other scholar-ship, R. D. Altick, *The Art of Literary Research* (New York, 1963); and H. T. Meserole, 'Literary Scholarship', in F. W. Bateson, *A Guide to English Literature* (1965, revised 1967).

8. LINGUISTICS

The foundation-work in modern linguistics is Ferdinand de Saussure, *Cours de linguistique générale* (Lausanne and Paris, 1916), which has been translated (New York, 1949); and the story since then may be studied in R. H. Robins, *A Short History of Linguistics* (1967). Works on structural linguistics are now extremely numerous, especially in English. C. F. Hockett, *A Course in Modern Linguistics* (New York, 1958) is a useful textbook, while *Readings in Linguistics*, edited by Martin Joos and others, 2 vols (Chicago, 1957–67) collects major articles since the 1920s by various hands. Roman Jakobson and M. Halle, *Fundamentals of Language* (Hague, 1956) is a notable introduction; many of Jakobson's works are now being collected as *Selected Writings* (Hague, 1967–). For the chief writings of the leader of the British school, J. R. Firth, *Papers in Linguistics 1934–51* (1957). Josef Vachek, *The Linguistic School of Prague* (Bloomington, 1966) describes the achievements of a flourish-ing inter-war movement. *Portraits of Linguists* (Bloomington, 1966), edited in two volumes by T. A. Sebeok, is an ample biographical dictionary of the subject; and Mario Pei, *Glossary of Linguistic Termi-nology* (New York, 1967) is a useful work of reference.

Formal attempts to reconcile modern linguistics with the study of literature became common only in the 1960s. A relatively early attempt is Leo Spitzer, *Linguistics and Literary History: Essays in Stylistics* (Prince-ton, 1948); see also T. A. Sebeok (editor), *Style in Language* (Cambridge, Mass., 1960), on the difficulties of reconciliation; and Roger Fowler (editor), *Essays on Style and Language* (1966), on the alleged rewards. Gustaf Stern, *Meaning and Change of Meaning* (Gothenburg, 1932) might be regarded as a pioneer attempt to put semantics to the service of literary studies; and Udny Yule, *The Statistical Study of Literary Vocabulary* (Cambridge, 1944) performs a similar function for statistics. Stephen Ullmann, *Language and Style: Collected Papers* (Oxford, 1964) is a lucid and well-documented account of the relation between semantics and stylistics, on the one hand, and literary studies on the other; also Charles Bally, *Traité de stylistique française* (Heidelberg, 1909), and P. Guiraud, *La stylistique* (Paris, 1954). From the other end of the scale, literary views of language may be studied in William Empson, *Seven Types of Ambiguity* (1930, revised 1947) and *The Structure of Complex Words* (1951); on poetic syntax, Donald Davie, *Articulate Energy* (1955); on the nineteenth- and twentieth-century English novel, David Lodge, *The Language of Fiction* (1966); and on metaphor, Christine Brooke-Rose, *A Grammar of Metaphor* (1958). For a brief guide to the evolution of English, W. F. Bolton, *A Short History of Literary English* (1967). The parallel, or perhaps converging, lines of linguistic philosophy may be studied in Ludwig Wittgenstein, *Philosophical Investigations* (Oxford, 1953, revised and indexed 1968), and in such successor-works as J. L. Austin, *How to Do Things with Words* (Oxford, 1962).

9. PSYCHO-ANALYSIS

The works of Sigmund Freud have been collected in translation as *The Standard Edition of the Complete Psychological Works*, translated by James Strachey and Anna Freud, 23 vols (1953–64). For a history of the orthodoxies and heresies of Freudianism, see J. A. C. Brown, *Freud and the Post-Freudians* (1961, enlarged 1964). The standard biography is by Ernest Jones, *Freud: Life and Work*, 3 vols (1953–7), condensed into one volume by Lionel Trilling and Steven Marcus (New York, 1961); the letters have been selected in translation by his son Ernst L. Freud (1961). A noted example of a literary essay by a convinced Freudian is Ernest Jones, *Hamlet and Oedipus* (1949), first published in brief in 1910.

An introduction to the work of C. G. Jung may be found in his dictated autobiography, published in English as *Memories, Dreams, Reflections* (1963); the *Collected Works* are appearing in translation edited by Sir Herbert Read and others (1953–).

There have been numerous attempts, hostile and admiring, to estimate the literary effects of the schools of Freud and Jung, including two notable essays by Lionel Trilling, 'Freud and Literature' in his *Liberal Imagination* (New York, 1950) and 'Freud: Within and Beyond Culture' in his *Beyond Culture* (New York, 1966); and Frederick J. Hoffmann, *Freudianism and the Literary Mind* (Baton Rouge, Louisiana, 1945), which includes a bibliography mainly on literary influences between the World Wars. Thomas Mann's Vienna lecture of 1936, 'Freud and the Future', which is direct evidence of his late but enthusiastic interest in psycho-analysis, is translated in his *Essays of Three Decades* (New York, 1947). On the stream-of-consciousness novel, Leon Edel, *The Psychological Novel 1900–50* (1955). Ernst Kris, *Psycho-analytic Explorations in Art* (New York, 1952), contains much of interest on both Freud and Jung as artistic influences. For more critical views, C. S. Lewis, 'Psycho-analysis and Literary Criticism' (1941), in his *They Asked for a Paper* (1962); and R. M. Adams, 'The Devil and Dr Jung' in his *Ikon* (Ithaca, New York, 1955).

10. SOCIOLOGY

Raymond Aron's history of sociology since Montesquieu began to appear in English translation in 1965 as *Main Currents in Sociological Thought;* also H. Stuart Hughes, *Consciousness and Society: the Reorientation of European Social Thought 1890–1930* (New York, 1958); Robert A. Nisbet, *The Sociological Tradition* (New York, 1966); and R. K. Merton, *Social Theory and Social Structure* (Glencoe, Illinois, 1951, revised 1957). Talcott Parsons, *The Structure of Social Action* (New York, 1937) is a study of sociology since Hobbes and Locke, mainly on Alfred Marshall, Pareto, Durkheim and Weber. There is a useful anthology of texts since Aristotle, *Class, Status and Power*, edited by R. Bendix and S. M. Lipset (New York, 1953, revised 1966); also Asa Briggs, 'The Language of Class in Early Nineteenth-Century England' in *Essays in Labour History in Memory of G. D. H. Cole*, edited by Briggs and John Saville (1960).

Max Weber, *The Protestant Ethic and the Spirit of Capitalism*, which first appeared as articles in German in 1904–6, was translated by Talcott Parsons in 1930 with an enlightening introduction by R. H. Tawney; Karl Jaspers's essay on Weber, from a German text of 1958, is translated in his *Leonardo, Descartes, Max Weber: Three Essays* (New York, 1964). For instances of the relation between social studies and modern historiography, G. C. Homans, *English Villagers in the Thirteenth Century* (Cambridge, Mass., 1942); Lawrence Stone, *The Crisis in the Aristocracy 1558–1641* (Oxford, 1965); and on seventeenth-century England, Peter Laslett, *The World We Have Lost* (1965). For attempts to relate social studies to the study of fiction, Lucien Goldmann, *Pour une sociologie du roman* (Paris, 1965), based on G. Lukács's earlier studies of European realism; and for a less speculative view, Diana Spearman, *The Novel and Society* (1966).

11. THE HISTORY OF IDEAS

For intellectual history in an established tradition, Basil Willey, *The Seventeenth-Century Background* (1938) and its sequels are distinguished examples. Sixteen of Arthur O. Lovejoy's papers arising from the creation in 1923 of the History of Ideas Club at Johns Hopkins University were collected as *Essays in the History of Ideas* (Baltimore, 1948); its first essay, 'The Historiography of Ideas' (1938), continues the argument in his introduction to *The Great Chain of Being* (Cambridge, Mass., 1936) on 'The Study of the History of Ideas', the book being an expansion of Harvard lectures of 1933. Lionel Trilling, 'The Meaning of a Literary Idea' (1949), collected in his *Liberal Imagination* (New York, 1950), was answered in 1954 by Ronald S. Crane in 'Philosophy, Literature and the History of Ideas', collected in his *Ideas of the Humanities*, vol. 1 (Chicago, 1967). The problem has been cautiously discussed by W. K. Wimsatt in 'History and Criticism: a Problematical Relationship' in his *Verbal Icon* (Lexington, Kentucky, 1954). For examples of Lovejoy's influence, the quarterly *Journal of the History of Ideas* (New York, 1940–), and especially the ninth volume (1948), where his achievement is admiringly discussed; and for examples of literary studies of English philosophical texts since Bacon, *The English Mind: Studies in the English Moralists Presented to Basil Willey*, edited by Hugh Sykes Davies and George Watson (Cambridge, 1964).

12. CULTURAL HISTORY

Heinrich Wölfflin, *Principles of Art History* was first published in German in 1915 and translated in 1932; and the present century has seen numerous attempts, mainly by Central European art historians resident in England and the United States, to relate the visual arts to literary and intellectual history. *The Journal of the Warburg Institute* (later *The Journal of the Warburg and Courtauld Institutes*) was begun in London in 1937, based on the achievements of Aby Warburg, some of whose articles were posthumously collected in two vols as *Gesammelte Schriften* in 1934. Erwin Panofsky's essays on art history have appeared in English collections as *Studies in Iconology* (New York, 1939) and as *Meaning in the Visual Arts* (New York, 1955), and in German (Berlin, 1964); his more extended works include *Gothic Art and Scholasticism* (New York, 1957) and, with R. Klibansky and F. Saxl, *Saturn and Melancholy* (1964). André Malraux, *The Psychology of Art* first appeared in French in 3 vols (Geneva, 1947–9) (translated New York, 1949–50), though it was largely written before the war and lost in manuscript; and his *Voices of Silence* (Paris, 1954) was later expanded in three parts, the first translated as *Museum without Walls* (1967). On the modern dissemination of the arts, Jean Seznec, *The Survival of the Pagan Gods* (New York, 1940), Edgar Wind, *Art and Anarchy* (1963) and Marshall McLuhan, *Understanding Media* (1964); and for examples of the marriage of artistic and intellectual history, Edgar Wind, *Pagan Mysteries of the Renaissance*

(1958, enlarged 1967). Rosemond Tuve, *A Reading of George Herbert* (Chicago, 1952), interprets the imagery of the *Temple* (1633) in the light of Christian iconography. John Summerson, *Heavenly Mansions and Other Essays on Architecture* (1949) includes essays on the sources of European Gothic and on the background of English architecture since Wren; and E. H. Gombrich, *Art and Illusion: a Study in the Psychology of Pictorial Representation* (1960) is an ambitious attempt to interpret the progress of imitation in the arts, continued in his essays collected as *Meditations on a Hobby Horse* (1963) and *Norm and Form* (1966). John Holloway, *The Story of the Night* (1961), attempts to relate anthropological studies to the interpretation of Shakespearean tragedy; for a history of anthropology, T. R. Penniman, *A Hundred Years of Anthropology* (1935, revised 1965). J. E. Cirlot, *A Dictionary of Symbols* (1962), translated from the Spanish, is useful handbook.

Literary interest in music has been spasmodic: Bruce Pattison, *Music and Poetry in the English Renaissance* (1948); Calvin S. Brown, *Music and Literature: a Comparison of the Arts* (1948); John Stevens, *Music and Poetry in the Early Tudor Court* (1961); F. W. Sternfeld, *Music in Shakespearean Tragedy* (1963); and *Shakespeare in Music*, edited by Phyllis Hartnoll (1964). On the visual arts seen from a literary standpoint, John Buxton, *Elizabethan Taste* (1964) is a study of all the arts under the first Elizabeth; B. Sprague Allen, *Tides in English Taste 1619–1800*, 2 vols (Cambridge, Mass., 1937) is a history of English fashions in architecture, painting and landscape gardening over two centuries; Jean Hagstrum, *The Sister Arts: the Tradition of Literary Pictorialism and English Poetry from Dryden to Gray* (Chicago, 1958) a history of the neo-classical doctrine of the parallel arts; and Ian Jack, *Keats and the Mirror of Art* Oxford, 1967) a study of visual influences on the poetry of Keats.

INDEX

Adams, R. M. 227
Addison, Joseph 207
Aeschylus 89, 169
Allen, B. Sprague 229
alliteration 115
Altick, R. D. 225
Alvarez, A. 171 and n.
anthropology 84 f., 88, 218 f.
archetypes 84 f., 162
Ariosto 96
Aristotle 29–30, 61, 105, 227
  on kinds 84 f., 223
Arnold, Matthew 19 and n., 20,
  40, 46, 71, 221
  'Sohrab and Rustum' 78–9
Aron, Raymond 227
Arrowsmith, William 224
art 209 f.
Auden, W. H. 129
Auerbach, Erich 85, 117
Augustine, St 49
Austen, Jane 123, 183–4
  Mansfield Park 187 f.
Austin, J. L. 226

Bacon, Francis 61, 81, 195,
  222, 228
Bald, R. C. 224
Baldensperger, F. 223
Bally, Charles 226
Balzac, H. de 180–81
Barber, C. L. 204 and n.

Barthes, Roland 222
Bateson, F. W. 225
Baudelaire, Charles 57, 58, 156
Beardsley, Monroe C. 67 f., 75 n.,
  196 and n., 223
Beckett, Samuel 91, 92
Bendix, R. 227
Bentley, Richard 34, 123
Beowulf 62
Bernstein, E. 173
Beum, Robert 222
bibliography 122
Blake, William 43, 44, 45, 64
Bloch, Marc 211 and n., 221
Bodkin, Maud 85
Bolingbroke (H. St John) 200
Bowers, Fredson 121 and n., 124
  and n., 125 n., 129–30, 130 n.,
  224–5
Bradley, A. C. 115, 124
Briggs, Asa 227
Brontë sisters 78, 178–9
Brooke-Rose, Christine 222, 226
Brower, R. A. 224
Brown, Arthur 130 and n.
Brown, Calvin S. 229
Brown, J. A. C. 226
Browning, Robert 71, 115, 196
Brunetière, F. 82, 186–7
Buckle, H. T. 67
Burckhardt, Jakob 67, 211, 213 f.
Burke, Edmund 23, 57

Bury, J. B. 192
Buxton, John 229
Byron 49, 53, 78, 115, 170
    English Bards 137–8

Cambridge English School 20–21
*Cambridge History of English
    Literature* 67
Carr, E. H. 221
Carter, John 224, 225
Casey, John 222
Catullus 42, 95
Chapman, R. W. 123
Chaucer, Geoffrey 73, 74, 81,
    113, 176
Chicago Aristotelians 87
Chomsky, Noam 150 and n.
Christianity 205 f.
Cicero 49, 56–7, 84, 104
Cirlot, J. E. 229
Cleveland, John 97
Clifford, James L. 223
Cobbett, William 176
Cole, G. D. H. 227
Coleridge, S. T. 45, 49, 53, 64, 76,
    83, 86, 126, 144
    Biographia literaria 30–31, 44, 52
    and n., 53, 126
    and Wordsworth 202 f.
Collingwood, R. G. 79–80
Collins, J. C. 221
comedy 91 f.
commentary 132 f.
comparative literature 102 f.,
    223–4
Comte, Auguste 31, 173 f.
conceit, metaphysical 98 f.
concordances 58
Constant, Benjamin 103
copy-text 125 f.
Corneille, Pierre 115
Cottle, B. 222
Cowley, Abraham 97
Cowper, William 86
Crane, Ronald S. 198 and n., 228
Croce, Benedetto 173

Croll, Morris W. 222
cultural history 209 f., 228–9

Dante Alighieri 41, 116, 205
    on translation 110, 197
Darbishire, Helen 128
Darwin, Charles 87
Davie, Donald 226
Davies, H. S. 228
Dawson, Giles E. 131 and n.
Dearing, Vinton A. 225
decorum 56, 84, 90, 93 f.
definition 36 f.
Defoe, Daniel 176–7, 183
Denham, Sir John 106–7, 110
Descartes, René 149, 227
Dickens, Charles 126, 151, 172,
    174, 178, 181, 184
    Bleak House 179
    Hard Times 179–80
    Our Mutual Friend 187 f.
dictionaries 36–7, 60
Disraeli, Benjamin 177–8, 181
Donne, John 55, 97 f., 145
    his text 137
Dryden, John 49, 57, 69, 71, 72, 73,
    89, 96, 105, 207
    his text 127
    on conceit 98–9
    on kinds 81, 83, 85–6
    on painting 211–12
    on translation 107, 110–11
Durkheim, Emile 173, 227

Eckermann, J. P. 103
Edel, Leon 223, 227
editorial art 120 f., 224–5
Eliot, George 174
    on class 180, 186, 190–91, 195,
    196, 217
Eliot, T. S. 16, 21, 31–2, 66
    Waste Land 144
Empson, William 41 and n., 66–7,
    118, 226
epic 86, 212
    mock-epic 95

Epicurus 200
Euripides 169

Fairfax, Edward 81
Fascism 28, 34–5, 40
Fielding, Henry 57, 74, 82, 86, 90, 177, 183
Firth, J. R. 225
Fitzgerald, Scott 127
Forster, E. M. 29 and n., 72, 182
Fowler, Roger 225
Frazer, J. G. 67, 84, 218 f.
Freud, Anna 226
Freud, Sigmund 156 f., 197, 210, 226–7
  Freudian slip 167 f.
Friederich, W. P. 223
Frost, Robert 113
Frye, Northrop 44 and n., 85, 223
Fussell, Paul 222

Gaskell, Elizabeth 178, 185, 186
Gaynor, Frank 148 and n.
Gibbon, Edward 31, 57
Gladstone, W. E. 20, 181, 221
Goethe, J. W. von 103, 104, 106, 113, 115, 157
Goldmann, Lucien 227
Goldsmith, Oliver 118–19
Gombrich, E. H. 157 n., 229
grammar 149 f.
Gray, Thomas 95, 106
Greg, W. W. 123, 125 and n., 126 f., 224
Grube, G. M. A. 223
Guiraud, P. 226

Hagstrum, Jean 229
Halle, M. 225
Hampshire, Stuart 32 and n.
Harrison, Jane 85
Hartnoll, Phyllis 229
Havelock, E. A. 221
Hegel, G. W. F. 198
Heminge and Condell 127

Hensler, A. 222
Herbert, George 97, 118, 126, 229
Hesiod 95
Higham, T. F. 224
Hill, Archibald A. 145–6, 146 n.
Hinman, Charlton 225
Hirsch, E. D. 223
Hitler, Adolf 40
Hobbes, Thomas 198, 199, 227
Hockett, C. F. 225
Hoffmann, F. J. 226
Hoggart, Richard 20 and n.
Holloway, John 229
Holmes, O. W. 108
Homans, G. C. 227
Homer 27, 29, 62, 71, 82, 95, 96
  Margites 94–5
  Pope's 107–8
Hopkins, G. M. 51, 146 n., 152
Horace 84, 89, 90, 93 f., 104
  on painting 211 f.
  on translation 110
Hough, Graham 223
House, Humphry 172
Housman, A. E. 34, 122–3, 224
Hughes, H. Stuart 227
Hugo, Victor 30
Hulme, T. E. 55, 56 n.
Hume, David 61, 194, 195

Ibsen, Henrik 93
iconology 214 f.
ideas, history of 192 f., 227–8
imagery 60 f.
imitation, literary 82, 100, 105
influences, literary 80 f., 84 f.
intentional fallacy 67, 70 f., 158
irony 144 f.
Isherwood, Christopher 182

Jack, Ian 229
Jakobson, Roman 222, 224, 225
James, Henry 35, 46, 71 and n., 120, 125, 145
  his revisions 129
Jaspers, Karl 227

Johnson, Samuel 39–40, 46, 57, 72, 81, 83, 97
  on editing 133 f., 224
  on Goldsmith 118–19
  on kinds 86, 89
  on Pope 200
  on translation 106 f., 110 f.
Jones, Ernest 158, 161–2, 226
Jonson, Ben 95, 97
  his text 127
Joos, Martin 146 n., 225
Joyce, James 159
  Ulysses 144
Jung, C. G. 84, 159, 162 f., 162 n., 165 and n., 168, 170, 226
Juvenal 137–8

Kafka, Franz 159
Kant, Immanuel 33–4, 103, 194, 204
Keats, John 25, 43, 86, 229
  his revisions 128–9
Ker, W. P. 68–9
kinds, literary 59, 73 f., 82, 84 f., 223
Kleist, Heinrich von 79
Klibansky, R. 228
Knights, L. C. 222
Koestler, Arthur 182
Kris, Ernst 227

Lachmann 122, 224
Langer, Susanne 31
Laslett, Peter 227
Lattimore, Richmond 224
Lawrence, D. H. 21, 40, 43, 44, 59
Leeman, A. D. 222
Leonardo da Vinci 157, 160, 214, 215, 227
Lerner, Laurence 222
Lessing 103, 115
  on painting 212
Lévi-Strauss, Claude 218 f.
Lewis, C. S. 50 and n., 64 and n., 114 and n., 223, 227
linguistics 141 f., 225–6

Lipset, S. M. 227
literal language 61
Locke, John 62, 109, 194, 202, 204, 227
Lodge, David 226
Longinus 104
Lovejoy, Arthur O. 37–9, 37 n., 192 f., 228
Lowes, J. L. 76
Lucan 82
Lucretius 41, 193, 201
Lukács, G. 227

Maas, Paul 127 n., 224
Machiavelli 112
McKerrow, R. B. 123, 125, 224
McLuhan, Marshall 228
Mahood, M. M. 118
Maitland, F. W. 214 n.
Mallarmé, S. 111, 112, 113
Malone, Edmond 34
Malraux, André 182, 225
Mann, Thomas 156, 159, 170, 226–7
Marcus, Steven 226
Marlowe, Christopher 91
Marshall, Alfred 227
Marvell, Andrew 41–3, 45, 98
Marxism 28, 34–5, 46, 77, 167, 173 f.
mass media 209 f.
Maxwell, J. C. 127 n., 224
Meredith, George 167
Merton, R. K. 227
Meserole, H. T. 225
metaphor 60 f., 98, 222
Metaphysicals 97 f.
metre 49 f., 115 f., 222
Michelangelo 214
Mill, J. S. 31, 44, 45, 172, 173 f., 204
Milton, John 26, 41 and n., 73, 75–6, 86, 103, 116, 193, 217
  and mock-epic 95 f.
  Dryden on 81
  his language 147

his text 128, 131
'Lycidas' 80, 198–9
Trinity MS 79
Molière 115
Montesquieu 173, 227
Moore, Henry 211
morality 39 f.
Morgan, B. Q. 224
Morize, André 223
Muir, Edwin 224
Murray, Gilbert 85
Musset, Alfred de 74
Mussolini, Benito 173

Nabokov, Vladimir 224
Nashe, Thomas 123
New Criticism 16, 67, 69, 75, 87,
    196, 221
Newton, Sir Isaac 61, 76
Nietzsche, Friedrich 50, 83, 215
Nisbett, Robert A. 227
novel 88, 90, 172 f., 227
    language of 57–8
    texts of 125
Nowottny, Winifred 222

Oedipus complex 156, 159,
    168, 226
Ogden, C. K. 62 and n.
Onions, C. T. 222
Orwell, George 33 and n., 39
Oxford English Dictionary 36–7
*Oxford History of
    English Literature* 67

Palmer, D. J. 221
Panofsky, Erwin 215 and n., 228
Pareto, V. 173, 227
parody 94–5, 100, 144 f.
Parsons, Talcott 227
Pasquali, G. 224
Pater, Walter 20, 113, 221
Pattison, Bruce 229
Pei, Mario 148 and n., 225
Penniman, T. R. 229
Petrarch 116

Pevsner, N. 216
philosophy 193 f.
phonetics 113–14, 151
Picard, Raymond 222
Plato 21, 38, 39, 46, 104,
    193 f., 221
    and Aristotle 29
Plautus 90–91
plot 87
Poggioli, Renato 223
Pope, Alexander 81, 85, 86, 89, 96,
    105, 207
    Dunciad 52, 95
    Essay on Criticism 51–2
    Essay on Man 200
    his text 127, 131
    on translation 107, 110 f.
Popper, Karl 221
Positivism 31
Posnett, H. M. 109
Pound, Ezra 113
prose 48–9, 55 f., 222
Proust, Marcel 72, 159
psycho-analysis 77 f., 156 f., 226–7
puns 118
Puttenham, George 61

Quiller-Couch, Sir Arthur 71
Quintilian 104

Racine, J. 53, 109, 115
Raleigh, Sir Walter 225
Read, Sir Herbert 226
Reynolds, Sir Joshua 207
rhetoric, Renaissance 152
rhyme 52–3, 222
Richards, I. A. 16, 31, 62 and n., 66,
    152, 158 f., 159 n.
Richardson, Samuel 57, 82, 85, 183
Righter, William 222
Rilke, R. M. 29 and n.
rime 52–3, 222
Robins, R. H. 225
Robson, J. M. 225
Rochester, second Earl of 105
romanticism 37 f., 86, 156, 205 f.

Rousseau, J.-J. 109, 156, 170
Ruskin, John 40, 67, 213, 214, 216
Rymer, Thomas 81

Sainte-Beuve, C. A. 67, 72, 102 f.,
    157–8, 195–6
Saintsbury, George 71, 222
Saint-Simon, Comte de 177–8
Sartre, J.-P. 56 and n., 195, 221
Saussure, F. de 142 f., 225
Saville, John 227
Savory, T. H. 224
Saxl, Fritz 214, 228
Scaliger 30
Schiller, Friedrich 30, 115, 167
schools, literary 80 f., 84 f.
Scott, Sir Walter 167
Scrutiny 40
Sebeok, T. A. 225
Seneca 57
Seznec, Jean 228
Shakespeare, William 24–5, 27, 33,
    39, 46, 47–8, 56, 73, 76, 77, 91,
    92, 97, 113, 115, 116, 124, 145,
    147–8, 157, 167, 176, 196, 205,
    225, 226
  his text 127–8
  Johnson on 133 f.
  Ernest Jones on 161–2
  verse and prose 54–5
Shapiro, Karl 222
Shattuck, Roger 224
Shelley, P. B. 30, 43, 71, 116, 201
Sidney, Sir Philip 30, 39, 46, 194, 200
Simpson, Percy 224
Smith, Adam 176
sociology 172 f., 227
Socrates 38
sonnets 116
Sophocles 27, 89, 163–4, 169
Sorel, Georges 173
Spearman, Diana 227
Spender, Stephen 193–4, 194 n.
Spenser, Edmund 74–5, 144, 216
  Dryden on 81
  his text 130, 131, 132

Spitzer, Leo 225
Staël, Mme de 103
Steinberg, S. H. 222, 225
Stephen, Leslie 32–3, 33 n., 193,
    200, 204, 207, 214 and n.
Stern, Gustaf 225
Sterne, Laurence 82
Sternfeld, F. W. 229
Stevens, John 229
Stevens, Wallace 63–4, 111–12
Stone, Lawrence 175 n., 227
Strachey, James 226
Stroh, Friedrich 221
structuralism 142 f.
stylistics 59–60
subconscious 156 f.
  subconscious intention 77 f.
subjectivism, literary 32 f., 165–6
Summerson, Sir John 229
Swift, Jonathan 75, 98–9, 144, 154,
    161, 196
  his text 131
symbol 64
syntax 56–7

Tawney, R. H. 227
Tennyson, Alfred 86, 115, 196
textual criticism 34, 121 f., 224–5
Thackeray, W. M. 174
Thomas, Dylan 75
Thompson, D'Arcy W. 211 n.
Thompson, John 222
Thomson, James 223
Thorpe, James 223
Tillyard, E. M. W. 221, 223
Tolstoy 33, 39, 43
tragedy 86, 91 f., 212
translation 107 f., 224
Trilling, Lionel 78 and n., 158 n.,
    166 and n., 182, 205 and n.,
    226, 228
Trollope, Anthony 35
Tuve, Rosemond 229

Ullmann, Stephen 222, 226
Upward, Edward 182

Vachek, J. 225
Valéry, Paul 36, 143
Vickers, Brian 222
Virgil 82, 100, 194
  and mock-epic 95 f.
Voltaire, 83, 103, 105, 111

Wagner, Richard 215
Walker, Alice 129 and n., 224
Waller, Edmund 81, 105
Warburg, Aby 214 f., 228
Warburton, William 81
Warren, Austin 221
Warton brothers 81
Watt, Ian 195 and n.
Weber, Max 173 f., 186, 187 f., 227
Weiss, Peter 92
Wellek, René 37 f., 37 n., 221, 223
Wilde, Oscar 63, 71
Wilkins, John 149

Willey, Basil 227–8
Williams, Raymond 91 and n.
Wilson, Edmund 163–4,
  163 n., 169
Wimsatt, W. K. 67 f., 75 n., 196
  and n., 222, 223, 228
Winckelmann, J. J. 212–13
Wind, Edgar 216, 228
Winters, Yvor 222
Wittgenstein, L. 222, 226
Wölfflin, Heinrich 213 f., 213 n.,
  217 and n., 218, 228
word-frequency 57
Wordsworth, William 38, 53–4,
  73, 197
  on kinds 86
  Prelude 30, 128, 202 f.

Yeats, W. B. 196
Yule, Udny 226